REAGAN AND THATCHER

REAGAN AND THATCHER

GEOFFREY SMITH

The Bodley Head
London

to
Elizabeth, Kate and Graham

First published 1990
© Geoffrey Smith 1990
Bodley Head Ltd, 20 Vauxhall Bridge Road, London SW1V 2SA

Geoffrey Smith has asserted his right
to be identified as the author of this work

A CIP catalogue record for this book
is available from the British Library

ISBN 0-370-31394-1

Photoset by Rowland Phototypesetting Ltd
Bury St Edmunds, Suffolk
Printed in Great Britain by
Mackays of Chatham PLC, Chatham, Kent

CONTENTS

	Acknowledgments	vii
1	Allies in Waiting	1
2	Thatcher Leads the Way	11
3	Partners in Power	23
4	In Reagan's Washington	38
5	Arms and the Leader	49
6	Reagan Sends a Signal	59
7	Nato in Disarray	68
8	The Falklands	76
9	At the Summit: from Versailles to Williamsburg	95
10	Testing the Bear	112
11	The Grenada Invasion	125
12	The Second Term Begins	136
13	A Coup at Camp David	146
14	In Churchill's Footsteps	161
15	Changing the Guard	177
16	The Libyan Gambit	189
17	Irangate: What Thatcher Knew	204
18	Reykjavik: 'It Was Like An Earthquake'	214
19	Doing Business with Gorbachev	227
20	Into the Sunset	242
21	The Balance Sheet	258
	References	271
	Index	279

ACKNOWLEDGMENTS

There is a particular fascination, but also a particular difficulty, in conducting the research for a book on the leaders of two different countries. One needs to spend considerable time in both of them. I have made frequent and often lengthy visits to the United States for many years; but it would have been impossible for me, as a journalist living in London, to have written this book if I had not become a Guest Scholar at the Woodrow Wilson International Center for Scholars in Washington DC. I spent altogether seven extremely happy months there, and received much kindness from many people. Theodore C. Barreaux, a member of the Board of Trustees of the Center, took trouble on my behalf that went well beyond the customary responsibilities of such a post. Charles Blitzer, the director of the Center, Samuel F. Wells Jr, the deputy director, and Robert Litwak, the director of the International Studies Program, did all that they could to make me welcome. I was extremely fortunate to have as my research assistant Carolyn Welge, who possessed the priceless asset of always doing everything more thoroughly than she was asked to do. Maria Holperin of the International Studies Program gave me invaluable assistance, especially with the transcription of tape recordings at a critical point. I owe a particular debt of gratitude to Ada McDill, who organised my files, my tapes and me with enthusiasm and unselfish efficiency throughout my stay at the Center.

When I went there I was still on the staff of *The Times*, and I am grateful to the then editor, Charles Wilson, for giving me leave of absence to take up the guest scholarship in the first instance.

Much of the material for such recent history must come from discussion with those who made it. I had the benefit of interviews, specially for this book, with both Mrs Thatcher and President Reagan. I had many, often very lengthy, conversations with a large number of those who served in their Cabinets or as officials in their administrations. Sometimes the discussions were on the record, as is evident from the quotations in the text; frequently they were, of necessity, in confidence.

I bear full responsibility for all the judgments I have made, but I would like to express my appreciation to all those who took the time and trouble to share their recollections with me.

Any book on Anglo-American relations has to take account of the well-known differences between the political systems of the two countries. There are also more subtle differences in the usage of political terms. In particular, the phrase 'right wing' has a sharp edge, perhaps an implication of extremism, in the United States which it does not possess in Britain. I have tried to respect this by applying the word sparingly to American politics and politicians. Where I have used it, this has been in a British sense. It is intended as a description, not an accusation.

In the early stages of this venture I owed much to the encouragement and helpfulness of my friends, Heidi and Alvin Toffler.

Throughout, I have benefited from the close interest of my publishers, Charles Elliott, my editor at The Bodley Head; Donald Lamm, the president of Norton, and his colleague Hilary Hinzmann. Nicholas Pearson of The Bodley Head has also provided the calm administrative support of which a hurried author always stands in need. I am grateful to them all.

My agent, Bill Hamilton of A. M. Heath, has been a tower of strength before, during, and after the writing of this book. His colleague, Sara Fisher, played an invaluable role at a critical moment. I know how much I owe to them both.

I also know how much I owe to my secretary for many years, Sally Knapp. She has given me exceptional assistance over this book.

Above all, I would like to thank my wife, Elizabeth, without whose active help and encouragement this book would not have been written; and our children, Kate and Graham. To all three of them this book is dedicated.

G.S.
London
September, 1990

1

ALLIES IN WAITING

On the morning of 9 April 1975 the recently retired Governor of California met the newly elected Leader of the Opposition in Britain at her room in the House of Commons. This first meeting between Margaret Thatcher and Ronald Reagan set the pattern for many more to come.

It was planned as a routine courtesy visit like so many others: two aspiring political leaders exchanging pleasantries and flattering each other's ego. From this modest beginning was to flower one of the most remarkable relationships between any president of the United States and any prime minister of Britain, and between the leaders of any two countries anywhere in the world in the 1980s. It was to be an extraordinary example of the interplay of personality and power.

Even this first encounter was different. It had been scheduled to last for forty-five minutes; looking back on that meeting fourteen years later, President Reagan recalled that it lasted for an hour and a half. 'We found,' he told me, 'that we were really akin with regard to our views of government and economics and government's place in people's lives and all that sort of thing.'

The success of that meeting was to be explained partly by personal chemistry. 'Ronald Reagan has a very soft spot for a lady,' Michael Deaver, one of his closest aides throughout the first Reagan term, remarked. Charles Price, the American Ambassador in London from 1983 until the end of the Reagan administration, made much the same point: 'Reagan is very deferential to ladies in general.' One of the reasons why Reagan liked Thatcher, according to Deaver, is that 'she carried a purse, and wore funny hats and she was a lady'. Although widely known as the Iron Lady, she did not lose, and indeed was prepared to use, her femininity.

Reagan, for his part, has the easy courtliness towards women that

Margaret Thatcher always appreciates. He brought into that rather drab room, which she had characteristically tried to enliven with flowers, a touch of glamour that was missing from most of her political visitors. It was not as a former actor, though, that she was welcoming Reagan. She cannot recall having seen him in any of his films. It was his reputation as the former Governor of California, a leader of the Republican Right, that counted with her.

During his time as Governor she had made some lecture tours to the United States for the English Speaking Union, and she had heard then of how he was running California. What really seems to have impressed her, though, was an address he delivered to the Institute of Directors, composed of top business leaders, in London in 1969. She did not attend it, but she must have read it carefully for it to have stuck so firmly in her mind twenty years later.

'I saw it in the newspaper,' she told me. 'I got it from the Institute of Directors. I think he was speaking there because he had been Governor of California and he was giving an account of how they had got rid of quite a lot of controls and a lot of expenditure, and how they were getting value for money in California. In a way he had the advantage of me because he was able to say: "This is what I believe! This is what I have done!" '

Reagan's speech won a standing ovation for only the second time in the history of the IOD's annual conference. The first occasion had been in 1962 when Lord Home received a similar reception the year before he became Prime Minister. The 1969 speech was a first taste for a British audience of what we have come to recognise as vintage Reagan: much humour, not too much substance, but a strong theme.

It was the theme that had the impact on Thatcher. She was still able to recall roughly the wording of his peroration: 'Will we spend our sunset years telling our children and our children's children what it was like when men were free? And what will our answer be if we are asked by those children, "Where were we when freedom was lost and what was it we found that seemed more precious to us than freedom?" ' So when he walked through her door in the House of Commons six years later she knew she was welcoming a kindred spirit.

In November 1978, six months before Thatcher became Prime Minister, Reagan was back in London once more. On the first morning of his visit, before he saw Thatcher again, the *Daily Telegraph* hosted a breakfast for him to meet a number of Conservative journalists at the Stafford Hotel.

The proceedings began with an improbable question from the

Telegraph editor, William (now Lord) Deedes, on the subject of garbage collection in California. For once Reagan belied his reputation as a man uninterested in detail. He knew a great deal about garbage collection in California, and was prepared to share his knowledge to a rather greater extent than his audience would have wished. The rest of the discussion went along more predictable lines. But as they were leaving one of the journalists remarked to his colleagues: 'Well, he's a nice old boy isn't he? But he's simply not up to being President.' The others shook their heads sagely in agreement.

The remainder of the day was not without its misadventures. Reagan was late for his meeting with Thatcher. He had been with the then Foreign Secretary, Dr David Owen. At one point the conversation focused upon China and Owen declared that he found Mr Ping rather reasonable. Puzzled glances were exchanged between Reagan and Richard Allen, who was to be his first National Security Adviser and who played an important role in strengthening the dialogue with Thatcherites before Reagan came to power. 'You mean Deng?' Reagan enquired politely, and no doubt with some inner satisfaction.

He derived still greater satisfaction as they were leaving Owen's office, when one of the tea ladies approached him. 'Mr Rygan is it?' she asked in broad cockney. 'Why yes,' was the pleased and perhaps slightly surprised response. 'Mr Ronald Rygan from Hollywood?' Again an acknowledgment. Then, from behind the pillars and out of the crevices, came what seemed like an avalanche of her colleagues, all fans. 'Tell us about *King's Row*. How did you lose your legs?'

Allen tried to drag him away. Thatcher was waiting. But Reagan was in his element. The instinct of the actor struggled with the obligation of the politician. 'Just a minute . . . take it easy. These are my friends.' So a little behind time, but in high good humour, Reagan shortly went off to his second meeting with Margaret Thatcher.

When they had first met, they were not just two highly ideological politicians who found themselves sharing the same broad philosophy. They also shared the same predicament. They were in the political wilderness. They were outsiders even in their own party.

That was more obvious in Reagan's case. Having served two terms as Governor of California, he had declined to run again. He retained his presidential ambitions, but the White House was in the hands of another and rather different Republican, Gerald Ford. So Reagan's first concern in early 1975 was to keep himself in the public eye after stepping down from office in California.

It was with this in mind that Peter Hannaford, the Governor's

Director of Public Affairs, and Michael Deaver, the Director of the Administration, decided to form a public-relations company centring upon Reagan when they returned to private life. One weekend in the autumn of 1974 they outlined their plans to Ronald Reagan and his wife, Nancy: speaking engagements, a newspaper column and regular radio commentaries, all of which would provide the ex-Governor with both an attractive income and publicity.

The 1975 visit to London was the first major enterprise in this programme of action. Reagan had received an invitation to address the Anglo–American Pilgrims' Society in London in April. He was eager to accept, even though by then he would no longer be Governor. So two days before his first meeting with Thatcher he was warning his distinguished audience that after what he termed 'the Communist takeover of Portugal' the Soviet Union was now in a position to alter substantially the political map of Europe. After the military coup which replaced half a century of right-wing dictatorship in April 1974, the Communists seemed for a time to be establishing control over that country. With the aid of the military they became dominant in the trade unions and the media, and more moderate politicians left the government before public protest forced a progressive decline in Communist influence. Reagan was rewarded for his remarks by *Pravda* with the description of a resurrected 'political dinosaur' of the Cold War, an assessment with which many on both sides of the Atlantic would then have agreed.

The meeting with Thatcher had been set up by Justin Dart, with whom the Reagans stayed in his small house in Culross Street, just behind the United States Embassy in Grosvenor Square. Dart was an ebullient businessman, the founder of Dart Industries, which he created from the Rexall drug chain, and the leading personality in what came to be known as Reagan's kitchen cabinet of wealthy conservative Californian backers, who years before had picked him out as someone to support as a potential president. It was he who suggested that Margaret Thatcher was someone Reagan ought to meet, and he arranged the occasion. So they were brought together by an old friend of Reagan's who saw them as ideological soul-mates.

Reagan was all the more inclined to see Thatcher in that light because of an episode a few nights before he set out for Britain. At a dinner party in the suburb of Potomac in Maryland, some miles outside Washington, a well-known liberal journalist criticised Thatcher severely. So much so, that in the car on the way home Reagan remarked that she must be all right if she upset someone like that so much.

Even before they met, comment in the American press was drawing a comparison between them. In an article in the *Key West Citizen* on 1 April 1975, the conservative columnist Kevin Phillips asked whether Thatcher's election to the Tory leadership in Britain might not contain a lesson 'for Americans prone to dismiss potential conservative opposition to Gerald Ford as the hopeless ideological extremism of a narrow fringe'. He argued that 'this may be the conservative opportunity: to assert principles of self-reliance, economic discipline, cultural tradition and nationalism that the Establishment has increasingly disregarded in the last decade'.

That was precisely how Reagan and Thatcher themselves saw their role. What was remarkable about Reagan's European visit, however, was not only how well he and Thatcher got on, but also how few other people of power and eminence he saw during the course of it. On his way to London he had stopped for a night in Zurich, where he met Alexander Solzhenitsyn. In London he saw one or two other leading Conservatives, apart from Thatcher. He paid a courtesy call on Roy Hattersley, now the Deputy Leader of the Labour Party and then a junior minister at the Foreign Office. But no meeting was arranged with any Cabinet minister. Only Margaret Thatcher treated him with the respect due to a potential president. According to Deaver, he never forgot that.

She was the closer to power at that time, having become Leader of the Conservative Party almost exactly two months before. But her election had been a surprise and she was not yet accepted by the party establishment. Only two members of Edward Heath's Shadow Cabinet had voted for her to be Leader, and to some she seemed virtually a usurper.

After the Conservatives had lost two general elections in 1974 under Heath they were determined to have a new leader. In February of that year Heath, as Prime Minister, had called a general election to answer the question: who rules Britain? Was it the government or the National Union of Mineworkers, which had gone on strike in defiance of Heath's statutory incomes policy? The dispute was crippling British industry, but the electorate returned an inconclusive verdict.

Neither the Conservatives nor Labour had an overall majority of seats in the House of Commons, where the smaller parties were unusually well represented. The Conservatives lost office. In effect they had been defeated by the miners. Labour formed a minority government and went on to win an overall majority in a second general election eight months later.

Thatcher won the leadership of the Conservative Party because she was the only senior member with the nerve to stand against Heath. It was a political coup rather than an electoral victory. Few would have taken her chances seriously a month beforehand. The old guard was stunned. Many of its members could not believe that she would last as Leader.

The essence of British politics is that it is a team game. No individual politician can achieve power alone. He or she has to be the leader of the party in power: without a strong party a British politician is doomed to be no more than an interesting maverick. Because the leader is elected by the party, not by the wider electorate, it is respect within the party that is the route to power – a seat in the Cabinet when the party is in power, or in the Shadow Cabinet when in opposition. This sharply distinguishes the British system from the American, with its primary elections. What took her colleagues aback was that Thatcher had not been a particularly senior member of the Shadow Cabinet when she was elected Party Leader.

It was not that she had been swept to the front by a tidal wave of right-wing sentiment in the party. Her ideological views were of no more than indirect importance. After the reverses of the Heath years many Conservatives were prepared to try something different. A new face and a new approach. She offered both. Her election nevertheless did not represent an ideological revolution. It was only gradually that Thatcherism was able to seize control of the party, and Thatcherite ideology has never been totally in command. The instinctive loyalty that Conservatives customarily give their leader was for some time withheld from her by many of them. She had seized the job, but she still had to fight for the power.

So the new Leader who greeted Reagan that first morning in 1975 was both an exhilarated and a beleaguered woman. She had advanced further towards her goal than he had. His eight years as Governor of California had established him as the most prominent conservative in American politics. This enabled him to mount a surprisingly strong challenge to President Ford for the Republican nomination the following year.

It was asking too much, though, to try to stop a sitting president, even an unelected president like Ford, from being his party's candidate. Ford had been nominated as Vice-President by Richard Nixon in 1973 when Spiro Agnew suddenly resigned over corruption charges. The following year Ford succeeded automatically to the Presidency on Nixon's resignation. He was installed in the White

House without ever having been elected president or vice-president. So the aura of the office was a bit thin in his case.

Even so, Reagan could be no more than the gallant loser of 1976, and most of those who heard his emotional speech of concession at the Republican Convention in Kansas City must have doubted whether at the age of 65 his chance would come again.

So it was still as an outsider that Reagan returned to London in November 1978. This second meeting went even better than the first. Confidence had already been established between them. But for that, Reagan might possibly not have come to London on this trip. His primary purpose was to visit Germany, where he was to meet Chancellor Helmut Schmidt; Franz Josef Strauss, the CDU–CSU candidate for Chancellor; Helmut Kohl, already leader of the CDU but still more than four years away from the Chancellorship; and a range of ministers and opposition figures.

His schedule suggests that in Bonn Reagan was treated as a politician of consequence. In both Paris and London he had to be content, on the government side, with meeting the foreign minister. Neither President Giscard d'Estaing nor the British Prime Minister, James Callaghan, saw him. What is more remarkable is that Kingman Brewster, then the American Ambassador in London, did not find time to see him either. This caused some distress among Reagan's advisers, even though Brewster was the appointee of a Democratic President, Jimmy Carter.

An hour had been allotted for Reagan's discussion with Margaret Thatcher, but once again it ran over time. Their first meeting had been concerned essentially with generalities, their philosophy of government and so forth. This second discussion could not be said to have dwelt on details – conversations with Reagan hardly ever did – but it was more substantive. As she sat on a high-backed chair to the right of her desk and he plonked himself down on a hassock near the centre of the room a warmth and animation developed.

Characteristically, he spoke a lot of his experiences as Governor of California. In all their discussions over the years he was more anecdotal and she more analytical. The conversation ranged across national and international policy, from President Carter to China and the Middle East, from the Soviet Union to taxation. But it was domestic policy on which both of them principally focused. Rather surprisingly at such an early date, they discussed privatisation at some length. This was not an occasion, though, to dwell too much on any single topic. What made the meeting such a success was that they liked the sound of each other's principles and prejudices.

By now Thatcher had moved from the somewhat cramped room in which they had met three years before into more spacious quarters. In 1975 she had been in the old Leader of the Opposition's room, looking out on to the Speaker's Court, which was often filled with chauffeurs waiting in official cars for their ministers. It is one of the less exhilarating vistas at Westminster. There the Party Leader had to work and receive her visitors in the same room as she would preside over the Shadow Cabinet. A visitor would wend his way past the long table with more than twenty chairs around it to the small space that was left at the end. Of necessity Thatcher and Reagan had to sit quite close together in those restricted surroundings.

In 1978, however, she was in what had previously been part of the flat occupied by the Sergeant at Arms. Here there was an outer office for secretaries with rows of false books, then the Shadow Cabinet room and, down the corridor, a room for the Leader of the Opposition herself. With a view over New Palace Yard, it was a distinct improvement, even if it was next door to the kitchen. The amenities were weighted on the side of tradition rather than luxury. Upstairs was a bathroom with an old iron bath. Thatcher was none the less more comfortably placed.

Her political prospects had improved as well. Not only had she held on to the Conservative leadership, against some expectations, but she was now poised for victory in the general election which could not long be delayed.

This was partly because of her own determination, but still more because of the difficulties of the Labour government. In order to obtain a large loan from the International Monetary Fund (IMF) at the end of 1976, so as to avert a disastrous sterling crisis, it had been forced to impose severe cuts on public expenditure. Inflation was held in check only by a stringent incomes policy – restricting the annual growth of pay with the agreement of the trade union leaders – which had aroused so much resentment among union members that it clearly could not be sustained for much longer.

These economic problems were compounded by political misjudgment. Only the month before Reagan's visit, in October 1978, James Callaghan, the Prime Minister, had refused at the last minute – to the astonishment of the country in general and his own supporters in particular – to call the election which everybody had expected. Labour's private opinion polls had suggested that it would be touch and go whether he could hold on to power.

Reagan was shortly to make his successful bid for the Presidency, but at that time he was running behind Ford in the opinion polls for the Republican nomination. He was handicapped both by his age and by his reputation as an extremist. Neither he nor Thatcher represented the mainstream of their party. This gave them a feeling of isolation even as they reached for the reins of power; it also gave a double determination to them and to their followers.

On the right wing of both the Republican and the Conservative parties there was a similar sense of frustration. Their policies were never given a sustained opportunity. Even if the electorate was prepared to accept them, neither party seemed to have the stomach to stick with them for long.

In the United States there had been the Goldwater fiasco in 1964, when the overwhelming defeat of Senator Barry Goldwater as the Republican candidate appeared to confirm the belief that an ardent conservative was doomed to defeat.

That conclusion was partially disproved by the election of Richard Nixon four years later. But there were always doubts as to whether Nixon was a true conservative. He was supported by that wing of the Republican Party, but simply as the best candidate on offer: Reagan's bid that year was no more than half-hearted. If conservatives had not backed Nixon they might have let in a liberal Republican. Once in office, Nixon began with conservative domestic policies, but then in 1972 resorted to wage and price controls. When these were removed the following year there was massive inflation. Both the controls and the inflation were anathema to the Right. If only, they thought, there was someone with the resolution to apply free-market policies for the necessary length of time.

Similar thoughts were nursed among British Conservative right-wingers. Edward Heath had been elected in 1970 on an openly right-wing programme, but after two years there came the celebrated U-turn when he sought a concordat with the trade unions and imposed statutory wage and price controls. Some on the Right could not even bring themselves to support him in the general election that was called in February 1974 in the midst of the miners' strike. All of them were deflated and determined that it must be different next time.

So in both countries the Right had been gathering its energies in preparation for a serious thrust for power, and in both countries first Thatcher and in due course Reagan were given the leadership by parties that did not really believe in the new leader's programmes. In each case the experienced professionals, the men accustomed to governing, assumed that the new, maverick leader would soon come to terms with the real world and move towards the centre. For some years, not just after Thatcher became Party Leader but even after she became Prime Minister, one of the favourite guessing games in British politics was just when she would make her U-turn. When would she show that she was just like the rest?

Thatcher and Reagan were united in the determination that they never would. Implicit in both their early discussions, before either of them obtained power, was a shared dream. They were not just politicians out of office. They were crusaders, and crusaders for the same broad objectives. They wanted to change the direction in which their respective countries had been governed for half a century, to diminish the power of government and to enlarge the role of the market.

This experience of being out in the cold together and then coming in from the cold together was critical to everything that came later. It was an experience that neither could share with any subsequent national leader. Those two early conversations laid the basis for their relationship in office. They had their disagreements, some of them deeper than is often appreciated; they had their misunderstandings and they had their blunders. There were occasions of disillusionment. But nothing impaired the personal friendship that they established then.

2

THATCHER LEADS THE WAY

When the Conservative Party under Margaret Thatcher won the general election of Thursday 3 May 1979, Ronald Reagan was the first leading foreign politician to phone her with congratulations. But he was not put through to her the first time. A mere former Governor of California and failed presidential candidate was not judged to have a sufficient call upon the time of the new Prime Minister. Fortunately, he persisted, and finally managed to speak with her on the Monday afternoon. Whereas many a lesser politician would have been affronted by such treatment, there is no indication that relations between Thatcher and Reagan were blighted for an instant.

The delay would never have occurred, however, if Reagan's original call had come to one of her personal officials rather than to an established civil servant. Those who had served her in the days of opposition knew not only of the connection with him but also of the importance attached by many Thatcherites to the relationship with the more conservative Republicans in the United States.

Transatlantic exchanges from right to right went back well beyond both Thatcher and Reagan. They plugged into a network that already existed. In the way of politicians down the ages, they took advantage – imperfectly, often haphazardly and always selectively – of ideas that had already been in circulation, sometimes for quite a while. But this was a very loose network. As was fitting for apostles of the free society, it was not deliberately planned. There was no blueprint for the Dawn of the New Right.

At an intellectual level the starting point can be traced to the establishment of the Mont Pelerin Society in 1947. This was started by F. A. Hayek, the Austrian-born economist, political philosopher, Nobel prize-winner and sage of the Right. The society's nature and purpose were indicated by the personality of its founder.

Hayek was later to win the fervent admiration of Thatcher, one of the most practical of politicians. Yet he is himself in a sense one of the least practical of political gurus. He is not interested in how power is to be won. Often he gives the impression of not being concerned as to how ideas are to be put into practice. Certainly he is not the man for navigating ideas round the inevitable political obstacles. It is the ideas themselves that matter to him. Milton Friedman, the Chicago economist and preacher of monetarism who has been involved with Mont Pelerin from the beginning, is seen on the Right as more of an intellectual problem-solver, the man who is fertile with practical answers to practical questions. Both approaches have played their part.

Three years before founding the Mont Pelerin Society, Hayek had published perhaps his most famous work, *The Road to Serfdom*, in which he warned that centralised economic planning would ultimately lead to the end of the liberal society. This book had such an enthusiastic reception that he decided to bring together for regular discussion scholars, businessmen and a few politicians committed to the defence and advancement of the free society. Originally they were drawn from Europe and the United States. Subsequently the catchment area has been extended, with a number of Japanese members in particular brought in at Hayek's personal instigation. But there can be no doubt that, especially in the early years, this was essentially an Anglo–American enterprise. Hayek was then at the London School of Economics and was soon to move to Chicago, and most of the inner core were either Americans or British.

The first meeting of the group was held at a hotel above Vevey in Switzerland. Hayek had one or two suggestions for a name – perhaps the Tocqueville or the Acton Society. Neither found favour. So they settled for the mountain on which they were meeting. The Mont Pelerin Society has no publications and no formal politics. It simply brings people together for international and regional conferences of a week to a fortnight at a time. But what happens when such a group of like-minded people are thrown together for that length of time, especially when they feel that they are out of step with the conventional wisdom? They exchange opinions and experiences incessantly; they invite each other to their respective organisations; they solicit articles and books to be published by their own think-tank or university. A process of informal, unstructured networking begins.

What Sir Rhodes Boyson, the bewhiskered former Minister for Higher Education, terms the spider's legs spread out from the Mont Pelerin Society to the think-tanks and the universities. In London there are particularly the Institute of Economic Affairs, the Adam Smith Institute and the Centre for Policy Studies. In the United States the leading examples are the Heritage Foundation and the American Enterprise Institute in Washington – though the latter ranges from the centre to conservative – and the Hoover Institution in California. The University of Chicago has played an important role and there are a number of other significant centres.

The Institute of Economic Affairs was founded in 1957. The Centre for Policy Studies was started by Margaret Thatcher herself and her political mentor, Sir Keith Joseph, after the Conservatives lost power in 1974. It was to be the voice of the pure right uncontaminated by the liberal notions and corporatism which they believed had infected the Conservative Party's official Research Department.

Then, in 1977, the Adam Smith Institute was founded by three men who were all working in America at the time. One of them, Madsen Pirie, who became director of the institute, was a colleague on the Republican Study Committee on Capitol Hill of Edwin Feulner, who has been Director of Heritage for most of its life. The two institutions have always been close and still hold a joint conference every year. The Adam Smith Institute specialises in devising policies for adoption by the government, though a good many Tories would have been sleeping more happily in their beds if the poll tax had not been one of them.

Among the very early members of Mont Pelerin was Allen Wallis, who became Under-Secretary of State for Economic Affairs under Reagan and was the official in charge of American preparations for all the economic summits from 1983 until the end of the Reagan era. For some years Wallis acted as treasurer of the society. Later members included Sir Alan Walters, who has moved in recent years between being Thatcher's personal economic adviser and Professor of Political Economy at Johns Hopkins University in Maryland. His closeness to Thatcher provoked the resignation of the Chancellor of the Exchequer, Nigel Lawson, which was then immediately followed by Walters's own resignation in October 1989.

This varied but vigorous process of thinking, speaking and writing provided something of a joint intellectual inheritance for both Thatcher and Reagan. But the transmission of this inheritance was uncoordinated. Neither Thatcher nor Reagan was ever a member of the Mont Pelerin Society, nor did either of them ever attend any of its meetings. Both of them felt instinctively what others worked out intellectually, and both of them had policy advisers who were well connected to the transtlantic network.

Politicians are forced by the nature of their trade to present a face of certainty to the general public. As Walter Lippmann once remarked: 'Men do not follow those who are themselves in doubt.' So those who aspire to leadership stifle their doubts as they present their case. But successful politicians are rarely original thinkers. They display their distinctiveness by the originality with which they shop in the market-place of other people's ideas. But even those who most proudly proclaim, as Thatcher does, that they are 'conviction politicians' need reassurance that their convictions have substance. The more daring their shopping the more they may need intellectual reassurance.

That, even more than specific ideas, was what the right-wing intellectual network offered the two leaders, giving them confidence that their convictions were not outdated, that there was a substantial body of thought that espoused those convictions and was eager for them to be put into practice. That the intellectuals on this network had such strong transatlantic connections was critical.

What was remarkable about the early speeches that both Reagan and Thatcher delivered in the other's country was how similar were the convictions expressed and how closely these beliefs accorded with the thinking on the Mont Pelerin circuit. The theme of Reagan's speech to the Institute of Directors in London – the one that had so impressed Thatcher with its talk of the encroachment of government – was in line with Hayek's conviction that a fundamental moral principle was at stake in the ordering of economic and social policy.

In September 1975, five months after her meeting with Reagan in London, Thatcher paid her first visit to the United States as Party Leader. The good publicity she received on both sides of the Atlantic bolstered her self-confidence and helped to strengthen her position in the Party at a difficult time. A favourable report in the *New York Times* referred to her 'passion for precision that enabled her to keep to the breathtaking schedule of her four-day visit to New York with the punctuality of a British Railways train'. This was no doubt intended as a compliment.

In London *The Times* published an approving leading article on her speech to the Institute of Socioeconomic Studies in New York which contrasted with its earlier criticism of her. This speech was characteristically more substantive and detailed than Reagan's in London, but the theme was similar. Entitled 'Let Our Children Grow Tall', it argued that 'the persistent expansion of the role of the state and the relentless pursuit of equality has caused and is causing damage to our economy in a variety of ways'.

This was one of the seminal speeches that she made during her days in opposition. The dangers of too large a public sector, of an over-extended welfare state, of excessive taxation and regulation; the need for everyone to have the opportunity to excel and to profit from their achievement – the main ingredients of what we have come to know as Thatcherism were all there. But what mattered just as much as what she said to Americans was what they said to her. She was gratified and stimulated by her discussions with such people as William Simon and James Schlesinger. The whole experience confirmed her enthusiasm for the United States.

It was very different from the attitude she had displayed towards Europe in the referendum a few months before on whether Britain should remain a member of the Community. As leader of the party that had taken Britain in she was obliged to support continued membership. There is no reason to believe that that conflicted with her considered, rational judgment. But her heart was not in it. She made only one substantial speech during the campaign and on her one visit to the headquarters of the Britain in Europe movement had a row with its Director, Sir Con O'Neill, who a few years before had been the official principally responsible for negotiating Britain's entry.

Her instinctive, emotional preference for the United States was set early. It was at the heart of her approach to world affairs and it made her all the more eager to collaborate with Reagan. 'She only has to step on to American soil,' one of her advisers remarked. 'She doesn't even have to kiss the earth like the Pope.'

Why is she so pro-American? In the first place, it is not at all unusual to find this sentiment held strongly among intensely patriotic British people of her generation. She was 13 when the Second World War began and 19 when it ended. The years of her political coming of age as she moved from Oxford to being a parliamentary candidate were the years of Soviet expansion into Eastern Europe, the establishment of Nato and then the Korean War. The years of shared danger.

In all these crises the Americans were Britain's closest and most powerful friends. The interests of the two countries seemed indistinguishable in these anxieties. To somebody inclined to see the world in sharp black and white terms, as Margaret Thatcher is, the Americans were most emphatically on the British side. To keep them there, to avoid their slipping back into the comfortable life within their own borders, had to be a priority of British policy. For without them what could be done?

But Thatcher's attachment to the United States does not come from wartime memories and post-war realpolitik alone. She is attracted by American society. She admired the United States before she ever exchanged a word with Reagan. She found it easier to get on with him because she was pro-American: she was not pro-American because she liked him.

It was the similarity of their views on domestic policy which was initially crucial. Thatcher took office with the determination not to become immersed in foreign affairs. Many heads of government come to power with this laudable intention, but hardly any take it to the extreme that she wished to do at first. She was not going to attend any summits or international conferences.

She was elected in May 1979. The following month the economic summit was to be held in Tokyo. In July there was to be the Commonwealth Conference in Lusaka at which independence for Rhodesia, now Zimbabwe, was to be the main item, and then in October the European Council was to meet in Dublin. Her original intention was to avoid them all. Let the Foreign Secretary handle them.

She went around declaring that she did not have the expertise, the background, or the interest. The thought of spending ten days at the Commonwealth Conference particularly appalled her. How could she keep her patience for that length of time in a gathering with which she did not have much empathy anyway? She wanted to concentrate all her energies on the economy.

It was not a position that any prime minister could have sustained. Too much offence would have been given. Too often it would have looked as if she was failing to speak up for Britain. In any case, sooner rather than later, she began to be interested. She recognised the importance of many of the issues, she enjoyed the hard bargaining and she sometimes responded unexpectedly to personalities.

On the way to the Tokyo summit her plane stopped to refuel in Moscow. About an hour before they got there a message came that the Soviet Prime Minister, Alexei Kosygin, was on his way to the airport and would like her to have dinner with him. She accepted without any of the enthusiasm that she subsequently lavished upon Gorbachev, and it was a somewhat disgruntled British party that filed into the VIP lounge in Moscow airport, where dinner had been laid on. But there was then a long and very serious discussion, mostly about East–West relations, in which Thatcher became more and more engaged. Against all assumptions, she found Kosygin interesting and enjoyed the argument.

This was all the more surprising because one of the speeches which attracted particular attention during her early days as party leader was a blistering attack in January 1976 on the military might of the Soviet Union, in the course of which she promised to build up Britain's defences. It was this speech which earned her the title of 'The Iron Lady' from the Soviet army newspaper *Red Star* – an insult that she accepted with relish.

An even stranger episode than her meeting with Kosygin occurred at the Commonwealth Conference at Lusaka. As soon as she arrived she characteristically wanted to see the Conference Chairman, President Kenneth Kaunda of Zambia. When he was not free right away she insisted on seeing someone else. Not a minute was to be lost, even if it was just a Commonwealth Conference.

So a meeting was hurriedly arranged with Julius Nyerere, the radical President of Tanzania and one of the Commonwealth leaders with whom she might be thought to have least in common. Yet she returned stimulated and saying that after all she thought she could do business with that man. The Conference as a whole was a dramatic success.

These incidents illustrate how quickly her interest in international affairs was engaged, even though she was very conscious of her inexperience at the start, and how swiftly she would form a judgment on personalities.

With President Jimmy Carter it did not take her long to form an adverse opinion. In some respects he was more like her than Reagan is: working obsessively hard, absorbed in detail and bringing a formidable analytical power to bear on any problem. It was Carter who began some of the policies that are especially associated with Reaganism and Thatcherism: the arms build-up and economic deregulation.

But he would have seemed indecisive to her, and he lacks the kind of debonair personality that she likes. She was careful, none the less, to allow none of her misgivings to appear in public, or to him or his entourage. The relationship with the United States was too important for her to allow personal predilections to get in the way.

The one visit she paid to Washington during the Carter Presidency went well. That was in December 1979, and in a sense she was doubly lucky in the timing. It was only the month before her arrival that the American hostages had been taken in Tehran, and she took the opportunity of her first public declaration as Prime Minister in the United States to state unequivocally on the White House lawn her backing for the President. She had told him, she declared, that if he asked for economic sanctions against Iran, 'you would expect nothing less and you would get nothing less than our full support'.

This was at a time when it was by no means clear precisely what attitude America's allies were going to take over Iran. So her remarks, offering categorical backing in a way that nobody else had yet done, were no mere formality. It gave her the opportunity to play the role of the reliable ally to maximum dramatic effect.

Yet she had needed some persuasion to make this statement. Her first instinct was that this was not an issue on which Britain could do anything useful, and she has never liked an empty diplomatic gesture. Over dinner at the British Embassy the night before, she had discussed the tactics for the visit with Lord Carrington, her highly respected Foreign Secretary; Sir John (now Lord) Hunt, the Cabinet Secretary; Sir Michael Palliser, Permanent Under-Secretary at the Foreign Office; Sir Frank Cooper, the Permanent Under-Secretary at the Ministry of Defence; and Sir Nicholas Henderson, the new British Ambassador in Washington.

Late in the evening Cooper mentioned to Carrington that he had seen on television the families of the hostages parading outside the White House and that it would be necessary to say something helpful on the question. Thatcher rounded on him: 'Don't be stupid!' Carrington took Cooper's side, but only after vigorous discussion did they prevail, and Cooper was sent away to draft the remarks that she would deliver the following day. She must have been surprised at how favourable an impression her words made in Washington.

She was also fortunate that in the middle of her visit to Washington the successful conclusion was announced of the negotiations for creating the new independent state of Zimbabwe. So she was able to bask in a diplomatic triumph.

Carter received her with every courtesy and gesture of friendship. He gave a splendid party for her at the White House and told the Ambassador that he attached unique importance to the relationship with Britain. None the less, she was hoping for Reagan's election in 1980, just as he had been hoping for her success in the spring of 1979. A month after her election he had paid an exceptionally warm tribute to her in his weekly radio programme. 'I couldn't be happier,' he declared, 'than I am over England's new Prime Minister. It has been my privilege to meet and have two lengthy meetings with Margaret Thatcher. I've been rooting for her to become Prime Minister since our first meeting. If anyone can remind England of the greatness it knew during those dangerous days of World War Two when alone and unafraid her people fought the Battle of Britain it will be the Prime Minister the English press has already nicknamed "Maggie".'

He went on in characteristic fashion to illustrate the decline in British industrial productivity by pointing to what he said was the fall in the output of bricklayers: 'I think "Maggie", bless her soul, will do something about that.'

There were two significant features of that broadcast. One was the personal feeling that went beyond the conventional compliments to be expected from one friendly politician to another. Reading that script years later, one feels that he really had been 'rooting for Maggie'. The other feature was his romantic concept of what he would no doubt have regarded as the true Britain.

Both of them looked at the other's country with a slightly idealised gaze. Indeed, that was how both of them looked at their own country. Not that either was satisfied with the condition it was then in. Both of them in somewhat dramatic fashion saw it as their mission to pull their country up from the slough of despond into which it had fallen under successive governments of the Left and Centre. In each case the focus was initially internal and domestic. What drew them together was that in each case it was the same kind of mission.

Just as Thatcher's first priority was economics, into which foreign policy gradually intruded, so it was with Reagan. One of his former senior advisers believes: 'His strongest ideological inclinations are economic. Yes, he's interested in the expansion of freedom, but for him that means very much market-oriented democracy. It is not enough to have socialist democracy. Let's suppose you have the Bill of Rights and all the freedoms we take to be precious, and one-person-one-vote democracy, and we all agree that it's totally representative and fair, and it's protected by law in all kinds of ways that we respect. And if it was socialist, would he be happy? Not one bit.'

The belief in the moral dimension of capitalism, the association of the free market with the free society, was common to Thatcher and Reagan. It was characteristic of the loose, transatlantic intellectual network to which they were both connected. But it was not only right-wing intellectuals on both sides of the Atlantic who were in touch with each other, nor the personal advisers of Thatcher and Reagan. So were those practical men of politics, the party managers.

Bill Brock, a former senator from Tennessee, became Chairman of the Republican National Committee in January 1977, when the party was at just about the lowest point in its history. After Vietnam,

Watergate, the resignation of Richard Nixon and the defeat of Gerald Ford, this was a time when serious political analysts were pondering whether the party had much of a future.

But in politics there is always something to be said for taking over at the bottom and for making a virtue of your misfortunes. That was what Brock did. In addition to rebuilding the party organisation at home, he deliberately set out to see what lessons the Republicans could learn from parties overseas. The principal inspiration he drew was from the successful Thatcher campaign of 1979.

He was immensely impressed with its quality: 'it was just so superior to anything I had seen in the States'. Two aspects of it struck him in particular: the general theme; and the technical skill of the advertising. Both were relevant for his purposes.

Immediately on his return he hired someone from Saatchi and Saatchi, the company that had made the television ads for the Conservatives, to do the same for the Republicans. A decade later Brock remembered vividly one of the British ads in particular. This showed a race in which Britain was represented by a 'strong, strapping, healthy young man and Great Britain was out in front of the whole world pack. Each time he came around they added a few more pounds for him to carry of taxes and regulations and government intervention and bureaucracy. Every time they put another of those burdens around his neck for him to carry obviously he had more and more trouble maintaining the lead. He began to falter and then, of course, he lost the lead. It was just a wonderful ad. I can see it right now.'

This was precisely the theme that Brock wanted for the Republican ads. But it was only after some agonising that it was decided to go ahead. Such an advertising campaign was unprecedented in American politics because it was related to the party, not the candidate. American politics revolve around personalities, not parties. It is the candidate who determines what the party's policy shall be, not the other way round.

But Brock was taking his decision towards the end of 1979, and the Republicans would not choose a presidential candidate until their convention in July 1980. So for once a party theme was being established well in advance of knowing who the candidate would be, and that theme derived much from the inspiration of Margaret Thatcher.

Nor was this the end of the British Conservative contribution to the Republicans in 1980. The Republican television advertising campaign was timed for the spring, but before it was ready they were presented with 'equal time' on television. That is when the President delivers a televised speech and the opposing party is given equal time to respond. As the Republicans did not yet have a candidate, Brock, as Party Chairman, gave the response; and as they did not yet have their own ads he used two of the British Conservative ones. He explained in effect that these would give a foretaste of the message in the Republican ads, but to borrow as explicitly as this from the campaigning of a foreign party was quite exceptional in American politics.

Michael Baroody, then Director of Public Affairs at the Republican National Committee, recalls: 'We aired them to show that the problems that we were feeling in this country, that government was putting on us entirely too much of a burden, did not make us unique. The feeling was shared elsewhere, in Britain for example. It was dramatised there in these ads and we intended to do the same here.' Baroody went on to indicate that another purpose of airing the British ads was, 'subliminally at least, to point out that in Britain people did something about it. The voters chose a change . . . and we ought to do the same thing here. No matter who the nominee was, we could vote for change.'

'By the time Ronald Reagan won the nomination,' Brock claimed, 'the issues were set and the Republicans were controlling the agenda.' Had the party nominated another candidate, who wanted to campaign on a very different platform, there could have been embarrassment. With Reagan there was no difficulty. 'What we didn't know,' Brock reflected, 'was that apparently he was in contact with Margaret Thatcher and was buying into the programme on his own. So the two happened to come together precisely at the right moment in time.'

The Thatcher example did more for the Republicans than help them to refine their campaigning tactics. The psychological effect of her election was even more important. Brock went so far as to say that it was absolutely crucial. 'We had the example of success . . . it gave us confidence. It gave our candidate confidence.'

For most of the 1980 campaign Reagan was still regarded, not only in Europe but also by many people in the United States, especially on the Eastern seaboard, as a wild cowboy from the West, an extremist whose finger ought not to be allowed to hover above the nuclear button. That a country as moderate as Britian, which seemed to much American opinion to have gone so far down the road to socialist ruin, was prepared to elect someone as right-wing as Thatcher seemed a reassurance. 'If Great Britain was able to do it,' as Brock put it, 'as far down as they were, I think we could make the case that we certainly could do at least as well.'

She became the Republican talisman. They could point to her. They could draw encouragement from her. In Brock's words, 'there was nothing that even came close to having the impact that the 1979 election in Great Britain had upon us.'

Curiously, Thatcher herself did not know many Reaganites at that time. For her 1975 visit she had sought the guidance of William Deedes, the *Telegraph* editor, as to whom she should see. He consulted the *Telegraph*'s man in Washington, Stephen Barber, who advised that it was not worth spending time at the Heritage Foundation, which he evidently considered too much of a fringe organisation. That was how the Republican Right was widely regarded at that time. The British Embassy, indeed, was slow to appreciate that Reagan was going to be elected in 1980.

By then almost everything was ready for the Reagan–Thatcher partnership. There was the personal rapport between them; their understanding was strengthened by a loose network of intellectuals on both sides of the Atlantic; there was cooperation between the party managers; and Thatcher was installed in office. All that remained was for Reagan to win his election.

3

PARTNERS IN POWER

When Reagan was elected, on 4 November 1980, Thatcher was one of the first to send him a congratulatory message, and she was more fortunate than he had been when the positions were reversed the previous year. Richard Allen, soon to become Reagan's first National Security Adviser, made sure that it was the first to be given to him. It made the desired impression. Reagan himself told the British Ambassador how much he appreciated it, and it pleased him so much that he read it out to a large gathering in California.

But could the pleasant relationship of the days of aspiration be translated into an active working partnership? Political history is littered with sad tales of those who were allies on the way up, but whose friendship crumbled under the pressures of power. Why should Thatcher and Reagan not suffer that fate? What was it that enabled them not only to sustain their relationship, but even to deepen it?

Both came to the leadership of a country whose self-confidence had been severely damaged and which wanted above all to walk tall in the world again. For the United States the seizure of the hostages in Tehran was but the latest in a series of national humiliations stretching back to the assassination of John Kennedy. For Britain economic decline seemed to have become a way of life.

The essence of both Reaganism and Thatcherism, even more than any economic doctrine, was a state of mind: a determination to change all this. They were going to resist decline, to restore confidence and to assert the national interest. They believed in less government, but they believed just as passionately in strong government. In this broad sense they shared the same approach to leadership. But their styles of leadership were very different because they are very different people.

23

Had Reagan been a British politician, Thatcher would never have had much time for him. In his understanding of the issues, his grasp of detail and his grip over his officials, she would have regarded him as sloppy. She has a relish for argument, often going on late into the night. He is uncomfortable with disagreement around him and prefers to keep regular hours. He is not, indeed, someone with whom it is usually possible to have a sustained, analytical argument. He operates more by instinct, by political feel. She is a workaholic, he has a gift for relaxation. He has a sense of fun, a love of anecdotes and a taste for jokes in general. His one-line quips are famous. Unusually for a successful British politician, she has no sense of humour. She can deploy wit, but as an instrument of combat rather than a means of enjoyment.

'Now that I am no longer a servant of the United States government,' a former American official remarked, 'I can say that it was never an equal contest.' Others, American just as much as British, have made the same point, with varying degrees of tact.

Ever since the decline of British power reduced the United Kingdom to a second-rank nation, it has seemed to successive British governments that one of the best ways of affecting what happens more broadly in the world is as the best friend, the wise and experienced adviser, of the most powerful country of all. The relationship is a matter of sentiment, reflecting much shared experience and identity of view. It is also a compensation to Britain for no longer being a great power itself. All the advantages of language and custom give the British a better chance than anyone else of becoming quietly and intimately involved in the process of American decision-making. That was what Harold Macmillan meant by his somewhat patronising reference to Britain being to the United States as the Greeks were to the Romans: the centre of an older civilisation using its accumulated wisdom to guide the new centre of power.

But the special relationship has really flourished only when there has been a close rapport at the top between president and prime minister. That is important not only because of the personal decisions which only they can take, but equally because of the signals they send down through their respective governments.

In trying to make the most of this opportunity Thatcher was following the tradition of all post-war British prime ministers with the sole exception of Edward Heath. Henry Kissinger records regretfully in his memoirs: 'Heath disdained the occasional telephone calls I urged upon the British Ambassadors to establish the personal relationship that Nixon craved lest he be accused by France, as his predecessor Harold Macmillan had been, of being an American Trojan Horse.' Thatcher had no such anxieties.

For her purpose it was crucial that she brought to the partnership a deeper understanding of issues, a wider intellectual range and a greater capacity to defend in argument the positions that they both held. This greater personal contribution helped to compensate for the disparity in power between the two countries. One has only to think of what would have happened if it had been the other way round, if the President of the United States had been the more formidable personally: there would have been no partnership of any consequence, because the British Prime Minister would not have had enough to contribute to make it worthwhile.

Reagan's administrative methods also had their advantage for Thatcher. It was inherent in his style of leadership that, having set the direction, there should be gaps in strategy which others would fill. That task would naturally fall to his advisers and Cabinet members. But this provided an opportunity for a foreign leader whom he trusted, who had ideas of her own and who was not afraid to argue for them.

This required from Reagan, however, a quality rarely found in those who have fought their way to high office. Four days after entering the White House he was being briefed by Kenneth Adelman, later Director of the Arms Control and Disarmament Agency (ACDA), who had been to Wiesbaden with President Carter for the release of the hostages from Tehran. In the room with Reagan were the Secretary of State, Alexander Haig; the Secretary of Defense, Caspar Weinberger; the National Security Adviser, Richard Allen; and the troika, as they were then known, of his most intimate White House advisers – James Baker, Edwin Meese and Michael Deaver. After Adelman's presentation, the questions started. Every now and then the President would sit up and try to say something, but as someone else got in a question first he would lean back waiting for another opening. After a while Adelman found it necessary to take the initiative himself: 'Mr President, do you have a question?'

There are two ways of interpreting this incident. One is to be appalled at a President apparently so lacking in authority among his senior officials. The other is to be reassured by a President so comfortable with himself and his office that he did not need to assert himself in this way. It was this quality of quiet assurance that was critical in his relationship with Thatcher.

She is what is termed in Britain a managing woman. There is some sensitivity in London at any suggestion that she ever hectored Reagan, and it is true that she was careful never to have a personal quarrel with him. She took infinite care to nurture his friendship wherever possible. But she customarily did most of the talking and would push her point, usually with tact but also with some vigour. Where a lesser man would have felt threatened, he did not. On the contrary, he seemed to relish her spirit. On one occasion, when he was being harangued by her at some length on the telephone, he took the instrument away from his ear, put his hand over the speaker, turned to his visitor and remarked with a smile: 'Isn't she marvellous?'

What others regard as her liabilities may not have been seen by him in that light at all. One of his former aides pointed out that throughout his life he has always formed good relationships with dominating women: first his mother, who was the powerful personality in his childhood; then his present wife; finally Thatcher. 'This is just my hypothesis,' he added, 'that Reagan saw Thatcher unconsciously as a favourable version of a mother figure . . . just even in the very manner in which she would say "now Ronnie" there was something that made her seem as if she were the senior partner.' David Gergen, Director of Communications in the White House during Reagan's first term, made a similar point: 'There were times during the Economic Summits and other occasions when I found her to be protective of him.'

Their different styles made it easier for them to get on with each other, given their respective roles. Margaret Thatcher would not have relished having to deal with another Margaret Thatcher. But that can hardly explain why they were elected at much the same time. Were they both swept to power on the same ideological wave of right-wing sentiment?

That is what they both seemed to believe. They were both right-wing crusaders and they therefore assumed that the voters had put them in office to pursue such a crusade. But there is always a danger of taking political leaders too much at their own valuation. The opinion polls at the time and the nature of their election campaigns suggest that the truth was more complicated.

Both attacked the pervasive sense of national decline. 'They say that the United States has had its day in the sun, that our nation has passed its zenith,' Reagan declared scornfully to the 1980 Republican Convention in Detroit. 'My fellow citizens, I utterly reject that view.' Just as the British Conservative manifesto stated flatly: 'Our country's relative decline is not inevitable.'

Both warned of the encroaching power of the state. 'This election may be the last chance we have,' Thatcher wrote apocalyptically in a foreword to the manifesto, 'to reverse that process, to restore the balance of power in favour of the people.' While Reagan told the Convention that 'government is never more dangerous than when our desire to have it help us blinds us to its great power to harm us'.

Both promised to cut personal tax rates so as to restore incentives, to control inflation, to curb public spending in general but to increase defence spending in particular and to uphold the family.

Yet it was not solely, probably not even principally, because of their commitments that they were elected. Gallup noted after the American election of 1980: 'An examination of political indicators and the views of voters on key issues shows that the Reagan landslide was not so much the result of an ideological shift to the right among the electorate as dissatisifaction with the leadership of the nation and a desire for change.'

Much the same had been true in Britain the year before. Opinion polls revealed unhappiness at the high level of taxation and waste in the welfare state, but certainly not a rejection of the welfare state itself. A MORI (Market and Opinion Research International) poll in April 1979, the month before the election, showed that 75 per cent of voters wanted to reduce income tax by reducing government spending. It is a safe bet that they did not mean reducing government services. Cut bureaucracy, weed out waste, slim down the Civil Service: those were the popular themes of the day. There was the implicit assumption that such policies would be enough to provide for lower taxes. It was Thatcherism without tears.

But Thatcher benefited because, while the electorate wanted both lower taxes and good services, it was more worried at that time by the level of taxes than the quality of the services. The main anxieties of the voters were prices, jobs, strikes, taxes, and law and order. With the possible exception of jobs, that was a Conservative agenda. It reflected widespread public disquiet at the record of the Labour government. With the oil-price shocks, the 1970s were years of inflation; direct taxes in Britain were among the highest in the world outside Scandinavia and were imposed at lower levels of income; and Labour's incomes policy collapsed in a flurry of strikes in the winter of 1978–9.

The vulnerability of their opponents was the key factor for both Reagan and Thatcher. Both benefited electorally from a national disaster for which neither bore the slightest responsibility. In the case of Reagan, it was the seizure of the hostages in Tehran which humiliated President Carter. In Britain, it was the industrial strife of the winter of discontent, which made the Labour government look toothless as its authority was defied, garbage was not collected and the dead were not buried.

That would have been the fourth phase of the incomes policy. In the first two years it had the full support of the union leaders. Indeed, they largely devised the restraints on pay increases. In the third year they felt able only to acquiesce in the government's policy, rather than give it their open approval. By the fourth year even that was impossible. Too much resentment had built up among union members who believed that they could get more money for themselves by free collective bargaining without restrictions. By then the government was losing twice over: the union leaders had been given undue influence over official policy in other fields, but they were no longer able to deliver their side of the bargain by curbing pay rises.

In both countries the electorate was naturally inclined to look for a replacement without regard for ideology. But it was no disadvantage for either Reagan or Thatcher that they offered something different from the prevailing orthodoxy. Their voters might not have been converted to the full doctrine of Reaganism or Thatcherism, but the trauma of the hostages gave point to the new Right's emphasis on national pride and strength, while industrial chaos in Britain enhanced Thatcher's case for trade-union reform.

Yet both had to allay specific fears. Reagan had to dispose of the charge that, if not exactly a warmonger, he would be unsafe as the guardian of the nuclear button. Thatcher had to erase memories of the previous Conservative government, which had been brought down in 1974 by a miners' strike. Would the return of the Tories bring back the three-day working week, when industry had been nearly paralysed by the conflict?

Thatcher oscillated a little uneasily between promises of trade-union reform and reassurances of the moderation of that reform. The issue probably cost her a larger majority. Reagan met his challenge more comfortably, with his relaxed and winning manner in his television debate with Carter which sealed his election. Yet neither Reagan nor Thatcher had entirely dispelled the anxieties before taking office.

They were not then the dominating personalities that they later became. If the British general election of May 1979 had been a personal contest like an American presidential election, Margaret Thatcher would never have become Prime Minister. Throughout the campaign the opinion polls showed her trailing well behind the

Labour Prime Minister, James Callaghan. Her party took her to victory, not the other way round.

Reagan scored ahead of Carter, as he had to do in an American election. But he did not yet have the magical hold upon public affection that he was to enjoy later. Yet there was one section of the electorate for whom, right from the beginning, he clearly had an unusual appeal for a Republican: the blue-collar vote. Gallup calculated that whereas 58 per cent of blue-collar workers had voted for Carter in 1976, only 48 per cent of them did in 1980, compared with 46 per cent for Reagan. But such broad figures tell only part of the story. Like Thatcher, Reagan never had much of a following among non-white voters. Among white blue-collar workers he was actually in the lead.

This was in line with the inroads that Thatcher had made in the traditionally Labour sector of skilled workers and their wives. In both Britain and the United States economic dissatisfaction was a principal factor. But the rugged assertion of the national interest that both leaders managed to convey on other issues, which repelled some voters, must have been significant for a section of the electorate that particularly dislikes seeing its country pushed around in the world.

Thatcher and Reagan came to power sharing not only the same ideology, but many of the same electoral strengths and weaknesses. This must have made it easier for each to empathise with the other. Each began the years in office together with the belief that the other was the most natural ally.

But this was not the first strong partnership between an American president and a British prime minister, nor was it even the one with the most fateful consequences. That distinction must belong to Roosevelt and Churchill. Their partnership was historic because the fate of their countries depended upon it. The outcome of the Second World War was determined by Anglo–American collaboration, which the Roosevelt–Churchill relationship both symbolised and made effective. There is, however, such an aura around the names of Churchill and Roosevelt that it is easy to exaggerate the personal warmth between them. In his memoirs Churchill wrote that: 'My relations with the President gradually became so close that the chief business between our two countries was virtually conducted by these personal interchanges between him and me. In this way our perfect understanding was gained.' That was presenting an essential truth in a somewhat romantic glow.

Churchill was referring here to the remarkable personal correspondence they exchanged throughout the war. Neither before nor since has there ever been anything like this sustained, sometimes daily, interchange over a period of years between two great national leaders under the most severe pressure in time of national crisis. Over a thousand written messages and telegrams went from Churchill and nearly eight hundred from Roosevelt. The written communications between Thatcher and Reagan, for all their friendship and understanding, never approached this. As a contribution to victory, it would be hard to exaggerate the importance of the Roosevelt–Churchill relationship which was reflected in the intensity of their correspondence.

Yet to speak of a 'perfect understanding' was to exercise rather more than an author's licence. Theirs was a limited partnership for the specific purpose of winning the war. It did not extend much beyond that. Their friendship waxed and waned according to how much they needed each other. Their views on domestic policy, even their broader approaches to world affairs, were very different. Had they not been brought together in such circumstances, it is unlikely that they would ever have become close friends.

According to Churchill's doctor, Lord Moran, a sharp if sometimes rather acid observer, who accompanied Churchill on most of his great wartime journeys: 'The cast of Roosevelt's mind – I am thinking of his preoccupation with social problems and the rights of the common man – struck no sparks in Winston's mind. The war was all they had in common.'

Their differences over how the post-war world should be ordered emerged quite early. Within two months of American entry into the war Roosevelt was pressing Churchill somewhat sharply to renounce discriminatory trade practices as part of the price for military aid under the Lend-Lease agreement. This was in effect demanding that Britain should give up the Imperial Preference system of tariff protection among the countries of the British Empire. Looking back with the benefit of nearly half a century's hindsight, the substance of Roosevelt's request does not appear unreasonable. The goal of international free trade is more widely accepted these days, at least in theory. But Churchill objected strongly to such advantage being taken of Britain's financial plight in wartime.

He reacted even more vigorously to Roosevelt's attempt to pressurise him into granting immediate self-government for India. Roosevelt was not deploying a light touch. 'American public opinion cannot understand why,' he wrote bluntly, 'if the British Government is willing to allow the component parts of India to secede from the

30

British Empire after the war, it is not willing to permit them to enjoy what is tantamount to self-government during the war.' But whatever the logic of the issue, this was a decision for the British government, and Churchill was brooking no interference.

The basic disagreement between them on British imperialism could be contained but never resolved. 'We mean to hold our own,' Churchill proclaimed defiantly in a speech in November 1942. 'I have not become the King's First Minister in order to preside over the liquidation of the British Empire.' But for Roosevelt the liquidation of all colonial empires, the British not least among them, was a principal post-war objective.

There were other post-war objectives that they did not hold in common, notably on the treatment of the Soviet Union and on such an apparently mundane issue as the organisation of civil aviation, which touched delicate commercial interests. The United States was pressing for free international competition, which the British feared would lead to American domination. Churchill argued in a long message to Roosevelt on 28 November 1944 that it had been 'agreed between us as a war measure that you should make the transport aircraft . . . and that we should concentrate our efforts upon fighting types. In consequence the United States are in an incomparably better position than we are to fill any needs of air transport that may arise after the war is over, and to build up their civil aircraft industry.' So the British government sought to safeguard its position by various restrictive practices. It was the familiar free-trade versus protection issue in a different guise. But more revealing than any specific differences on policy was the changing nature of the exchanges between the two leaders.

When Roosevelt, with remarkable prescience, began the correspondence, little more than a week after the outbreak of war, he was generous, sympathetic, but not uncalculating. Churchill in the early stages was inevitably in the position of the supplicant. The warm, personal touches were evident even then. With Roosevelt they were probably part of the instinctive equipment of the incomparable politician. With Churchill they were part of the essential strategy for the survival of Britain. Knowing that Roosevelt had a deep love of naval matters, he took care to provide him whenever possible with the details of naval engagements, especially those in which the British had had the better of the battle.

Then, after Pearl Harbor, when the two countries were fighting side by side, Churchill could afford to be more assertive. No longer did he need to try to coax Roosevelt into the war. They were in it

31

together, and comradeship flourished. But by the time of the Tehran conference in November 1943, the balance of power between them was changing once again.

Churchill was eager for Anglo–American discussions in Cairo before going on to see Stalin and his advisers in Tehran. Roosevelt repeatedly and deviously fobbed him off. 'In regard to Cairo,' he remarked jauntily in the message telling Churchill that Stalin (whom they both rather archly referred to as Uncle Joe) would go to Tehran, 'I have held all along, as I know you have, that it would be a terrible mistake if U. J. thought we had ganged up on him on military action.' That was hardly an accurate understanding of Churchill's position, but it was a theme to which Roosevelt was to return not only in Tehran but still more damagingly at Yalta. It indicated not just a passing misunderstanding, but a basic difference between them.

Roosevelt went to Yalta with the overriding purpose of securing the partnership among the great powers for managing the post-war world. The critical question was whether Stalin could be coaxed into a spirit of cooperation when the defence of the Soviet Union was no longer in jeopardy. Roosevelt did not therefore share Churchill's concern to limit Soviet expansion into Eastern Europe. For the larger objective of post-war harmony, the President was prepared to placate the Soviet leader. Whether the balance of military and political power at that stage would have made it possible for Roosevelt and Churchill together to press Stalin more effectively over Eastern Europe remains in dispute. Roosevelt's strategy made it certain that the attempt would not be made.

Before Yalta Churchill tried persistently to secure Roosevelt's agreement first of all to a preliminary meeting in Malta between the two of them, together with their military staffs, to prepare for their discussions with Stalin. When Roosevelt maintained that his travel plans made that impossible, Churchill suggested that the American and British Chiefs of Staff should go on ahead for talks in Malta and then proposed a preparatory meeting of foreign ministers.

Brief, almost token, conversations were finally held at all three levels in response to Churchill's pressure before they flew on to Yalta. But there was not the Anglo–American meeting of minds that he had wanted. Roosevelt was still determined not to give any impression of ganging up against Stalin. So it was hardly surprising that Churchill should feel isolated at Yalta itself.

By then Roosevelt was a sick man, but it was more than his health that had deteriorated. So too had Britain's relative position. It was now clearly the junior partner and this affected the personal relationship. Roosevelt could afford sometimes to be dismissive, even peremptory in tone. Churchill was once again seeking his favour, occasionally resentfully.

None of this diminishes the historic significance of the partnership. But it is a romantic myth that the personal bonds were impervious to the fluctuations in national power. This distinguishes it from the Reagan–Thatcher relationship. Reagan and Thatcher were not tested by challenges of such magnitude, but the personal ties between them were stronger and more consistent.

When Churchill became Prime Minister again in 1951 he got on quite well with Truman for the year that remained of his presidency, though that relationship never approached the Churchill–Roosevelt partnership. Then Churchill's old wartime friend Eisenhower was elected to the White House. Because it revived memories of wartime comradeship there is a natural tendency to attribute too much to the Churchill–Eisenhower relationship in the 1950s. Although the personal friendship remained, Eisenhower felt that by that time the old war leader was beginning to be past it. Nor could dealings ever have been particularly easy when the Secretary of State, Foster Dulles, was on bad terms with the British Foreign Secretary, Anthony Eden.

Eden's premiership will forever be associated with the disastrous souring of Anglo–American relations over the Suez fiasco. Harold Macmillan managed to restore the national relationship with the aid of his own wartime friendship with Eisenhower. The Macmillan–Eisenhower relationship was also notable for the restoration of Anglo–American nuclear cooperation, which had been abruptly terminated at the end of the war. Britain would not have the independent nuclear deterrent that it possesses today without the agreements that were reached then.

But this was not the closest partnership that Macmillan was to enjoy with an American president. There is no reason to question the judgment of his official biographer, Alistair Horne, that when Kennedy succeeded Eisenhower, Macmillan 'was in fact about to enter into a relationship that – although totally different in kind – would be even closer than that which he had had with Ike'. It was the Kennedy–Macmillan relationship that was the closest between president and prime minister in the post-war years before Thatcher and Reagan.

'There isn't any doubt,' according to McGeorge Bundy, Kennedy's National Security Adviser throughout his Presidency, 'that Macmillan was the most important head of government for Kennedy from a number of points of view. He became closer to him personally. That wasn't true in the spring of sixty-one, but it was very clearly true in the summer of sixty-three.'

Ted Sorensen, who was perhaps Kennedy's most intimate adviser, with the exception of the President's brother, Robert Kennedy, confirms that the relationship with Macmillan was important and that it grew progressively stronger. But while Sorensen stresses the friendship – 'don't minimise friendship; that's important and relatively rare among world leaders' – he adds a reservation. Kennedy 'regarded Macmillan as a friend and as a counsellor whose advice he didn't always take'. In the Berlin crisis, the Cuban missile crisis and over the Nuclear Test Ban Treaty, 'in each case Macmillan counselled more of a path of accommodation than Kennedy was willing to pursue'. For all the friendship, Kennedy thought Macmillan was inclined sometimes to be a bit too soft.

Macmillan himself tended on occasion to exaggerate his role. In his memoirs he reflected with pride on his government's part in the Cuban missile crisis: 'We were in on and took full part in (and almost responsibility for) every American move.' That was not true. Lord Harlech, who as Sir David Ormsby-Gore had been the British Ambassador in Washington at the time, discussed Britain's role in the crisis a year before his death in 1985. He had been quite exceptionally close to Kennedy, having been related to him by marriage. Ormsby-Gore's cousin, Lord Hartington, had married Kennedy's late sister, Kathleen, when their father, Joseph Kennedy, had been Ambassador in London.

It was on 16 October 1962 that the President was first informed of the presence of Soviet missiles in Cuba and it was on that day that he set up ExComm, the special group of advisers to discuss the handling of the crisis. Throughout that week they deliberated. Ormsby-Gore was not told anything at that stage, though by Friday 19 October he realised that something strange was happening. A joint Anglo–American meeting of intelligence officers was taking place in Washington that week, and senior members of the CIA kept cancelling their appointments. Ormsby-Gore reported to London on that Friday that the excitement in Washington was probably about missiles in Cuba, but his information did not come from the administration.

The following evening he met Robert Kennedy at a reception and received a pretty clear hint that this supposition was correct, but still no specific confirmation. It was only on the morning of Sunday 21 October that the President called in Ormsby-Gore and gave him a full briefing on the situation, telling him that he would be telephoning Macmillan that evening.

The British were the first of the allies to be informed, and thereafter there were frequent telephone conversations between President and Prime Minister. But this was only after the critical decision had been taken to impose a blockade on Cuba rather than launch an immediate air strike or invasion. So the British were not 'in on' the most important decision at all. They never even knew of the choice until after it had been made.

One should also be cautious about accepting Macmillan's impression of the subsequent telephone talks. Whether it is even accurate to speak of consultation is debatable. Both Bundy and Sorensen believe Kennedy's purpose was to keep Macmillan informed rather than to get advice. 'I make a distinction,' Sorensen cautions, 'between Kennedy's relationship with Ormsby-Gore and Kennedy's relationship with Macmillan. David Ormsby-Gore was a very old friend, a very close confidant. I would say there was consultation with David Ormsby-Gore.'

Bundy also doubts whether the Kennedy–Macmillan discussions led to many specific changes in policy, but adds that such conversations 'do give courage both ways, and that was important to both men and not just to Macmillan'.

So Macmillan acquitted himself over Cuba as a good friend and reliable ally. Kennedy, while making it quite clear that he was keeping the reins of decision in his own hands, treated his allies with courtesy and consideration. Although Britain was the first of the allies to be notified, Kennedy sent the former Secretary of State, Dean Acheson, to inform de Gaulle personally and to brief the Nato Council in Paris. Konrad Adenauer of Germany, John Diefenbaker of Canada and Amintore Fanfani of Italy, were all notified before the President made his first public disclosure of the crisis on television the day after telling Macmillan for the first time.

Macmillan was treated as the first among equals. No other allied leader had regular telephone conversations with Kennedy after the public announcement, but the formalities were observed in each case. The episode has gone down in history as a golden example of allied harmony under pressure. That was partly because the policy worked and it was in everyone's political interest to emphasise how closely they had cooperated.

Two months later the two leaders met in Nassau to resolve another crisis which, though less momentous than Cuba, posed a more direct threat to Anglo–American relations. One of the agreements that

Macmillan had made with Eisenhower was that Britain should be able to purchase the American ballistic missile system, Skybolt. But Kennedy had been persuaded by his military experts to cancel Skybolt without really appreciating the political significance of depriving Britain of what was going to be its independent nuclear deterrent.

It was then that Macmillan's frienship with Kennedy paid dividends. According to Sorensen, Kennedy did not really want to go to Nassau at that time with so much on his agenda in the immediate aftermath of Cuba. But he recognised that Macmillan was in some political trouble and as a friend he agreed to meet him. Once Kennedy grasped the full implications, and that he could be the American president who destroyed the British deterrent by reneging for merely technical reasons on an agreement reached by his predecessor, the matter was settled without too much difficulty.

Britain was enabled to purchase Polaris instead, which today remains the British deterrent. But the outcome was not as self-evident at the time as it might seem with hindsight, and without Macmillan's personal relationship with Kennedy and his persuasive arguments the President might never have been forced to come to terms with the issue.

The international development on which Macmillan's influence with Kennedy was most significant and most beneficial was the Limited Test Ban Treaty of 1963. 'Now Macmillan,' Bundy recollects, 'had an important part in this and I think Kennedy always felt that Macmillan had urged him to have one more try at a time when he himself was not optimistic.' That was a telling and perhaps a decisive contribution. But Sorensen also recalls that at one delicate point in the negotiations Kennedy suspected that Macmillan had weakened the American bargaining position by suggesting to Krushchev that the United States would be prepared to compromise. Whether Kennedy's suspicion was justified or not, the fact that he held it implies that trust between the two men was less than total.

But it was much greater than any British prime minister enjoyed with Kennedy's successor, Lyndon Johnson. For most of Johnson's Presidency Harold Wilson was the British Prime Minister, and it was perhaps revealing that on one occasion Johnson greeted him at the airport in Texas by the name of Pearson, confusing him with the Canadian Prime Minister, Lester Pearson.

If Johnson had a special relationship with another head of government it was probably with Harold Holt of Australia. 'He felt very drawn to Harold Holt,' according to Harry McPherson, Johnson's Special Counsel in the White House. 'One of the main reasons, of course, was that Harold Holt put troops into Vietnam and Harold Holt ran on a ticket of "All the Way with LBJ" in Australia.' There is nothing like unstinted support to convince one politician of the wisdom of another. Wilson did not offer enough of it over Vietnam to satisfy Johnson, who always suspected that the British Prime Minister was about to undercut him with peace initiatives. It was not a high point in Anglo–American relations.

4

IN REAGAN'S WASHINGTON

On 17 November 1980, less than two weeks after Reagan's election, former President Richard Nixon wrote him a memorandum of eleven pages on a subject that must have been very much on the minds of Margaret Thatcher and her colleagues. She had got the president she wanted. But every American administration is like a family business. Its very existence depends on the man at the top, but he cannot do it all himself. Much of the work has to be done by those whom he appoints, and if there were going to be strong Anglo–American cooperation at a practical level Reagan's key appointees would have to play a critical part. Whom would he choose?

The Nixon memorandum was designed to help him answer that question. Its tone suggests that it had a broader purpose as well: to establish Nixon's credentials as a reliable adviser and potential confidant. 'As far as my own personal situation is concerned,' Nixon reassured the new President, 'I do not, as you know, seek any official position. However, I would welcome the opportunity to provide advice in areas where I have special experience to you and to members of your Cabinet and the White House staff where you deem it appropriate.'

This was part of his sustained campaign for political rehabilitation. He was quickly off the mark in offering his thoughts, so it is ironic that there can be no certainty that his memorandum ever reached Reagan's desk.

Certainly the original was still in Edwin Meese's files some years later. But that was not unique. In the early years of the administration everyone believed that the sure road to Reagan's attention was through Meese, his Chief of Staff when he was Governor of California and now Counsellor to the President. So everyone sent their letters to Meese if they were particularly anxious for the President to take their representations seriously. Meese is a notably friendly and personally helpful man, which may have increased the tendency for people to approach him; but the outcome was a bad case of traffic congestion. For some time a letter from King Fahd of Saudi Arabia nestled in Meese's bottom drawer alongside one from the Pope on the opening of full diplomatic relations with the Vatican.

So one cannot be sure what influence, if any, Nixon's memorandum had. He was not attempting to secure reemployment for all those who had served in his administration. Only for the State Department and Defense did he stress the need for experience: 'You cannot afford on-the-job training for your Secretaries of State and Defense.'

He might have been expected therefore to recommend the reinstatement of Henry Kissinger. Whether Kissinger would have been his first choice is impossible to say because Nixon had concluded that Reagan had ruled out such an appointment: 'Based on press reports, I understand that Kissinger is not under consideration for Secretary of State.' So he contented himself with the suggestion that Kissinger should be called upon for advice and for specific negotiating assignments: 'unlike most intellectuals, he is a superb operator and negotiator and is a national asset which should not be wasted.'

Rather than Kissinger, Nixon proposed Alexander Haig for Secretary of State, and endorsed him with ringing testimony:

> He would reassure the Europeans, give pause to the Russians, and in addition, because of over five years as Henry's deputy in the White House and two years at NATO, he has acquired a great deal of experience in dealing with the Chinese, the Japanese, the various factions in the Mideast, the Africans and the Latin Americans. He is intelligent, strong, and generally shares your views on foreign policy. Those who oppose him because they think he is 'soft' are either ignorant or stupid.

This judgment would have been supported in London at the time, though with less surging enthusiasm. Thatcher subsequently found Haig very trying during the Falklands conflict. She did not regret his resignation. Later, when he was to come through London, she was always ready to see him, but purely as a gesture of courtesy. Nevertheless, back in 1980 his appointment did indeed 'reassure the Europeans', not least the British, who remembered his days as Nato commander in Europe. In what was expected to be primarily a West Coast administration, he was one senior figure who would know his way around Europe without difficulty.

It was with Haig's successor as Secretary of State, George Shultz, that Thatcher got on particularly well, which makes Nixon's comments on Schultz's credentials for the post all the more remarkable: 'George Schultz has done a superb job in every government position to which I appointed him. However, I do not believe that he has the depth of understanding of world issues generally and the Soviet Union in particular that is needed for this period.'

Nixon favoured making Shultz either Defense Secretary, where he 'could do an excellent job', or Secretary of the Treasury, where he 'would be superb if you could prevail upon him to take it again'. But Nixon's first choice for the Treasury was William Simon, who had held the post under both Nixon and Ford and had subsequently made a fortune on Wall Street. Thatcher would certainly have preferred the appointment of Simon, with whom she had got on well on her 1975 visit to New York and whose thinking impressed her, to that of Donald Regan, the man Reagan in fact appointed. Regan remains a Thatcher admirer, but they did not enjoy a close rapport during his Treasury days.

It is interesting that Nixon never considered another Thatcher favourite, Caspar Weinberger, for Defense, where he was to contribute so much to Anglo–American relations. Nixon would either have given him responsibility for the Budget again, which he had under Ford, or sent him to the Treasury.

Another name which cropped up frequently in the Nixon memorandum was that of John Connally, the former Governor of Texas (and former Democrat), who had been alongside John Kennedy when he was assassinated. Although Connally had subsequently earned a reputation for a somewhat rough approach to allies as Nixon's Treasury Secretary, he seems to have been rather more favourably regarded in London in the early 1980s than might have been expected. That is probably because at the beginning of a new administration there are so many unfamiliar faces around, and Connally was at least a known quantity to Europeans.

In recent years he has attracted attention for a rather spectacular bankruptcy in 1987 more than for his political activities. He is largely forgotten. But back in 1980 he had been one of Reagan's rivals for the Republican nomination and Nixon suggested him as first choice for Defense, a possible Secretary of State – though 'his appointment might send many in the American–Jewish community up the wall' – Treasury Secretary or Director of OMB (Office of Management and Budget). He was Nixon's man for all offices, but Reagan's appointment for none.

As it was, Thatcher must have felt broadly satisfied with Reagan's principal foreign-policy appointments. Apart from Haig at State and Weinberger at the Pentagon, there were Richard Allen as National Security Adviser and William Casey at the CIA. Allen never established his position effectively within the Administration, but that was an internal matter. He had taken particular care to create links with the Thatcherites before Reagan's election, and both he and Casey were anglophiles.

So Thatcher looked forward to her first visit to Reagan's Washington. Well before his inauguration on 20 January 1981 the British Ambassador had been told by Meese at a party given by Katherine Graham, the proprietor of the *Washington Post*, that Reagan wanted Thatcher to be his first major foreign visitor. So she was. At the end of February, little more than a month after Reagan had settled into the White House, Margaret Thatcher became the first foreign head of government to pay a state visit to Washington in that Administration.

Reagan greeted her in what was described in the *Washington Post* as an unusually warm welcoming ceremony on the south lawn of the White House, and throughout her visit he showed her every consideration. Not only did he host the customary White House dinner, but against all precedent he attended the return dinner at the British Embassy the following evening. Usually on such occasions the President is represented by the Vice-President, but this time Reagan insisted on going himself, a move by no means to the liking of the State Department, who feared that other embassies would in future expect the President to grace their dinners when their head of government was in town. It need not have worried; Reagan refused to allow that occasion to become a precedent, declining other embassy dinners.

At the British Embassy that evening he gave every impression of enjoying himself hugely, staying much later than he normally did at any function. Later, indeed, than Mrs Reagan would have liked, as she was always eager to go home fairly early; and later than some other guests would have wished. Contrary to protocol, some of them even left before the President.

The following morning, surprisingly, the two leaders met once again, this time for tea in the yellow oval room of the mansion in the White House, accompanied by Nancy Reagan and Denis Thatcher. It was a mark of special respect and may have been designed to give the impression of a family friendship. But it was never that. Even though this meeting was largely a social occasion, nearly all the talking was done by the President and Margaret Thatcher. Nancy

Reagan and Denis Thatcher were there as loyal and dutiful spouses, nothing more and nothing less. 'They were just there,' as Deaver put it, 'and they left it to the other two to get on with the business.'

The relationship between Margaret Thatcher and Nancy Reagan never became close, but was never difficult either. It was not close because, as Deaver remarked, 'Nancy isn't a woman's woman anyway. The chemistry was wrong. It was not anything other than that.' It might be added that Thatcher is not a woman's woman, either.

But the relationship never became difficult because that would have been against the interest of both of them. Thatcher must have known that it would have been hard for her to have maintained a warm friendship with the President while being on prickly terms with his wife. She would soon have appreciated what some others came to realise too late: that Mrs Reagan is a woman of decided opinions on the personalities with whom her husband has to deal.

Nancy Reagan, for her part, according to Deaver, 'knew that this was somebody whom her husband liked; whom she could learn something from, maybe; and who would be helpful to him as he dealt with the allies and the rest of the world, to have a partner'. There was, he went on, this bond that Mrs Reagan could clearly see. 'There was no need for her to get involved in that relationship at all. Besides that, she was more interested in the Royals than she was the government part of it.'

That naturally predisposed her towards Britain, while Thatcher was happy to entertain her at Chequers when she did visit England. But Margaret Thatcher seldom spoke of Nancy Reagan in private conversation. For Mrs Reagan what mattered was that Thatcher was supporting the President. One member of the Thatcher entourage once remarked that if Ronald Reagan had married Nancy, rather than Jane Wyman, as his first wife, he would not have become President. Nancy would have made sure that he became a major film star, and he would never have left Hollywood.

That first visit had all the signs of a triumphant success. The public tributes went far beyond the conventional coinage of diplomatic compliments. 'It is widely known that I share many of your ideals and beliefs,' Reagan told Thatcher at the state dinner in the White House. 'My admiration for you was reinforced at today's productive meeting. I believe, however, that our relationship goes beyond cordiality and shared ideals.'

The following evening at the British Embassy he paid her the kind of compliment that every politician likes to receive from another.

'You are a hard act to follow,' he remarked as he rose to reply to her speech.

The admiration was genuine, and it was all the more striking because it did not reflect the conventional wisdom in Washington at that time. In so far as her experience was considered relevant to the United States, it tended to be more as an awful warning than a shining example.

A long article of comparison by Caroline Atkinson in the *Washington Post* at the beginning of February had pointed out:

Today the British economy is in the grip of the worst slump since World War II, with output forecast to fall still further this year. Unemployment, which traditionally has been well below US levels, has surged relentlessly for the past 16 months and is set to continue climbing sharply for the next year ... While there are important differences between the British and American economies, the Reagan administration was nevertheless voted in on a platform very similar to that of the British Conservatives ... Could the Reagan administration, too, preside over economic carnage in the next two years?

Nor was this a lone voice on the Washington scene. David Broder, one of the most distinguished and respected of all American columnists, greeted Thatcher with the bleak comment that 'she has come to Washington at an opportune time. Her presence is a reminder to President Reagan and the nation that good intentions do not always produce desired results.'

A passing comment from Evans and Novak, the right-wing columnists, was perhaps even more telling. They quoted one of Reagan's advisers rejecting an increase in the gas tax: 'It could be the first step towards Thatcherization. Better not to touch it.' The casual use of 'Thatcherization' as a term of opprobrium reveals the general attitude in Washington in those days.

So it should not have been altogether surprising in an administration so attentive to immediate media reactions that Reagan's spokesmen were trying to avoid his being too closely associated with her. James Brady, then the President's press secretary, who remarked privately during that visit that 'it took a crowbar to get them apart', was reported to have offered journalists at one stage a White House staff paper listing the differences between the economic situations in the two countries. 'Don't be afraid that Reagan will go the same way as Thatcher,' was the unspoken message. It provided a sobering contrast to the rhetoric of the formal dinners.

Two members of Reagan's Cabinet spoke more publicly and more bluntly. David Stockman, Reagan's youthful Budget Director and the strongest influence on economic policy in the early days of the administration, told a Congressional committee that under Thatcher 'taxes and government spending have increased, not decreased. The growth of the money supply has been high not low. What has been implemented has failed, as one would have expected.'

The Treasury Secretary, Donald Regan, was even less tactful in his testimony. Also criticising her failure to make deeper tax cuts, he pointed out that 'they raised the Value Added Tax so that the Government is still taking 70 per cent of the income of those in the higher tax brackets'. He added for good measure that she had also done a poor job of controlling the foreign exchange market. (Regan's statement might have been more tactfully timed; just after delivering it, he left for lunch with Thatcher at the British Embassy.)

Of course, Regan's and Stockman's judgments were shared by many people in Britain at that time. Thatcher was going through a bad spell. Her popularity at home had fallen. Her Cabinet was divided. The economy was in difficulties and her Chancellor was about to introduce the most controversial Budget of all her years in office.

Indeed, she would never have been able to go to the United States at all just then if she had not chosen to duck out of a confrontation with Britain's coalminers. This was the Prime Minister who had been elected to stand up to the unions, and here she was being defied by the very union which had brought down the previous Conservative government seven years beforehand. Was this not the moment for Thatcher to prove her determination in deeds not words? But, as she was to say so often in a different context later on, the time was not ripe.

There were some who believed that she had put off the decisive battle with the miners because that would have interfered with her cherished visit to Washington and her ambition to be the new President's closest ally. In fact there was another reason: the government could hope to defeat the miners only if it could face a long strike without industrial production being brought close to a standstill. That meant having large stocks of coal at the power stations, a situation that would not exist for another three years.

So Thatcher gave way to the miners in February 1981, and set off to tell the Americans what a strong government Britain now had. It was understandable that some Americans had their doubts. That Regan and Stockman expressed those doubts as openly as they did was a clear early indication that internal cohesion was not to be the Reagan administration's secret weapon.

These divisions were sometimes a problem for Thatcher, but they also presented an opportunity. It was where the administration was itself divided, where she would have friends in Washington eager for her to use her influence on their side, that she would have the best chance of tilting the balance in her favour on the great international issues.

That Reagan was not deterred by these criticisms of her from associating himself so publicly with her and her policies showed the strength of his personal commitment. It also demonstrated another characteristic which, to some extent, he shared with her: a strange capacity to divorce himself, when it suited him, from the very government he was leading. If he wanted to go along with her in defiance of the advice he was being given, and against what some other members of the administration were saying, then he would do so without agonising, or so much as a backward glance.

Yet, successful as Thatcher's first visit was, there was one great disillusionment. She became aware for the first time of Reagan's intellectual weaknesses. She was dismayed by what seemed his total lack of interest in detail. On the two occasions they had met before, they had both been crusaders without the responsibilities of office. It had been a time for bold hopes and broad objectives. They were humming the same battle tunes, they were marching to the same drummer's beat. But once in power something more is required to cope with the complexities, and she feared that it was not there.

Instead, she found Reagan drawing out from her the practical political experience of putting Thatcherite policies into operation. What problems had she encountered? How had she dealt with them? What had she learnt, and by inference what might he learn from her example? All this was at a political not a substantive level.

At the same time, the President indicated his misgivings that she had not been cutting taxes. Was she really going down that road, as he hoped? 'Well, I am,' she told him, 'but you have to do it in stages, piece by piece. Otherwise you upset the equilibrium.' It was the first indication of their disagreement on the timing of tax cuts and their impact on the budget deficit, but it was hardly the great intellectual engagement she had been expecting on a range of issues. No cut and thrust. No serious debate. She was shocked.

Her response was not to reveal the slightest disappointment to any

American, nor to lose sight of the larger picture. She never forgot, in her occasional private irritation, the prime importance that she attached to the United States. Sometimes she may have been tempted to underestimate Reagan, especially his political skills, but she was well aware of his other attributes. She once remarked to Robert McFarlane, Reagan's National Security Adviser from 1983 to 1985, that the President was unique in his generation in what some call stubbornness and she called the strength of his conviction. He would not bend to opposition as easily as most.

So her rhetoric on this visit was as fulsome as his. This was not mere ritual. 'The message I have brought across the Atlantic,' she announced in that opening ceremony on the White House lawn, 'is that we in Britain stand with you. America's successes will be our successes. Your problems will be our problems, and when you look for friends we will be there.' In saying this she was casting herself in the role she was to play for the next eight years, and indeed would wish to play for as long as she held office.

There are different ways in which an ally can handle its relationship with a superpower. It can be the awkward partner, whose agreement is always liable to be withheld. To be won it has to be wooed. De Gaulle was the supreme example of someone who went so far in that direction that others often wondered if he was still an ally at all. Thatcher played it differently. She was signalling that February morning that she was to be the most reliable friend.

She had her first tangible reward, beyond mere expressions of friendship, before she left Washington. Back in 1979 Nato had agreed to follow what was known as a dual-track policy for intermediate nuclear forces (INF) in Europe. The alliance would prepare to deploy these missiles in five Western European countries (Britain, Germany, Italy, Belgium and the Netherlands) at the same time as pursuing arms-control negotiations on INF with the Soviet Union.

But a debate was now raging within the new administration in Washington as to whether to accept the negotiating part of this policy. Would it not be simpler and more straightforward just to go ahead and deploy, without waiting for the outcome of what might turn out to be prolonged negotiations? That was what the Pentagon wanted. Weinberger, the Defense Secretary, and his influential Assistant Secretary, Richard Perle, argued this line with some vigour.

Perle is believed to have done so with all the more confidence because he had not been convinced by the military case for the programme. He was in favour of deployment because he believed in a strong defence posture. But he had not been persuaded that the missiles were militarily essential. So if their European allies were so foolish as to reject weapons for which they had earlier asked, that would be a pity but not a catastrophe. The State Department, however, was convinced of the necessity to honour both parts of the commitment, to negotiate as well as to deploy, as was Thatcher.

Their view was that this was established Nato policy and that it would be disastrous for the cohesion of the alliance for the new administration to walk away from the commitment, even if it had been undertaken under Carter. It would also have scuppered the chances of European governments being able to proceed with deployment because their public opinion would have been outraged.

It was because of this risk that the dual-track strategy had been adopted in the first place. The case for deploying intermediate-range missiles in Western Europe had first been made in effect by Chancellor Helmut Schmidt in a celebrated speech to the International Institute for Strategic Studies in London late in 1977. He pointed to the build-up of Soviet SS-20s and indicated that Nato needed to have weapons of its own to balance them.

But over the next year, as discussions proceeded within Nato about siting Pershing Two and cruise missiles in Western Europe, the German government and others began to have qualms about the political reaction. So, in order to avoid frightening the voters, the lines of a convoluted Nato compromise were agreed at the economic summit that was held in Guadaloupe in January 1979. Then in December that year the dual-track strategy was formally accepted by Nato. The readiness to negotiate was the price to be paid for deployment. To have unstitched that compromise would probably have made deployment politically impossible.

How widely that was appreciated within the new adminstration in Washington may be doubted. Certainly the argument seems to have been conducted along the simple lines of observing alliance agreements.

Officials in the State Department alerted the British Embassy to the internal debate that was going on. Without ever needing to say so explicitly, they were in effect enlisting Thatcher in the struggle against the Pentagon, knowing how much Reagan would respect her view. It was the first but by no means the last time that one side or another would seek to deploy her in the interagency battle in Washington. Such a tactic obviously suited them. It also suited her, provided it was not overdone, because it maximised her influence on American decisions.

In this instance, neither the British, nor indeed other European governments, seemed to appreciate quite how sharp a dispute was going on in Washington. Otherwise Thatcher would have pressed the question even harder in her conversations with the President. It was not at the top of her priorities. But she did discuss it, he appeared to go along with her and that was enough.

The issue was settled by getting him to endorse the dual-track policy in a public statement after his talks with her. It was Lawrence Eagleburger, then Assistant Secretary of State for European Affairs, and James Rentschler, of the National Security Council staff, who put this undertaking in the statement. Presumably they would not have done so without the approval of their superiors, and certainly they would have found it much harder to get the insertion accepted without Thatcher's advocacy. Whether Reagan himself appreciated the controversial nature of his endorsement may be doubted. But Thatcher had told him that she wanted it, he trusted her judgement, so it was all right by him.

This was the first of a number of decisions which Thatcher managed to swing her way through this powerful combination: Reagan's personal confidence in her and the presence of allies elsewhere in the administration.

As she left Washington to make a speech in New York, Thatcher must have felt that her mission had been accomplished. She was in relaxed mood. After her speech she recalled with pleasure the dancing at the embassy the previous evening – it is one of the few pastimes she really enjoys. 'I wish,' she said, 'we could go dancing again.'

In New York she received a popular reception that contrasted astonishingly with the criticisms of the opinion-formers. When her car was stopped at traffic lights she was cheered on the streets. No doubt this enthusiasm owed much to her being the first woman prime minister in the Western world. But it was none the less a pleasing conclusion to a highly successful visit. Foundations had been laid.

5

ARMS AND THE LEADER

In the early afternoon of 30 March 1981, barely two months after his inauguration, Ronald Reagan nearly joined the ranks of assassinated presidents. As he came out of the Washington Hilton Hotel, where he had been speaking to more than three thousand trade-union representatives, six shots were fired from the crowd. The gunman, a 25-year-old named John Hinckley who had been receiving psychiatric care, seriously wounded both the President and his press secretary, James Brady.

Reagan was immediately pushed into his waiting car by one of his secret-service agents and driven to George Washington Hospital. With some assistance he was able to walk into the hospital where doctors operated to remove a bullet from near his heart. His one-liners as he lay awaiting treatment became famous: 'I hope you're all Republicans,' he told the doctors about to operate on him. 'Honey, I forgot to duck,' he said to his wife, who had rushed to the hospital on hearing the news.

The episode struck a particularly sensitive cord in the American nervous system because of the traumatic memories it evoked. The near-tragedy naturally brought a wave of personal sympathy. But it also did something of greater and more lasting political significance. It aroused admiration for Reagan's courage and a new awareness of his style.

He displayed, as one commentator remarked at the time, grace under pressure. That was the mark of a president more telling than intellectual competence. It was from this time that he established his extraordinary hold on the affections of the American people, which explains so much about his Presidency.

Thatcher immediately sent a strong message of sympathy. She is a much more emotional woman than is generally appreciated, and there is no reason to doubt that this was a spontaneous and genuine expression of her feelings. But, just as the shooting gave Reagan an unpredicted political boost, so did her swift reaction have some political consequences for her.

Thatcher's was one of the first messages to be received in the White House situation room. Allen, the National Security Adviser and a Thatcher ally, immediately sent it to Nancy Reagan and put it at the top of Reagan's folder so that the President would see it as soon as he opened his papers the next day. It was one of those personal gestures which strengthened the bond, and which showed once again the benefit for Thatcher of having well-wishers in the administration.

Reagan was in fact more badly wounded than was made known at the time. This was smoothly covered up by the White House staff. Public attention focused on Haig's performance at a White House press conference on the afternoon of the shooting. Appearing some-what breathlessly in the press room he declared in answer to a question: 'As of now I am in control here, in the White House, pending return of the Vice-President.' The unfortunately excited impression he conveyed as he tried to instil a sense of calm and order dealt a severe blow to his prestige. But the way in which the President's closest White House advisers, especially the Chief of Staff, James Baker, coolly sent out the signals that it was 'business as usual' was no less significant politically. It confirmed their authority within the administration and allowed time for the President to recuperate without too much political anxiety.

The first major event that he attended after his recovery was the Ottawa economic summit in July. That marked not only his return to fitness but also a critical development in his partnership with Thatcher.

There is a tendency among a number of officials to be somewhat dismissive of these annual gatherings of the heads of government of the seven leading industrial nations (the United States, Germany, France, Italy, Canada, Japan and Britain). As a rule not many specific decisions are taken there, the communiqué is largely prepared in advance and some officials readily persuade themselves that they could accomplish whatever of substance might be done there without troubling their leaders.

One former official believes that he could take a class of American seniors in high school, give them the assignment of representing different countries, allow them two weeks to prepare, using only news magazines, and then be able to get a discussion out of them of roughly equal quality to the summits themselves. But then, it is a professional temptation for officials to believe that the business of government would be so much easier if it were not for the people who have been elected to do the job.

Those who do value the summits are the leaders themselves. For them it is a unique opportunity to get together and to test their skill in argument with each other. Certainly Reagan appreciated these meetings. It is striking how much he refers to them in conversation as he looks back on his partnership with Thatcher. In his letter of thanks to her for her message of goodwill after his operation in September 1989, following his fall from a horse, he mentioned that they were one of the aspects of the Presidency that he missed.

The summits were particularly important in solidifying the partnership between the two of them. 'When there were disagreements between the seven,' he reflects, 'we found we were always on the same side.' That was especially so at Ottawa. Time and again on that occasion the two of them were shoulder to shoulder against the rest, and Thatcher won his renewed admiration for the forceful and articulate manner in which she was able to present the positions that they both held. He was new to the occasion, he might not fully have recovered his strength, and spontaneous debate against formidable adversaries never displayed him at his best. At one point he was sitting with a large yellow legal pad in front of him, and on that pad there was nothing but doodles of a series of heads wearing large cowboy hats.

This was also the first summit for President Mitterrand of France, who was then in his strongly socialist phase. The German Chancellor was still the formidable Social Democrat, Helmut Schmidt. The Canadian Prime Minister was Pierre Trudeau, who seems to have been a constant irritant to both Thatcher and Reagan. So it was hardly surprising that Reagan and Thatcher felt a beleaguered duo. The exchanges sometimes became quite heated. Trudeau, the host and conference chairman, told the press at the time, 'I wouldn't think I would go so far as to say it was all sweetness and light.' Indeed not; at one moment Thatcher exploded: 'Pierre, you're acting like a spoilt schoolboy.'

It was a meeting that could have been politically embarrassing for Reagan, and to a lesser extent for Thatcher. His advisers were acutely aware that this was a time when he was still, as one of them put it, 'viewed as a country bumpkin, a cowboy, or a fool or a danger'. A communiqué strongly critical of American policies, which could easily have emerged from that gathering, would have made it appear that

Reagan had commanded little respect at his first international conference. He had not, indeed, carried much weight personally and would have been in difficulties without Thatcher at his side.

The disagreements ranged across both economic and security issues. There was the basic economic question of whether it was more important to fight inflation or unemployment. Thatcher and Reagan believed in principle that the conquest of inflation was the prerequisite of general economic health. Most if not all the others were more worried by the threat of rising unemployment.

The communiqué that emerged at the end was a masterpiece of diplomatic compromise. 'The fight to bring down inflation and reduce unemployment must be our highest priority and these linked problems must be tackled at the same time.' So the leaders chose not to choose between these priorities. Nothing there for Reagan to worry about. Indeed, the following sentence was an implied endorsement of the monetarist argument that the creation of secure jobs required low inflation: 'We must continue to reduce inflation if we are to secure the higher investment and sustainable growth on which the durable recovery of employment depends.'

Most of the other governments, especially the French and Germans, were indignant at the impact on their economies of high American interest rates. Schmidt was reported to have complained that real interest rates in Germany had been forced up higher than at any time since Jesus Christ. Again there was a compromise in the communiqué, and again it inclined to Thatcher–Reagan: 'We see low and stable monetary growth as essential to reducing inflation. Interest rates have to play their part in achieving this and are likely to remain high where fears of inflation remain strong.' Almost as a consolation prize the next sentence offers the reflection that 'we are fully aware that levels and movements of interest rates in one country can make stabilization policies more difficult in other countries'.

There was another economic issue to which Reagan, looking back to that summit, attaches special importance: 'there were things that all of them did not see as a couple of us thought they should, and that was with regard to free trade and fair trade and the elimination of protectionism between countries.' On this point the communiqué registered a distinct success for the couple with a firm commitment to the principle of maintaining liberal trade policies and an open multilateral trading system.

But Reagan had come to power as a foreign-policy hawk as well as an economic hardliner, and in contrast to previous economic summits much time and energy were devoted to relations with the

Soviet bloc. The sharpest point of contention was over trade and the transfer of technology to the East, and especially over the plan to build a pipeline to bring gas from Siberia to Germany and other Western European countries. The United States feared that this would leave Western Europe vulnerable to economic pressure, as well as providing the Soviets with additional high technology. The issue of the pipeline was to prove a source of some friction between Reagan and Thatcher. But that battle lay in the future. At Ottawa her interest was to save him from political embarrassment without endorsing his entire position on East–West trade.

The final communiqué was a masterpiece of circumspection. 'We also reviewed the significance of East–West economic relations for our political and security interests. We recognised that there is a complex balance of political and economic interests and risks in these relations,' it declared with surpassing blandness. 'We concluded that consultations and, where appropriate, coordination are necessary to ensure that, in the field of East–West relations, our economic policies continue to be compatible with our political and security objectives.'

That phraseology was a fine example of the diplomatic art of avoiding a commitment on any side while saving face on all sides. A promise to consult carries no commitment as to the result of those consultations. It was one of a number of occasions in putting together that communiqué when delicate draftsmanship was required.

At the time Reagan publicly gave credit to Thatcher for coming up with compromise language when they were in difficulties. This revealed an unexpected aspect of her skills to those who do not believe that she was born to compromise. She is also credited by some with another unlikely achievement at Ottawa.

One of Reagan's former officials maintains that she took the initiative there in getting the heads of government to use each other's first names, thereby injecting a greater informality and warmth into the proceedings. His story is corroborated by Michael Deaver, who was also there. According to this version, Thatcher even went so far as to address the President as 'Ronald', a name by which he is never known. It is always 'Ron', 'Ronnie' or, to those who knew him years ago, his old childhood nickname of 'Dutch'.

Donald Regan claims in his memoirs that, on the contrary, it was Reagan who suggested the use of first names. But in conversation his version is much the same as the story that Reagan tells. As he sat there, 'the new boy in school', the President heard the others all talking to each other on a first-name basis. So he 'spoke up and said my name is Ron'. Reagan adds the thought that it was probably at

Margaret Thatcher's instigation that the others were using first names.

But another, more experienced, member of that summit points out that first names had always been the practice before either Thatcher or Reagan were there. The episode serves as a small reminder that even those who attend summits are sometimes not altogether sure what is going on.

On military security the Thatcher–Reagan team obtained a firmer statement than might have been expected, especially as previous summits had been reluctant to get involved in this field. But now the heads of government declared that they were seriously concerned about the continued build-up of Soviet military power and endorsed the need for 'a balance of military capabilities'.

This was combined with an equally strong statement in favour of 'working towards balanced and verifiable arms control and disarmament'. Such words were in line with the commitment to the dual-track strategy for INF which Reagan had given during Thatcher's visit to Washington in February. But that commitment, unequivocal though it was, had not put an end to the argument.

After Reagan had announced his acceptance of Nato policy 'to pursue arms control efforts at the same time' as going ahead with the deployment of INF, it might have been thought that the United States would then be ready to set a date for opening negotiations with the Soviet Union. But it was not quite as simple as that.

Right from the beginning of his Presidency Reagan believed that it would be a mistake to negotiate with the Soviets too soon. During the election campaign he had spoken of negotiations that would *reduce* the number of arms, not simply control their expansion. Hence, when negotiations on strategic arms did begin, they were given the title START (Strategic Arms Reduction Talks) instead of the previous SALT (Strategic Arms Limitation Talks). But American military strength had to be built up first.

This was partly Reagan displaying the instincts of the trade-union negotiator he had been – according to one of his aides, a more formative experience than his acting because he had been better at it. His inclination was strengthened by intelligence reports that the Soviet Union did not believe that the Americans would sustain their defence expansion beyond the first year. Reagan wanted to prove them wrong and to have a couple of annual defence increases adopted before negotiating seriously.

Thatcher would have been sympathetic to much of that reasoning. She was still 'The Iron Lady' in her speeches about the Soviet Union. Within days of her election in 1979 she had told *Time* magazine that 'the domination of the world by the Communist system' remained the Russian objective. At the Conservative Party Conference that October she said that the dangers were greater than they had been since 1945. British defence expenditure was also being increased.

But she was more exposed than Reagan to the political pressures in Europe. That was why she had wanted the dual-track strategy to be accepted by the new administration when she visited Washington in February. This second battle, for a date to be named for the beginning of negotiations, was won only after further intense wrangling in Washington, and between the United States and its allies.

It was at the Nuclear Planning Group (NPG) meeting in Bonn on 7 and 8 April 1981 that Nato defence ministers first became aware of the extent of American doubts about the negotiating track. Weinberger and Perle did not renege on the President's commitment, but they made it very clear that the deploying track had total priority.

As Weinberger and the Pentagon were much more influential within the new administration than the State Department under Haig, this gloss on the President's words had to be taken seriously. The communiqué at the end of that meeting reflected the American insistence on deployment by stating that this was the primary aim of TNF (Theatre Nuclear Force) policy. But in quiet discussions at Bonn it was made clear that in the eyes of the allies the two tracks went very much together.

Even that did not resolve the matter finally. But at the ministerial meeting of the Nato Council in Rome on 4 and 5 May 1981 the decisive undertaking was given. The five deploying allies 'welcomed the intention of the United States to begin negotiations with the Soviet Union on TNF arms control within the SALT framework by the end of the year'.

Behind that formal diplomatic language lay a political drama that illustrated the difficulty of dealing with the Reagan administration in its early days. When Haig arrived in Rome he produced a text and said, in effect, to his fellow foreign ministers: here is the paragraph for the communiqué on dual track. When amendments were suggested he responded: 'Gentlemen, I sweated blood on this, night after night over the last week, and this is the best text I have been able to wrench out of my colleagues in the administration. I am bound to tell you I have had the gravest difficulty in getting anything as good as this. If you want me to change it I shall have to go back to Washington, and telephone overnight, and it will be very difficult to get words changed. But I will do my best if that is really your wish.'

It was their wish. So Haig spent quite a bit of that night on the telephone to Washington clearing the revised wording. In demanding this, his Nato colleagues were not indicating their lack of confidence in him personally. On the contrary, whatever difficulties may later have developed with the British government, Haig was regarded then as the best advocate Nato had in Washington. His problem lay within his administration. Almost from the very beginning he was an outsider in his own team, and relations got progressively worse. That inevitably reduced his value to the allies, but the episode does illustrate how they could be used to win battles within the administration in Washington.

They were insistent on this occasion partly because they were not prepared to have the wording of a Nato foreign ministers' communiqué simply presented as a *fait accompli* from Washington, and partly because they were determined to have a firmer commitment to negotiation than appeared in the original text.

This was not a mere technical detail. The reference to beginning negotiations 'within the SALT framework' was an indication that they were to cover strategic arms as well as intermediate weapons. What was at stake was the whole process of arms talks in Reagan's first term, and all that that implied for European–American relations.

The role of Thatcher and the British government in this particular episode was not as a separate, independent player. But the fact that the British, under a leader who was known to be so tough towards the Soviet Union, was at one with the other allies was bound to carry special weight in Washington.

She did not, however, win every battle on arms control. There remained the critical question of what the Nato negotiating position would be once talks were opened. The original Nato dual-track decision of 1979 had not envisaged the elimination of intermediate missiles from Europe, merely their reduction to lower levels than would otherwise have been the case. But the German and Dutch governments in particular were becoming progressively more nervous in the face of mounting popular protest against deployment. So the German Foreign Minister, Hans-Dietrich Genscher, floated the idea with the Americans that the best outcome would be to have no missiles on either side in Europe, East or West. This would become known as the zero option.

The proposal was first discussed more widely at a Nato Nuclear Planning Group (NPG) meeting at Gleneagles in Scotland in October 1981, when it was put forward by the Germans, with backing from the Dutch and others. A reservation was expressed at senior British official level, with the evident support of the major Nato commanders. But there was not at that stage strong British ministerial opposition and Weinberger responded favourably, undertaking to put the idea before the President when he returned to Washington.

The proposition had immediate appeal to the Pentagon. It did not believe that Europe would ever have the stomach to go ahead with deployment. Therefore it would make sense to extract as much as possible from the Soviets in return for the West undertaking not to do what it would be unable to do anyway. At the first National Security Council meeting in Washington to discuss the administration's negotiating position on INF, Haig recalls, Weinberger stated categorically that 'Western Europe is unreliable and will not deploy the Pershings. Therefore, Mr President, you must come forward with a public relations ploy to deflect what is happening.'

The zero option had all the greater attraction to Weinberger and Perle as a public-relations ploy because neither they nor anyone else at that time thought there was the slightest chance of the Soviets accepting. Nobody was anticipating Gorbachev in 1981.

This was a time when the case for some public-relations initiative seemed pressing. Popular protest was mounting in a number of Western European countries. It was fanned by the peace movements, but was not confined to them. Reagan seemed a threatening figure to many Europeans, who found the coincidence of new missiles and the new administration in Washington particularly disturbing. Zero–zero appeared a smart way of countering these anxieties because nobody could then accuse the United States of not going far enough. It would simultaneously put the Soviet Union on the defensive, take the momentum out of the peace movements and reassure moderate, but nervous, members of the general public – or so it was hoped.

But both the State Department and the British government were opposed to the West becoming tied to a zero–zero formula. A pure public-relations ploy did not appeal either to Haig or to Thatcher, for fear that the Soviets might accept at some stage in the future. If that happened it would destroy what to the British and to a number of others was the basic rationale for the missiles.

From the beginning two not entirely compatible arguments had been advanced for deployment. One was to counter the Soviet SS-20s. That purpose would be achieved by a zero–zero agreement. Away would go the SS-20s in return for keeping the American Pershing Two and cruise missiles out of Western Europe. But the other objective was to couple the United States more firmly to the defence of Europe by having American nuclear missiles on the ground there. The Soviets would have to calculate that in any war these missiles would be brought into play, thereby involving the full potential of the American nuclear armoury, before the conventional defences of Europe were overrun. The difficulty was that this second line of reasoning required American missiles to be deployed in Western Europe irrespective of whether the Soviets had any SS-20s.

So the issue finally went to the President with the diplomatic and political forces neatly balanced: the British ranged against the Germans, and the State Department against the Pentagon. He came down in favour of zero–zero. It was the kind of bold, sweeping and engagingly simple proposal that Ronald Reagan liked, and it possessed an additional attraction. He had an innate horror of nuclear weapons: getting rid of one category of them was always likely to appeal to him.

It is often thought that Reagan's ambition for a nuclear-free world was an old man's dream, one that came to him much later in his Presidency. That is not so. It is something he wanted right from the beginning, though his advisers managed in those days to talk him out of moves that they regarded as exceptionally dangerous.

This conviction of his was to prove a source of recurring difficulty with Thatcher. Indeed, she balks at the word 'conviction' in this context. 'I would have said it was an aspiration,' she remarked. 'It cannot be a conviction. It is unrealistic. It was one of the few times, you know, when I think his aspirations left the reality of human nature.'

When she put the case for nuclear deterrence 'he accepted that, when one started to talk to him'. Yet the conversion would be no more than temporary. 'From time to time, he would come out again with his "world without nuclear weapons". It is a world which I cannot foresee existing because there have always been evil people in the world.'

Reagan's decision to go for zero–zero in November 1981 was the first time she suffered from Reagan's idealism. But once he had decided, there was nothing any ally could do about it. They were, after all, his missiles.

6

REAGAN SENDS A SIGNAL

Ever since Franklin Roosevelt's first hundred days of frenetic activity in the White House, incoming presidents, and prime ministers as well for that matter, have appreciated the need to send an early signal to the country. The message that Ronald Reagan delivered in August 1981 reverberated not only throughout the United States but much further afield, not least in Britain.

He responded to an illegal strike by air-traffic controllers by sacking all those who had walked out. The dispute over pay, pensions and the length of the working week had by that time dragged on for nearly five months. After its members had overwhelmingly rejected an interim agreement, and further negotiations had collapsed, the Professional Air Traffic Controllers' Organisation (PATCO) called a national stoppage on 3 August in violation of the law against strikes by federal employees. When the air controllers ignored Reagan's warning to return to their jobs in forty-eight hours, he dismissed the lot.

An emergency programme was instituted for the swift training of new controllers and the better use of existing ones. Controllers from the military service were used as strike-breakers. Air traffic continued. Eleven months later the union, which had been fined severely in the courts and deprived of its right to represent workers, went bankrupt.

'We cannot as citizens pick and choose the laws we will or will not obey,' the President reminded the country. His action had been tough, decisive and effective. It demonstrated how a readiness to take big decisions without agonising can sometimes matter far more than intellectual sophistication.

He impressed the American public: an NBC News poll in mid-August found that 64 per cent of them approved of his handling of the dispute. For the British government it was an inspiration. This was not because British ministers faced precisely the same challenge; circumstances were different in the two countries. But Reagan had demonstrated that it was possible for a government with nerve to take on a union which seeks to exploit its position in a vital industry, and to win.

That was just the kind of message that Thatcher and her colleagues needed to receive. They had come to office pledged to curb the power of the unions. They knew they would have to do so over a period of time or see themselves driven from office, as the last Conservative government had been overthrown by the miners – another union which had exploited its control of a vital industry. But could they win a showdown this time? Reagan's example gave them more encouragement than anything else. If a month beforehand Thatcher had been guiding him in Ottawa, now it was his turn to show her how.

Reagan, of course, had asserted his authority with one stroke. Thatcher was forced to move a step at a time. This gradualist approach was dictated by political factors. The country was nervous after so much industrial strife and the Prime Minister was out of sympathy with her Secretary of State for Employment, James Prior. If each had been able to follow their instincts, she would have alarmed the country by plunging ahead too fast and he might not have moved perceptibly at all. He put the emphasis on establishing a good working relationship with the trade-union leaders. Between them Thatcher and Prior managed to move at just about the right pace to bring about real reform while maintaining public confidence.

The first Thatcherite reform of trade-union law had been passed in August 1980, a full year before Reagan dismissed the air controllers. The second instalment of this legislation came along in 1982. These were the first, cautious beginnings of a lengthy process. The decisive challenge was not to come until the miners' strike of 1984–5. It was the outcome of that dispute which conclusively marked the reduction of trade-union power.

Thatcher and Reagan had felt that they were kindred spirits in the first place because they had the same ideas on the role of the government at home. So it might have been expected that once they were both in office they would be continually trying to draw ideas from the other's experience. Reagan had been eager to hear how Thatcher had fared politically when he saw her in Washington in February 1981. One of the ironies of the President's first year in power, however, was how little the two governments looked to each other for inspiration on the substance of domestic policy. David Stockman, the young and energetic Budget Director, had instituted one study to examine what had been done about the tax structure and taxation rates in Thatcher's Britain. But that was all that the incoming administration evidently had time or inclination for.

There were three reasons for this neglect. Stockman and his colleagues very quickly found their hands more than full trying to cope with the problems that came rushing upon them: there simply was not time for the orderly examination of relevant examples. Second, there was by then the widespread feeling in Washington that Thatcher was messing up her economic policy. Finally, despite all their philosophical agreement, a sharp difference had emerged between Thatcher and Reagan over when to cut taxes. Both agreed on the principle of lower taxation, but they diverged sharply about the right time to do it.

The first Budget introduced in Britain under Thatcher – by her first Chancellor of the Exchequer, Sir Geoffrey Howe, within weeks of her coming to office in 1979 – had sharply reduced the rates of income tax, but had nearly doubled the principal indirect tax, Value Added Tax. The 1980 Budget made no dramatic changes. But then, in March 1981, came a Budget that was bitterly disputed within Thatcher's own Cabinet, was highly controversial throughout Britain and seemed almost sacrilegious to Reaganite supply-siders. Her Chancellor actually increased taxes, and did so in the midst of a recession. For her pains she was savaged by the *Wall Street Journal*, the public voice of supply-side economics in the United States. Hers, it proclaimed, was a Budget of despair: 'Mrs Thatcher seems to have given up on bringing the British government's spending and borrowing under control.'

It is true that she had failed to persuade her Cabinet colleagues to cut public spending as she would have wished. But it was the response to that failure that was revealing. Taxes were raised rather than allow the deficit to go up. This was a Budget that displayed her priorities.

She was characteristically ready to assert them in discussion. In early February 1981, a month before that contentious Budget, Congressman James Jones, the newly elected Chairman of the Budget Committee in the House of Representatives, took his colleagues on a fact-finding mission to London. As Reagan had been talking so much about the Thatcher experiment, Jones thought they should examine the evidence on the spot.

He was apparently less enchanted at the time than his mellow recollections would suggest. Nowadays he is a Thatcher admirer. Then he wrote a somewhat tart article in the *Washington Post*, in which he accused her government of over-promising, of depending too much on monetary targets, of failing to cut spending enough and of allowing unemployment to rise too much. But she gave the committee one piece of advice that lodged firmly in his mind: before you cut your taxes, cut your spending.

It made such an impression on the Congressman that he quoted it in a debate on the United States Budget in the committee back in Washington some months later. But one person who was not prepared to heed this admonition was the President himself. One of the central features of Reagan's election campaign had been his support for the Kemp–Roth Bill, which was to become the largest tax-cutting legislation in American history.

After his election Reagan maintained his backing for the measure, but a debate broke out among his advisers over when it should be implemented. Should tax cuts be delayed until mid- or late summer, as the new Treasury Secretary, Donald Regan, and the Budget Director, David Stockman, preferred? Or should they be put into operation as soon as possible, and backdated to the beginning of the year, as Congressman Jack Kemp, the main inspiration of the legislation, wanted? This was not a trivial, technical detail. It symbolised a fundamental division between two different kinds of conservative. The former group were the more cautious monetarists. The latter were the dash-for-growth supply-siders.

In order to get the Kemp–Roth bill through Congress Reagan was forced to compromise on timing and on the size of reduction in the first year. But instinctively he was in the latter camp. Thatcher was firmly in the former. It was a difference that was never reconciled, though it came to matter less in future years.

Precisely this difference between two kinds of conservative was to separate Thatcher years later from her second Chancellor, Nigel Lawson. Well before his dramatic resignation in October 1989 she had become uncomfortable with his approach. Her reluctance to run any risk with inflation is one of her most basic economic instincts. In retrospect, it is not surprising that it brought her into conflict with Lawson. What is significant is that it did not undermine her relationship with Reagan.

The bill passed by Congress on 4 August 1981 provided for a reduction of 25 per cent in personal income tax over thirty-three months: 5 per cent from October 1981; another 10 per cent from July 1982; and a further 10 per cent from July 1983.

But Reagan also insisted, at the same time, on massive increases in defence expenditure. In theory, these losses in revenue would be more than compensated for by cuts in other spending programmes and the stimulus to economic growth that would come from the tax cuts. That was good supply-side philosophy. So Reagan came to power with a commitment to balance the federal budget by 1984.

It turned out very differently. Various allowances were reinstated in the tax bill on its passage through Congress, so that it gave away more money than originally intended. Nor was Stockman able to secure spending cuts as large as he had hoped.

The consequence was a succession of sharply rising budget deficits, which was a cause of anxiety to Thatcher, and of recurring argument, for some years. Throughout most of 1981, however, despite her warnings about not cutting taxes before cutting spending, she seemed to think that Reagan's progamme was reasonably on course. Presumably she was taking at face value what she was hearing about the spending cuts. Indeed, non-defence spending, apart from the social entitlement programmes, was being reduced quite sharply in real terms.

It was not enough. By November the President was confessing not only that he would be unable to balance the Budget in 1984, but that he hesitated to 'set a date or an amount with regard to budget deficits or when a balanced budget would take place'. When it came to withdrawing from a commitment Reagan did not go in for half-measures.

The difference between them was essentially on fiscal policy, but that had implications for monetary policy as well. As the federal deficit rose, so the Federal Reserve Board under the chairmanship of Paul Volcker – which exercises its responsibility for monetary policy in the United States independently of the federal government – felt it necessary to raise interest rates still further to control inflation. In the autumn of 1981 Donald Regan told Geoffrey Howe that there was no connection between the deficit and interest rates. It was an assurance that was received with marked scepticism on the British side.

Thatcher's advisers accepted that higher American interest rates were inevitable in the cirumstances, but they would have changed the circumstances by cutting the deficit. In any case, they believed that the United States was going too far in the right direction by making monetary policy excessively tight in the teeth of the worst recession since the 1930s. Squeezing economic activity so much had the effect of reducing the flow of revenue to the Treasury and therefore indirectly enlarging the deficit still more.

It was also bound to depress the international economy at a time when it was already in considerable difficulty. Thatcher would never have joined the chorus of criticism against Reagan on this point at the Ottawa summit. But she became progressively more concerned over the international repercussions of American economic policy. There was relief in Britain when the Federal Reserve began to reduce interest rates early in 1982, but that did nothing to assuage Thatcher's anxiety on the basic problem of the deficit itself.

She was the only foreign head of government to visit the United States Treasury in those years and engage its senior members in lively discussion on the merits of their policy.

The Treasury had in fact accepted the tax package only with reluctance, suspecting correctly that the spending cuts would not be so large as predicted and that the deficit would rise. In defending administration policy to her, however, they appeared to be arguing that the United States would be able to grow out of the deficit. So Dr Beryl Sprinkel, then a senior Treasury official and later Chairman of the President's Council of Economic Advisers, who prided himself on being a firm monetarist, found himself to his astonishment being accused by Thatcher of being a Keynesian. This left Sprinkel himself speechless and spluttering, and his colleagues highly amused.

In these discussions Thatcher did not presume to tell the administration how to run its economic policy, tempting though that might have been. Her line was rather that the United States had a responsibility on the deficit which it was failing to meet. Precisely how it should fulfil that obligation was for the United States to decide. Had she been forced to be more specific, she would no doubt have argued that if the deficit could not be reduced enough in any other way it would be better to raise taxes. That was her belief, but she was careful to avoid being accused of interfering in the details of American domestic policy.

Thatcher had come to power not very knowledgable about international affairs, or indeed particularly interested. In this field her ideas were few, strong and simple. Her ambition was not to waste too much time on foreign policy. But the United States never seemed to be foreign in her mind, perhaps because of the language. (Although she has a bit of French, she is not really a linguist.) And because she felt so much at home dealing with Americans she may well have thought that she understood the United States better than she really did. Certainly, on the question of economic policy she did not take full account of how different the American political system is. Why, she used to wonder irritably, did they not just put through a sensible budget package of tax increases and spending reductions?

For Reagan it was never as simple as that. One of the justifications for his pressing ahead with such extravagant tax cuts right away was that, if he did not seize the mood in Congress, he might not get another chance. The separation of powers between the President and Capitol Hill makes it much harder to pursue an orderly range of policies in neat sequence.

Moreover, Reagan had another consideration in mind. The elimination of the deficit would have made it more difficult to restrain the spending instincts of Congress, especially of the House, which then as now was under apparently perpetual Democratic control. An atmosphere of alarm about the budget has its value to a president whose purpose is to reduce the level of governmental activity in economic and social life. So he never shared Thatcher's concern over the deficit.

She came subsequently to have a greater appreciation of Reagan's point, that if you increase taxation, you depress the level of economic activity. At a later stage the British government was much influenced by the American record of cutting taxes, but in 1981 Thatcher was afraid of the United States going the way of the British economy in the 1970s, with balance of payments problems being combined with stagflation. In that case, both American stagnation and inflation would be exported.

So during Reagan's first year in office both Reaganites and Thatcherites looked askance at the economic record of the other. Thatcher was too cautious about cutting taxes, and Reagan was too careless about the deficit. But over the next few years each did better than the other had expected, though neither had by any means an ideal record. Both managed to bring down inflation significantly, with Britain doing so first. The British balance of payments improved sharply, output began to rise again, though unemployment did too, at a record-breaking rate. The United States recovered well from the 1981–2 recession and inflation was contained better than expected – but the deficit went on soaring out of control.

Towards the end of Regan's time at the Treasury, which broadly coincided with Reagan's first term, the financial authorities in other countries were increasingly alarmed by the rising dollar. They wanted active American intervention, which Regan resisted. He did not believe in attempts by governments or central banks to manage exchange rates. Their proper level should be left to the market to decide. That was precisely Thatcher's view as well, and Howe did not press for a policy of managed exchange rates. So, although British Treasury officials were more nervous than ministers about the

American strategy at this stage, there was less disagreement on international economic policy with Britain than there was between Regan's Treasury and most other members of the Group of Five (Japan, Germany, France, Britain and the U.S.A.).

Howe did provoke a protest through the American Embassy in London for a public attack on American economic policy in late 1982. He and Regan were never close friends, but they got on better than Regan did with many other finance ministers. Some of Howe's dealings with Regan aroused amusement as much as irritation.

In February 1983, Howe as Chairman of the IMF Interim Committee managed for the first time to secure the agreement of Saudi Arabia to an increase in the size of the fund. This was vigorously resisted by Regan. Finally, at a dinner for ministers alone at the F Street Club on the corner of 20th Street in Washington, Regan conceded – but only after a phone call to the White House, to secure the President's agreement, in which he explained how hard he was being pressed by the British. This did not deter Regan from asking Howe to accompany him to the White House the following day to see the President so that the new arrangement could be presented as a joint triumph. Howe agreed, but a heavy snowfall prevented the ceremony.

The Regan–Howe relationship must have benefited from the closeness of Sir Alan Walters, Thatcher's personal economic adviser, to a number of American Treasury officials. Dividing his time as he did between Britain and the United States, Walters was well placed to continue in office the transatlantic conservative intellectual dialogue that had been begun in the years of opposition. Oddly enough, however, whereas Walters was in touch with Thatcher personally whenever he wished, there was no sign that the American Treasury officials had a similarly direct line to the President.

Thatcher and Reagan regarded each other as natural allies on one economic issue that deeply concerned both of them: protectionism. When they met they would always talk about trade discrimination. They would both complain about Japanese practices and the European Common Agricultural Policy. She knew that he gave a certain amount of ground to protectionist forces at home. But on the whole, taking into account the strength of those forces during recession, he was regarded as being on the side of the free-traders. She understood his difficulties and appreciated his resistance.

That resistance can never have been easy, but it may not have been quite so difficult as a traditional view of American politics might suggest. The Republicans used to be the party of protection, because they were reflecting the anxieties of the business community.

Nowadays, the pressure for protection in the United States comes more from unions worrying about jobs than from employers worrying about profits. Partly for that reason, and partly as the opposition party in presidential politics, always eager for an issue on which they can attack the White House, it is the Democrats these days who are more the party of protection. So, in ranging himself alongside Thatcher on this question, Reagan was not defying his party as he would have been doing in the past.

A belief in free markets was one of the principles that brought Thatcher and Reagan together in the first place. That principle was applied in some of the earliest actions of the Thatcher government: the removal of exchange controls and of legal restrictions on pay, prices and dividends. It was evident in the United States in the programme of deregulation that had been begun under Carter and was taken further by Reagan. Airline deregulation in 1978 was followed, for example, by trucking and rail deregulation in 1980, and by bus deregulation in 1982.

On both sides of the Atlantic there was the development of enterprise zones, areas that would enjoy tax concessions and freedom from the normal planning controls. This was a good example of how ideas did travel across the Atlantic between Reaganites and Thatcherites. Sir Geoffrey Howe put forward the concept in a speech in 1978, and introduced them in his 1980 Budget. The proposal was taken up in a pamphlet by Stuart Butler of the Heritage Foundation in Washington in 1979, and adopted by Congressman Jack Kemp.

Reagan was then persuaded to commit himself to it in a major speech in the South Bronx before his election. It became an important part of his campaign programme, although as President he never managed to get the legislation passed by Congress. The idea was, however, taken up by a number of state governments. Nobody would suggest that it has become a major item of economic or social policy on either side of the Atlantic, but its history shows how in an undramatic way the lines of economic communication were open.

Later on, the programme of privatisation would become one of the principal achievements of Thatcherism. It started slowly, but even in the early years both governments were in their different ways trying to reduce the role of the state in economic life. In that sense they retained the same aspirations. They had not forgotten their basic philosophy, even when they differed on specific policies.

7

NATO IN DISARRAY

In the autumn of 1981 Margaret Thatcher found herself facing the same kind of dilemma that had brought her predecessor, Harold Macmillan, rushing to Nassau nineteen years before. Once again the Americans were changing their own nuclear weapons programme, and once again this would have serious implications for Britain's independent deterrent.

In 1962 Kennedy had decided to scrap Skybolt, which Eisenhower had previously agreed to sell the United Kingdom as the new British deterrent. At Nassau, Kennedy and Macmillan had agreed to replace Skybolt with Polaris. But by the time Thatcher came to power the British government was looking ahead to the mid-1990s when Polaris was expected to become obsolete. So in July 1980 Thatcher had exchanged letters with President Carter agreeing to buy Trident C-4 missiles from the United States on generous terms. The British government heaved a sigh of relief that it would be able to stay in the nuclear game for another generation. But then Reagan decided, within a few months of taking office, to develop a new, larger, more accurate, but more expensive Trident missile, the D-5, and to phase out the C-4.

This decision could not have come at a worse time for Thatcher. No British government has believed more passionately in keeping an independent nuclear deterrent for the United Kingdom. To have given it up would have gone against her deepest convictions. It would also have been damaging politically. She would have been exposed to the taunt that she had been let down by her closest ally. Even worse, her policies would then have been made to look unrealistic, the dreams of a woman clinging to a bygone age.

She had to keep the deterrent, but she could not afford to pay too much for it. As all too many of her hosts in Washington had pointed out in February 1981 the British economy was performing less than brilliantly. Public spending was proving a stubborn problem, preventing her from cutting taxes as she would have wished. In September she switched her Secretary of State for Defence, replacing Francis Pym with John Nott, in the hope of curtailing the large section of the budget spent on defence. So this was not the moment to commit large additional sums for a change of missiles.

What was Britain to do in these circumstances? It could have insisted on the existing agreement and stuck with the C-4. But that would have meant being saddled with a missile that would soon become outdated and for which it would become progressively more difficult to get spare parts. It would be more logical to switch to D-5 with the Americans, but would that be too expensive? The D-5 threatened to be much more costly for Britain largely because it requires larger submarines, but also because the dollar had been rising against the pound since the 1980 agreement was made.

This was an instance where Reagan's friendship did indeed pay off for Thatcher. The atmosphere of the discussions between the American and British teams was very different from the hard bargaining that characterises most international deals. That had been true of the 1980 negotiations as well. But a renegotiation, with the extra expense that the British faced, could have presented special difficulties. Instead, one of the American participants recalls: 'I can just see us sitting there in the White House situation room, Coca-Colas all over the place, people bringing in jelly doughnuts and it just being perfectly warm.'

There was a special reason for that. The American team – Robert McFarlane, then Deputy National Security Adviser, Richard Perle and Richard Burt, then Assistant Secretary of State for European Affairs – knew that the President expected them to reach an amicable settlement. When they did so he sent personal letters of thanks to his negotiators, which was by no means his customary practice on such occasions.

This was one of the early examples of the importance for Thatcher of the signals that Reagan sent down within his administration. His negotiators felt sure, as Perle recalls, that if the discussions ran into difficulties, and there was an appeal to the President, he would take the British side. To have pushed the British too hard would not have been the way to win points in Washington on this occasion.

Nor was this an isolated episode in this respect. Perle, who was regarded as the American hard man in any negotiation, believes that in all dealings with the British during the Reagan–Thatcher years there was an incentive for the Americans to settle at a lower level. If the matter reached the President he was likely to yield to her preferences. It is a refrain that is heard time and again in Washington as officials look back on that period.

Not that the American negotiators over Trident *wanted* to be hard on the British. That was important because an unsympathetic bureaucracy, even when under instructions to be sympathetic, still has a considerable capacity to cause delay without actually being disloyal. Delay might have been nearly as bad for Thatcher as disagreement in this instance, because she needed to have the matter sealed, settled and out of the way well before the next general election in June 1983.

Much of the negotiation was concerned with financial detail, so that Britain would not find it too expensive to continue with its own deterrent. The Americans were happy to extend the arrangement which had previously been made for C-4, whereby Britain's contribution towards research and development would be offset by the purchase of the British Rapier air-defence system, to be manned by British forces, for the protection of American bases in Britain. This turned out to have a double advantage for Britain. The Rapiers proved so satisfactory that the Americans bought more of them for the protection of their Turkish bases.

But the American negotiators did demand something in return. They wanted an assurance from the British that the money saved on Trident, through American generosity over research and development, would still be spent in the defence sector. They were determined not to make an unexpected and unintended donation to British social welfare or to the British road-building programme. Nor were they going to be satisfied with a general assurance of British good intentions. They were seeking a more specific commitment than that.

American defence planners had become worried by the extent to which the Secretary of State for Defence, John Nott, planned to run down the Royal Navy as part of his 1981 defence review. So they hit upon the idea of correcting at least part of that damage as part of the Trident deal. The British would be required, as evidence of good intent, to keep two amphibious ships in service longer than previously planned. The 15-year-old *Intrepid* and the 17-year-old *Fearless* were to have been phased out in 1982 and 1984 respectively, according to the government's defence review of 1981. The American proposal was that the British should reconsider that plan in return for the Americans being helpful over the research and development charges.

The British negotiators did not leap at the suggestion. How could they? It did not accord with the Nott strategy of focusing the British defence effort in the North Atlantic area, and officials must not appear too eager to modify the policies of their ministers. Nor could they be sure of winning the battle that would have to be fought in Whitehall before they could agree to keep the ships in service. Looking back on the episode, McFarlane, the chief American negotiator, believes that 'they resisted out of a realistic concern over whether they could really turn the tide back home and come up with the money'. He had no sense of pressing them to do something that they did not really want to do. On the contrary, 'these were good men and true, rather like-minded about the nature of the threat' and he felt that his pressure was helping them to secure the approval that they wanted from the British Treasury.

Had they refused to accept the American terms, they would almost certainly have been able to secure an agreement without this concession. But not so quickly, and they could not afford to delay for political reasons. Nor, probably, did they have any desire to do so. So they gave the assurance, and agreement was reached relatively quickly without any need for political intervention. Both sets of negotiators – the Americans as well as the British – knew that both Reagan and Thatcher would have been displeased if that had been necessary.

Ironically, both *Intrepid* and *Fearless* were to play a critical role in the Falklands War only a few months later. 'Without these ships, an armed landing on the Falklands would have been literally unthinkable,' according to Max Hastings and Simon Jenkins in their authoritative study *The Battle for the Falklands*. When Nott told the House of Commons in March 1982 that the terms for D-5 were even more advantageous for Britain than those for C-4 he was more correct than he can have realised. On 11 March Thatcher once again exchanged letters with a president of the United States, giving the British deterrent another lease of life. This time she must have felt doubly grateful because Reagan had not allowed grave disagreement on another issue to get in the way.

That disagreement was not only with Britain. It presented the most serious threat to the harmony of the whole Nato alliance during Reagan's first term. At issue was the pipeline that was to be built to bring natural gas from Siberia to West Germany, a project on which Reagan had expressed misgivings at the Ottawa summit. At the end of 1981 a difference of opinion became a crisis.

Throughout the year Nato anxiety had focused upon Poland as Solidarity gained momentum through a series of strikes. Memories of Hungary in 1956 and Czechoslovakia in 1968 inevitably arose. For how long would the Soviet Union stay its hand this time? The United States and other Western governments sounded diplomatic warnings and the alliance began a major process of consultation.

All Nato governments had very much in mind at that time their failure to keep in step after the Soviet invasion of Afghanistan in December 1979. The Carter administration in the United States had wanted the alliance to impose a joint programme of sanctions as swiftly as possible. In American eyes the Soviet action had turned East–West *détente* into a pretence and a delusion. But for many Western European governments *détente* remained the first priority, and one which ought not to be sacrificed for the sake of causes outside Europe. It was a basic difference of perspective which not surprisingly brought a disunited response.

The whole episode was handled disastrously by Nato. The sanctions ultimately imposed were disjointed and hardly intimidating. Although the Soviets were indeed embarrassed by their Afghanistan venture, this was more because of the force of international opinion and their inability to control the country than because of the resolve of Nato governments. The allies were determined, as the Polish drama developed, that they must not be caught in disarray again. So they planned assiduously for every eventuality except what actually occurred.

The fear had been of Soviet invasion. How was that to be deterred or, failing that, punished? Instead, on 13 December, the Polish Communist government itself imposed martial law. It was at this point that the Polish and pipeline issues intersected.

Up to then the Reagan administration had been unhappy about the pipeline, and it had tried to persuade its allies to give up the project, but it had not taken action to try to stop it. The West German government had resisted pressure to call off the deal, and Chancellor Helmut Schmidt had endorsed it as recently as late November at a meeting with Brezhnev in Bonn. The Americans did not believe the assurances they had been given – that the supplies from Siberia would never exceed 25 per cent of the Federal Republic's natural gas and 5 per cent of its total energy – but they had not felt that they could do anything about it.

After the imposition of martial law in Poland, however, the United States decided that it must retaliate. The difficulty was that the unacceptable action had been taken by the Polish authorities, not by the Soviet Union as expected, and the allies had not prepared any collective response to that. So for the first month Nato, having worked carefully to present a united front, was once again hopelessly divided. The Europeans wanted to concentrate on the Polish government and the United States believed that the Soviets were the real culprits.

At the end of December, before that difference could be resolved or at least papered over (which it was in January), Reagan announced a range of sanctions against the Soviet Union. The unexpected twist was that the last item on the list was a ban on licences for the sale of gas and oil equipment, including pipe-layers, to the Soviet Union. This was clearly an ingenious manoeuvre to take advantage of the Polish crisis in order to prevent the construction of the pipeline. Rather than acting in concert with the allies, the United States was trying to block a development on which they were set.

The principal architect of the pipeline sanctions was Richard Perle, who obtained the full backing of Weinberger. It was a characteristic Perle move, an example of swift lateral thinking that took his adversaries totally by surprise. For many people in Europe – and quite a number in the United States – Perle became a demon figure in the Reagan administration. Denis Healey, Labour's Shadow Foreign Secretary, called him 'The Prince of Darkness'. Perle was credited with blocking all serious moves towards disarmament for the first two-thirds of Reagan's term. Negotiations might proceed, but Perle would always be there in the end, so it was alleged, to block any threat of agreement. Heavily built, formidable in argument, to some he appeared downright menacing.

In fact, Perle was an anglophile, a great admirer of Thatcher and a man who won many friends among British officials for his charm, his intellectual powers and the sheer challenge of doing business with him. Those who negotiated with him found him straight: once he made a deal he stuck to it. But he was tough with friends as well as with foes, always played to win and sometimes had very much his own idea of what constituted victory.

On the pipeline issue, the victory he sought seemed to the British government positively perverse. Thatcher was not opposed to introducing some sanctions in protest against Polish martial law. In early January the Nato foreign ministers managed to compose their differences as to whether the Polish government or the Soviet Union should be the target. They recognised the importance of economic measures against both, while not actually promising any further action, which was a mark of European caution. The following month, though, Britain did impose some diplomatic and economic restrictions. The British government played its part in securing further economic sanctions later in the month by the European Community against the Soviet Union. But all these measures were relatively modest, and above all they did not damage Western interests in the attempt to punish the Soviet and Polish governments.

Thatcher shared some of the American unease about the pipeline itself, in particular the worry that it might make parts of Western Europe too dependent on Soviet energy. But she did not share American indignation, and she was convinced that the Germans and other Western European countries were determined to go ahead anyway. On the merits of the pipeline project she rather distanced herself from the argument. Where she was fully engaged was on the question of how far the American government should be allowed to apply pressure in order to achieve its aims.

The initial action taken by the United States at the end of December 1981 was directed only against American companies. But overhanging the ensuing debate throughout the first half of 1982 was the threat of sanctions against foreign companies which were not prepared to follow American instructions. It was the assertion of extra-territorial authority, to which the United States did indeed resort six months later, that outraged Thatcher.

It has sometimes been suggested that Thatcher was so eager to nourish the special relationship with the United States that she became Reagan's obedient servant, that she compromised British independence by toadying to the larger and more powerful partner. That was not an impression she created on anybody during the pipeline crisis. She was formidable in her fury.

What was the point, she wanted to know, of damaging Western European economies as a gesture of protest against the Soviet and Polish governments? Was the United States seriously considering calling in the Polish debts and putting the country into default? Had it considered the effects on the German and ultimately on the whole Western banking system? If sacrifices had to be made by the West to demonstrate its outrage, why was there no mention of restoring the embargo on wheat sales to the Soviet Union?

This last was a particularly sore point with European governments. The embargo had been imposed by Carter after the Soviet invasion of Afghanistan. But it bore heavily upon the grain farmers of the American Midwest, so in the 1980 election campaign Reagan promised to drop it. After his election it was a commitment which the new President acted upon with what many regarded as unseemly haste and with the minimum of consultation with the allies. American politics ruled.

So the argument raged within the alliance in the early months of

1982. Diplomatic efforts by the United States to persuade European governments to take stronger measures against the Soviet Union were unsuccessful, and the Reagan administration was itself divided over how much pressure to apply to the allies. In his memoirs Haig makes clear his general sympathy with Thatcher's position and his acceptance that the Europeans were not going to be deterred from building the pipeline. But his influence within the administration, which had never been high, was now in sharp decline.

In the minds of his more aggressive colleagues there was a direct choice. Either the Europeans would restrict credits to the Soviet Union or further action would have to be taken against the pipeline. But before that issue could be resolved there came a tempest in the South Atlantic that would be momentous for Thatcher and for her friendship with Reagan.

8

THE FALKLANDS

In the early hours of Friday 2 April 1982, Argentine forces invaded the Falkland Islands in the South Atlantic. After putting up a gallant but hopeless resistance for two hours the handful of British marines surrendered and Argentina had achieved its cherished ambition of controlling the Malvinas, as the Argentines describe the islands.

It is an article of faith, held with passionate fervour in Argentina, that the Malvinas are rightfully theirs. The claim is based on Argentina's position as the inheritor of Spain's colonial possessions. Although an English ship had first discovered the islands in 1690, Spanish control of them had been confirmed at the Treaty of Utrecht in 1713.

There had traditionally been no similarly emotional British attachment to the Falklands. Most British people did not care about the islands until they lost them. Yet the Falklands have been in the possession of Britain since they were taken in 1833 after a period of anarchy on the islands; and the islanders themselves are of British stock with a strong determination to remain under the jurisdiction of the United Kingdom. It was a dispute that had gone on for well over a century and attempts in the years before the invasion to find a diplomatic solution had been ineffectual.

When the military junta, under General Leopoldo Galtieri, decided to settle the matter by force they were seizing the one issue on which a brutal and repressive regime could hope to unite the Argentine people. They cannot have anticipated the sudden explosion of British feeling. So strong was the British resolve to recapture the islands that the Anglo–American relationship was presented with its most severe test since the Suez venture of 1956. Then the British Prime Minister, Anthony Eden, had presumed that President Eisenhower would at least acquiesce as Britain and France colluded with Israel in a bid to retake the Suez Canal after it had been seized by Nasser. Eden presumed in vain. Eisenhower denounced the action. American economic pressure was brought to bear. Within months Eden's health had broken and he was out of office. Only long sad years of retirement lay ahead for him.

Now, a quarter of a century later, another British prime minister was presuming on rather more than acquiescence from another American president as she prepared to respond to the Argentine invasion. Margaret Thatcher did not consult Ronald Reagan before deciding to send a task force to recapture the islands eight thousand miles away in the South Atlantic. She would need his practical help, but she was counting on their friendship.

Had the task force failed, Thatcher would have been out of office. Had Britain been forced by American pressure to give up the attempt, the blow to Anglo–American relations would have been much more severe than Suez. Then the British public, Parliament and even the Cabinet were bitterly divided. Now British territory had been invaded. British pride was mobilised.

Never was the personal relationship between a president of the United States and a prime minister of Great Britain put to a sharper test. Roosevelt did not need to be alerted to the threat of Hitler in 1940. He formed his friendship with Churchill, but he did not cooperate with Britain because of that friendship. It was rather the other way round. Before the outbreak of war he had met Churchill only once, many years before.

But now Washington did not immediately see any threat to anyone in the seizure of the Falklands. The islands were so small and so far away. Thatcher simply had to trust that Reagan would not let her down.

Neither Britain nor the United States was prepared for the Argentine invasion. Britain was unprepared militarily, the United States diplomatically. There was more justification for the Americans. They could hardly have been expected to make contingency plans for the fate of a group of islands that a great many people even in Britain had some difficulty in finding on the map when the crisis broke.

For some days most Americans in and out of government could not take the matter seriously. It seemed more suited to providing the libretto of a light opera than an international incident of any consequence. So perhaps it was not so surprising that, when the American Ambassador to the United Kingdom telephoned the State Department to ask if he should return to his post from his holiday in Bal Harbor, Florida, he was told not to bother.

John Louis, like all American ambassadors to Britain, was a political appointee. Although personally liked, he had no diplomatic experience and was generally regarded as one of the weakest holders of the office within memory. A member of the Johnson Wax family – he was the great-grandson of the company's founder – he came from Illinois and was the heir to a considerable fortune. The manner of his appointment did not suggest that Reagan was attaching much importance to the post. During the transition Reagan spent a weekend at the home of Walter Annenberg, the former Ambassador to London, who introduced the President-elect to Louis saying that he would be a good man for Annenberg's old post. Reagan agreed apparently without a second thought.

Louis' deputy, the white-haired Edward Streator, was a much respected figure on the London diplomatic and political scene. It was no disadvantage to either country that he remained in charge of the embassy at that time. But the incident reflected the initially casual response of official Washington to the crisis.

The response in London was anything but casual. There was public outrage and humiliation. Somehow the seizure of these remote islands seemed the final mark of British decline. It implied a disdain for British power, an assumption of British feebleness. An inability to protect its own people from outrage, no matter how small the number involved, is a blow to a nation's psyche, as Americans had discovered for themselves when their diplomats were taken hostage in Tehran.

In an emergency sitting of the House of Commons on the Saturday morning the atmosphere was emotional and explosive, even by the standards of that less than genteel body. It needed the resignation of the Foreign Secretary, Lord Carrington, to make Parliament and the country feel that the government had paid the price for being caught napping. Whether Carrington was indeed the culpable minister was by no means clear, but his resignation had the required effect in Washington as well. More than any other single event, his dramatic departure brought home to American public opinion that in British eyes this was no trifling affair. National pride was at stake and the government was in the gravest jeopardy.

Thatcher had first asked Reagan to use his influence to persuade the Argentine leader, Galtieri, to call off the invasion the day before it was launched. On that Thursday Reagan had spent much of the day having a medical check-up, so it was not until the evening that he was able to get through to Galtieri. When he did so he spent nearly an hour trying to dissuade the Argentine leader.

But it was hopeless. Galtieri gave the White House the impression of being drunk. It was too late to stop the attack, and probably whatever the President had said at any time would not have prevented it. The Argentines believed that he was simply going through the motions for the sake of his British ally. When it came to the point, so they thought, he would never do anything about an invasion.

When Haig asked the British Ambassador, Sir Nicholas Henderson, what in those circumstances the British wanted the Americans to do, he was told: 'Come on out on our side and stop supplying the Argentines immediately.' Haig was able to respond that the sale of arms to Argentina was already forbidden by Congress according to the rule linking arms sales to human rights violations. The American response was, however, more subtle and more confusing than the British would have wished. Part of the confusion was deliberate because the United States did not want the Argentines in particular and the Latin Americans in general to know how much assistance was being given to the British. But part of it came about because the administration was itself bitterly divided and because, from beginning to end of the dispute, there was a public and a private American policy. They never coincided, but both changed. So what began as the public policy became the private, and vice versa.

On the eve of the invasion the British Ambassador was giving a dinner party in honour of his birthday. When Vice-President George Bush arrived, he announced that he might have to leave early because the President wanted him to fly down to Buenos Aires to step up the pressure on Galtieri. This was the idea of William Clark, the National Security Adviser, a tall, relaxed Californian, who had much earlier been Reagan's Chief of Staff during the President's days as Governor of California. Judge Clark had been Haig's first deputy as Secretary of State, but by this time he was certainly not a Haig admirer.

The suggestion of using the Vice-President on this mission must have been designed to keep Haig out of the action. Haig and Bush were not on good terms, and right at the beginning of Reagan's Presidency there had been a dispute over Bush's being placed in charge of crisis management. This time Haig was determined that he must conduct the diplomacy.

When Henderson returned to his dinner table, after being called away to the telephone, he was heard to tell Bush: 'Now you can stay for some birthday cake!' Galtieri had rejected the suggestion of a visit from the Vice-President in his conversation with Reagan.

This did not immediately quash all thought of sending Bush to Argentina, but Haig subsequently telephoned the President and made clear his wish to undertake a mediating mission himself. This would be more ambitious than the task envisaged for Bush. Haig would not simply try to bring Galtieri to his senses. It would be a dramatic, Kissinger-style exercise in shuttle diplomacy designed to bring both Argentina and Britain to a compromise as he flew to and fro between London and Buenos Aires.

The logic of the operation was that bloodshed had to be avoided without allowing Argentina simply to keep the rewards of aggression. Some diplomatic settlement had to be found if at all possible. Mediating would also relieve the United States of the painful task of having to choose sides between its traditional ally and an important country in Latin America, at a time when Washington was becoming increasingly sensitive about the southern hemisphere.

Reagan gave his consent, but not without misgivings. He was never convinced that there was really such a role for the United States to play. Moreover, Haig by that time had lost the confidence of the White House officials, and some of their attitude must have rubbed off on the President himself. The endless internecine warfare between Haig and the White House staff in general, and James Baker in particular, had undermined Haig's authority and weakened his hold on office. The mistrust was deep on both sides, and in the White House there was the fear that Haig was desperately seeking a spectacular diplomatic success for himself as a means of reestablishing his political position. He gave the impression of wanting total authority to conduct the negotiations as he thought best.

This the President would not concede. While authorising Haig to go ahead with his attempt to mediate, Reagan indicated that the normal channels of decision must not be bypassed. This meant that the guidelines for his operation would have to be approved. How far this restricted Haig in practice is doubtful. He kept in regular telephone communication with Reagan and his guidelines were debated with some frequency in the National Security Planning Group (NSPG). But there is no evidence that he was prevented from taking any negotiating initiative that he wanted to try.

There was immediate anxiety on the British side as to what the Haig mission implied for them. On the very day of the invasion the British Cabinet had decided to send a task force to the South Atlantic. The atmosphere of shock in London made such action politically imperative, even if not all ministers at that stage acknowledged the likelihood of military conflict. But Britain had clearly signalled that it was not prepared tamely to accept the seizure of the islands as a *fait accompli*.

How then could the United States both mediate in the dispute and support its closest ally, whose territory had been violated? Was mediation not in fact simply a device to avoid having to take sides? The British government's reservations were conveyed to Washington, and it was not only among the British that Haig's initiative was criticised. In the week after the invasion two members of the Reagan Cabinet with responsibility for domestic policy expressed their misgivings in private conversation. Weinberger, whose responsibility for defence was more directly relevant, is also known never to have been in favour of mediation.

Haig always intended, if necessary, to come out in favour of the British. That is not just what he says with the benefit of hindsight. It is what he told a number of people privately at the time. But he hoped it would not be necessary. British anxieties were not allayed by his decision to go to London before Buenos Aires. That looked like an attempt to screw what concessions he could out of the British to place before the Argentines as the basis for a deal.

At the beginning of the crisis the administration, including the White House, seemed to be equivocal. Its statements were weasel-worded. There was more disappointment in official circles in London than was ever allowed to surface. It was compounded by American conduct at the United Nations.

The United States Ambassador to the United Nations, Jeane Kirkpatrick, had aroused British fury by attending a dinner in her honour at the Argentine Embassy in Washington on the evening of the invasion. She did not have a warm relationship with the British Ambassador to the UN, Sir Anthony Parsons, and her unpopularity in British eyes was to increase as the conflict progressed.

Although she was widely suspected of being anti-British, that is not in fact the case. She came to government from academic life with a fixed belief that the best diplomacy pursues the national interest, not some general international sentiment. She also came from the Democratic Party, becoming a Republican only in April 1985, and has the certainties of a political convert. Her tall, assured figure and forthright manner reflected her style. She knew her mind, would express it forcibly and had a distaste for bureaucratic compromise. Realpolitik was her guiding star, and realpolitik guided her towards establishing a closer relationship with Latin America in general and Argentina in particular. The United States had to pay more attention to a troubled area on its own doorstep. 'I do wish you people would look more at the map,' she remarked in justification to me during the crisis.

She watched the dispute unfold with mounting distress and irritation. Her preference throughout would have been to keep the United States out of it and to preserve the friendship which she had struggled hard to develop with Argentina. This did not make her anti-British, but it did make her exceedingly inconvenient to Britain.

On the day before the invasion Parsons, knowing that there was an imminent threat of Argentine action, called an emergency meeting of the Security Council. Kirkpatrick expressed her displeasure with characteristic vigour and refused to attend. At first the American seat was left empty. Then a fairly junior member of the delegation appeared with instructions neither to help nor to hinder Britain. That was the American role as Parsons proceeded to accomplish what is generally considered a diplomatic *tour de force*.

On Saturday 3 April, the day after the invasion, Parsons put before the Security Council Resolution 502, which demanded an immediate withdrawal of Argentine forces from the islands and instructed both governments to seek a diplomatic solution and 'to respect fully the purposes and principles of the charter of the United Nations'. This last phrase was designed to allow Britain to justify sending a task force to the South Atlantic under the terms of Article 51, which allows self-defence in response to armed attack.

To get this passed as a binding resolution needed two-thirds of the votes in the Security Council, which meant obtaining the support of a number of non-aligned nations. The way in which Parsons mobilised that majority, by a herculean exercise in lobbying and persuasion, has passed into British diplomatic folklore. Of the ten votes required on the Council, Parsons could count on five – France, Ireland, Japan, the United States and Britain. The United States was bound to vote for such a resolution, otherwise it would have been openly condoning outright aggression, but it did nothing to assist its passage.

As the deadline approached Parsons had managed to secure another four – those of Togo, Zaire, Uganda and Guyana. The outstanding one was Jordan. In this case Parsons's options were narrowed because the Jordanian delegate at the United Nations had been instructed by his government not to support Britain. So Parsons telephoned Thatcher and persuaded her to appeal direct to King Hussein. The approach worked, Jordan's vote was secured and Parsons had his majority.

On the Monday and Tuesday, 5 and 6 April, the first parts of the British task force sailed from Portsmouth and Southampton, with crowds cheering, bands playing and families weeping. For the rest of that month, as the force proceeded on the long journey to the South Atlantic, the public policy of the United States was to mediate, to be even-handed, to do whatever it could to avoid bloodshed and to keep its distance from both disputants. If that had been all that the Americans were doing, Thatcher would have been outraged. Her friendship with Reagan would not have passed the test. It was not in her nature to have much time for neutrality at the best of times, and she might well have echoed Churchill's words of almost half a century before: 'Surely we must have an opinion between right and wrong? Surely we must have an opinion between aggressor and victim?'

But there was also a private American policy and it was very different. This was quietly to provide Britain with all possible practical assistance short of military involvement. While Haig was accumulating what must have been a record dose of jet-lag in the shortest possible time, Caspar Weinberger was sitting in the Pentagon speeding up the supplies that the British task force would need. It was, indeed, one of the ironies of the crisis that Weinberger, who had so recently been the thorn in the British government's flesh over INF – the intermediate-range nuclear missiles in Europe – arms control negotiations and pipeline sanctions, was Britain's principal champion in the Reagan Cabinet on the Falklands. Whereas Haig, who had been so well attuned to British thinking on INF, and was far more sympathetic over the pipeline, seemed ambivalent over the Falklands.

Whatever the case for Haig's mediation, it was Weinberger who was doing what the British wanted. On Monday 5 April, only three days after the Argentine invasion, a small coordinating committee was set up within the Pentagon under the chairmanship of Dov Zakheim, Richard Perle's special assistant, to cut through the normal bureaucratic procedures.

This committee was working with the White House, the Joint Chiefs of Staff and the politico-military section of the State Department. So, while the momentum was coming from the Pentagon, this was not an entirely secretive operation unknown to anyone else in the administration. But it was not divulged to the outside world, and even in the senior ranks of the administration most people were unaware of all that was being done. The theory at first was that the Pentagon was simply facilitating the supply of items that had already been ordered and paid for by Britain. But even during that first month the coordinating committee was not pedantic about the distinction between old and new orders. Critical decisions were taken then: that Britain could use the American base on Ascension Island; that American aircraft fuel there would be made available; that more fuel and a wide range of supplies would be flown in; that Britain would be able to obtain further items in the United States itself and that special arrangements should be made to pay for all these resources.

From the very first, intelligence information flowed freely to the British. Intelligence cooperation between the two countries is in normal times so close that it would have been difficult to prevent this without taking drastic steps. It is more intimate than the cooperation either country has with any other. Nearly all electronic intelligence is exchanged. Not quite all. Just occasionally one or the other finds that it has started reading a new book on page three. But all SIGINT (signals intelligence) that goes into the American National Security Agency (NSA) system is transmitted to the computers at General Command Headquarters (GCHQ) at Cheltenham in England.

Beyond this there is regular, frequent contact between the personnel of the American and British services. There is also close cooperation in the examination of intelligence material. A representative of the CIA sits in on the weekly meeting of the Joint Intelligence Committee in London, and a diplomat in the British Embassy in Washington is assigned full-time to keep in touch with the security services there. 'You were so much in our intelligence breeches anyway,' Lawrence Eagleburger remarked, 'that had we decided to turn it off, we would have had to send every Brit home from Washington to accomplish it.'

The decision to pass to Britain during the Falklands conflict all intelligence information at American disposal was taken initially within the intelligence community as soon as the British request was made. This was ratified by the National Security Council staff within hours, but the final decision was taken by the President himself. The gesture was important, but the information itself, initially at least, was limited. The South Atlantic was not an area that had been well covered by American intelligence. There was at first no day to day satellite information available. Later on, a satellite was moved from the North to the South Atlantic for the express purpose of helping the British operation.

So throughout April there were three distinct approaches within the administration. There was the Weinberger line: the British are our closest friends and allies, they are the victims of aggression, give them what they need as quickly as we can.

There was the Kirkpatrick line: let us think first of the American national interest, good relations with Latin America are vital to us, British claims to sovereignty in the Falklands are dubious, so friendship with the British should not drag us into the conflict and break our ties with Argentina.

Then there was the Haig line, which was more subtle, and inconsistent, than either of the others. It was to mediate in public, but also in private to do at least some of the things that Weinberger was so eager to do. Haig did not object in principle to some practical assistance for the British. He appreciated the wider issues involved: that aggression must not be seen to have paid dividends, that the West must not appear incapable of meeting a challenge. He knew that a diplomatic solution might not be possible and wanted the British then to be in a position to win. Some evidence of British strength might even make Argentina more willing to negotiate.

But Haig had assumed the role of mediator, and, as he declares in his memoirs: 'The honest broker must, above all, be neutral' – or, one might add, appear to be neutral. This led him into some diplomatic contortions. He records that on 13 April he gave an assurance to the Argentine Foreign Minister, Costa Mendez: 'Since the outset of the crisis, the United States had not granted British requests that would go beyond the scope of our customary patterns of cooperation.' That statement was clearly carefully phrased. A great deal could be covered by that broad definition of the 'customary patterns of cooperation' between such close allies. But not everything that was happening.

A television report in mid-April on ABC's *Nightline* nearly wrecked his negotiations with Argentina, he states, again in his memoirs, because it alleged that the United States was 'offering extraordinary intelligence support to Britain. This report was false.' It is true that it was not 'extraordinary' for the United States to give Britain all the intelligence information it had. But one wonders if Haig's denial can even have been technically correct. Even though the United States was later to do more for Britain in the intelligence field, with the movement of the military satellite from the North Atlantic, additional measures were taken from an early stage.

Despite public denials and justifications, Haig was not happy with all that the Pentagon was doing. As he looks back now on those tumultuous days, he believes that Weinberger was acting along the policy lines approved by the President; but 'he pushed those lines to the limit in terms of direct support to the forces of Britain – and beyond those limits'. Did that undermine his mediating operation? 'Well I regarded it as more of what I had become accustomed to, and highly dangerous because it could have – and almost did on some occasions – derailed it. It is my view that whoever is charged with the diplomatic task has got to speak the truth to both parties within this mediation.'

At one level, that last statement is self-evidently correct. At another level, it points to the contradictions inherent in the policy itself and in a divided administration. Sir Nicholas Henderson wrote subsequently, after his retirement as ambassador, that Haig 'never wavered in two convictions: that the Argentines had been guilty of aggression and must not be allowed to get away with it or there would be dire consequences for the rest of the world, not least the American hemisphere; and that no good would redound to either side in the long run from a military solution which would also cause great difficulties for the United States.'

It was in trying to be faithful to both convictions that Haig ran into difficulties. How could he be open with both sides? He was both conducting American public policy, which required the honest broker to be neutral, and half supporting the private policy of helping one of the contestants. Such a strategy would have required the utmost ingenuity at the best of times. It was complicated still further by being attacked from both sides within the administration.

In these circumstances the attitude of the President himself was crucial. He upset the British early in the crisis by saying to the press on 6 April: 'It's a very difficult situation for the United States because we're friends with both of the countries engaged in this dispute.' That sounded to British ears too like the moral equivalence which rightly so enraged Americans when Europeans seemed to regard the United States and the Soviet Union of Brezhnev in the same light.

In retirement Reagan still recalls the complexity of the dilemma that the United States was in: 'We did not want suddenly to throw a fist at Argentina, although we did feel in our hearts that right was on the side of England.' This puts his position fairly and in a way that few people in Britain have ever appreciated. Latin America has always been something of a blind spot for British opinion, informed and otherwise. The gnawing anxiety of the United States about the southern hemisphere has never been truly understood in Britain, or in other Western European countries for that matter.

Kirkpatrick was not alone in arguing that 'people should look more at the map'. The Latin American section of the State Department, under Tom Enders, the Assistant Secretary for Inter-American Affairs, was also concerned about the damage that could be done to relations in the hemisphere. Quite a number in the administration who opposed Kirkpatrick at the time, and would do so again, are none the less prepared to concede that she had a point. The United States had been put on the spot. In deciding to help Britain it did not act without some genuine trepidation. That made the assistance, in a way, all the more significant.

Thanks largely to Weinberger, the practical help was massive. It included not only the use of the Ascension Island base and aircraft fuel, but a wide range of supplies and weapons, from ammunition to equipment for instant runways, from the latest Sidewinder missile for aircraft to submarine-detection devices and a complete helicopter engine. The United States supplied not only intelligence information but also made available to the British the use of some of their military satellite channels, which made a vital contribution to communication between the task force and headquarters in Britain.

Weinberger would never have pursued the policy he did without the authority of the President. This does not mean that Reagan gave his approval for each decision, each transfer of supplies. That was not his way. But he gave his broad authorisation, which in all probability Weinberger interpreted somewhat liberally throughout that month of April. There can be little doubt that further down the line Weinberger's sanction was interpreted even more liberally by the services themselves. That was especially true of the navy. There is traditionally a particular closeness between the American and British navies. In this instance, American naval officers did all they could to help their British counterparts, with enthusiasm but without fuss. Britain was fortunate that so much of the cooperation required was naval.

The crisis totally preoccupied the British government, as was inevitable. It had to see that the task force was assembled and equipped for a hazardous operation far from home. Looking back, its success may seem inevitable; but that was not how it appeared at the time, to either the British or the Americans. Thatcher and her ministers knew the risk they were running. Had it failed, she at least would have been finished.

The British Cabinet also had to maintain political confidence at home and secure diplomatic support abroad. It was a time of fervour, of mounting patriotic spirit at home, but of great tension too as the task force steamed south towards the Falklands.

The crisis took up quite a bit of the Reagan administration's time as well. Not only was the Secretary of State spending the month shuttling between London and Buenos Aires, but when the President was given his daily briefing on international developments by the National Security Adviser at about nine o'clock every morning he always wanted to hear what had been happening about the Falklands. There were also frequent discussions in the National Security Planning Group.

This is the inner group of the National Security Council, where most of the substantive debates on foreign policy took place. Unlike the NSC, which meets in the larger Roosevelt Room upstairs, meetings of the NSPG are confined to principals only and are held in the White House Situation Room in the basement. The membership under Reagan consisted of the President, the Vice-President, the National Security Adviser (then Judge Clark), the Secretary of State (Haig), the Defense Secretary (Weinberger), the CIA Director (William Casey), the UN Ambassador (Kirkpatrick), the Chairman of the Joint Chiefs of Staff (General David Jones) and the triumvirate of Baker, Meese and Deaver, who attended all important White House meetings during Reagan's first term.

One of the curiosities of their discussions on the Falklands was that their divisions on that issue did not follow the normal personal alignments. Weinberger and Kirkpatrick were at opposite poles, but personal relations between them were good – far better than either of them enjoyed with Haig, who obviously could not be present at those meetings because of his mediating mission and was represented either by his immediate deputy, Walter Stoessel, or by Lawrence Eagleburger, later Deputy Secretary of State in the Bush administration.

Casey broadly supported Britain, but did not want to damage relations with Kirkpatrick. Clark, who was on particularly good terms with both Weinberger and Kirkpatrick, was sympathetic to Kirkpatrick on the issue but concerned above all to hold the NSPG together. The Chiefs of Staff were generally helpful to Britain: that was where all their sympathies lay, but there were some occasions when they objected to certain items which were in short supply going to Britain and had to be overruled by the Pentagon coordinating committee.

Personal relations on the NSPG did matter. Possibly because Weinberger and Kirkpatrick usually got on well together, the arguments were not bitter as they might have been. Weinberger was able to act all the more effectively because he and Clark were the oldest and closest of friends. As a Californian, Clark was known to be sensitive to Central and South America. As someone with a deep respect for Kirkpatrick's skills and judgment, he could easily have thrown his full weight behind her. He might have tried to block Weinberger. But Weinberger was able, on the occasions when he did not deal with Reagan directly, to call Clark on the secure telephone whenever he needed any fresh presidential authorisation, and get it without delay. As one member of the NSPG put it: 'Cap proposed, the President approved.'

What mattered to Britain was that Reagan did approve. With such a divided administration that could not have been a mere formality. Certainly the British authorities never took American support for granted. Always there was the haunting memory of Suez.

While the NSPG deliberated, and while Weinberger did his best to speed the flow of material support for Britain, Haig was trying to bring the British government and the Argentine junta to a compromise. Their positions were so far apart that it is hard to see how logically they could have agreed. Yet, looking back, what is remarkable is how close Haig came to success.

Argentina wanted the concession of sovereignty over the Falklands in one form or another. Either negotiations that would be settled in their favour, or a share in administration that would enable them to acquire sovereignty, probably through the movement of Argentine nationals to the islands. On his first visit to London as a mediator on 8 April Haig found Thatcher in spirited mood. The discussions were tough and she left him in no doubt of her determination to recover the Falklands. He found the search for a compromise no easier in Buenos Aires, but for a very different reason. The junta were impossible to deal with. Nobody seemed capable of a decision.

After further flights by Haig to London and Buenos Aires, and a visit to Washington by the British Foreign Secretary, Francis Pym – clearly not on good terms with Thatcher, who dismissed him after the general election a year later – Haig produced what were supposed to be his final proposals near the end of April. By then the British task force had recaptured the neighbouring islands of South Georgia and was approaching the exclusion zone of 200 miles which the United Kingdom had drawn around the Falklands. Within that limit, the British warned, enemy ships were liable to be sunk. The time for diplomacy was running out.

The British government cunningly delayed its final verdict on Haig's terms until they had been rejected by Argentina. So, on 30 April, on Haig's recommendation, Reagan agreed that mediation had failed and that the United States should formally declare its support for Britain. The government and public opinion in Britain were delighted. The administration had come off the fence at last. When Pym went to Washington again that weekend he remarked joyfully that the last time he had come as a negotiator, whereas now he had come to visit an ally.

Not only had mediation failed to produce a settlement, but American public opinion had been moving sharply towards Britain. Gallup found at the end of April that 66 per cent believed Britain to be 'more nearly in the right', compared to only 12 per cent who thought that Argentina was. It is true that a note of caution was struck: while 38 per cent wanted to help Britain, 54 per cent preferred not to take sides. Of course, in such a poll everything depends on how the respondents interpret the word 'help'. American public opinion would certainly have been against any direct military involvement, but that was never contemplated.

What could not be recorded in any opinion poll was the atmosphere of positive enthusiasm for the British cause that was encountered so widely, at least on the East Coast, as admiration developed for the nerve of Britain's response. Congressional opinion – which is more immediately responsive to public opinion than is the House of Commons because of differences between the political systems – had also swung increasingly towards Britain. It is at such a time that the American instinct for the special relationship, indefinable, sentimental, but real, becomes evident and decisive.

The trend of both Congressional and public opinion had been aided by a superb performance by the British Embassy, and Henderson in particular. Eagleburger even goes as far as to say: 'I have never seen an embassy perform as well anywhere.' Henderson was perpetually putting the British case on television and around the corridors of Congress. He and his staff were using their knowledge of the Washington bureaucracy to get things done. 'They knew where to push the buttons to get decisions made,' Eagleburger remembers. 'When we slowed down on something, they caught it right away and someone would be zapped in to my office, rattling my desk.'

Now that the United States was publicly on Britain's side the flow of material could be increased considerably. There was less inhibition in giving practical support. Yet there was still a private policy which was different from the public policy. The attempt to mediate had not in fact been given up, just withdrawn from public view. American pressure for a compromise solution was to be kept up throughout May, and indeed almost up to the Argentine surrender on 14 June.

In public the diplomatic running was now taken up by Peru and by the United Nations Secretary-General, Perez de Cuellar. It was in their names that the next peace plans were put forward. But Haig and his officials were there in the wings, prompting, encouraging and pressurising, still preoccupied by their desire for a negotiated settlement. The Peruvian peace plan, which was put forward at the beginning of May, was little more than the repackaging of Haig's own last abortive proposals.

One of the most remarkable features of the whole conflict is that the Peruvian plan was accepted in principle by the British Cabinet. It provided for an immediate ceasefire, the mutual withdrawal of forces, the temporary involvement of third parties in administering the islands, acceptance by both sides that a dispute over sovereignty existed, acknowledgment that the views and interests of the islanders must be taken into account in reaching a definitive settlement, and the formation of a contact group (Brazil, Peru, West Germany and the United States) which would be responsible for securing a conclusive settlement by 30 April 1983.

In other words, Thatcher was prepared to concede negotiations on sovereignty with no assurance on their outcome. The views and interests of the islanders would be taken into account, but they would not necessarily be decisive. Such an agreement would have given Argentina a good chance of gaining the essence of its objective. The result could have been extremely embarrassing for Thatcher, but the junta rejected the offer. Whether the British Cabinet felt confident that they would, and could therefore afford to take a calculated gamble for the sake of appearing reasonable, or whether the nerve of British ministers had been shaken for a moment by the sinking of the destroyer *Sheffield*, is one of the imponderables of the war. But it shows how close Haig came to the compromise he wanted.

On 1 May, in the first major engagement of the war, the British had sunk the Argentine cruiser *General Belgrano* in what has remained one of the most controversial actions of the conflict. The cruiser was outside the exclusion zone and steaming away from the task force at the time; but it took the British War Cabinet, which was meeting at Chequers, less than twenty minutes to approve the decision to attack it on the grounds that it still presented a threat to British ships. Three days later the Argentine Navy had its revenge when the *Sheffield* was crippled by an Exocet missile.

It was the worst moment of the war from the British standpoint, partly because of the loss of the destroyer and partly because the episode revealed the deadliness of the Exocet. Argentina had been buying the missile from France, but supplies were halted within a week of the invasion. This was an example of the prompt cooperation received by Britain from France during the conflict. Whatever differences Thatcher has subsequently had with Mitterrand, she has never forgotten this backing.

Throughout May one set of proposals or another kept appearing out of somebody's hat, always with Haig's hopes attached. One set came from the British government itself, but before the month was out there was rising British irritation with the incessant diplomatic initiatives as it became clear that there was really no alternative to the military recapture of the islands.

That was accomplished with less time to spare than has ever been made public. Major-General Jeremy Moore, who accepted the Argentine surrender, had been instructed from London to demand unconditional surrender. The Argentine commander insisted that while he was ready to surrender, he was not authorised to make it unconditional. Moore decided on his own authority to accept the simple surrender because he knew that his forces had ammunition left for no more than a day or so, and winter was about to close in. Had the war not been concluded then, had it dragged on through the winter, would Anglo–American relations have stood the strain? The pressure from the United States for Britain to accept an unsatisfactory compromise would have become formidable and possibly irresistible.

It is arguable that Haig's mediation during April had served Britain's interest because it demonstrated Argentine intransigence and therefore made it easier for the United States to come out in favour of Britain. That is what Henderson has written, but not everyone shares that view. McFarlane tends to believe that, because of the Prime Minister's intervention, Reagan would probably have been prepared to back Britain from the first if it had not been for the mediation. Whether or not mediation was to Britain's advantage during April, it became a troublesome diversion from then on. By the end Haig, who had had some tense sessions with Thatcher, was regarded with annoyance approaching resentment by the British government.

Once the United States had formally declared its support, Britain felt that the time had come for the Americans to concentrate all their energies on providing the maximum practical assistance. Every new attempt to force a compromise seemed to put the American role in question once again.

In retrospect, Haig believed strongly that, even without American assistance, Britain would still have won, though 'in a far more anguishing way'. Others, British as well as American, thought that American practical help was decisive. What cannot be disputed is that it was of the utmost benefit, whether or not it actually tipped the scales. Without it, Britain would have been in grave difficulty. If the United States had actually used its power to thwart the British operation, as it did at Suez, that would have been devastating.

This brings into relief Reagan's personal role. Any idea that he and Thatcher were on the telephone together night after night planning the next moves in a great Anglo–American collaboration would be well wide of the mark. He points out that frequent telephone calls between them were not necessary 'because the understanding was there. She knew where we stood with each other'. One must doubt if she really did know where she stood with the administration throughout the dispute. There were moments when Reagan did wobble, particularly over whether Britain might have drawn the exclusion zone around the islands too wide and whether the use of force might on occasion be jeopardising the chances of a negotiated settlement – though it is worth noting that he evidently did not waver over the sinking of the *Belgrano*.

Not all the telephone conversations between them were successful. On 13 May he telephoned Thatcher in the mistaken belief that the Argentines were after all prepared to negotiate seriously. After this conversation, or another at about this time, one of his aides remarked with feeling that it was the last time they would allow that to happen: 'He couldn't get a word in edgeways.' That was not a unique complaint where Thatcher was concerned.

Yet, despite such irritations, despite recurring evidence that he never really quite understood why the islands mattered so much to Britain, despite many indications that he certainly did not appreciate the details of the dispute, Reagan never let Thatcher down over the Falklands.

Churchill wrote of Lord Jellicoe, the Commander-in-Chief of the British Battle Fleet in the First World War, that: 'He was the only man on either side who could lose the war in an afternoon.' Much the same might be said of Reagan over the Falklands. The decisions he had to take were simple, but critical. On a number of occasions he might have changed the whole complexion of the conflict by just saying no.

The pressures on him to do so were considerable. Pushing him strongly in that direction was Kirkpatrick, another strong woman of powerful personality and intellect, with formidable debating skills, whom he much respected. At his elbow in the White House was a National Security Adviser with appreciation for Kirkpatrick's case, although Clark was not trying to push any particular line. Other members of the NSPG had their doubts, or were not prepared to push too hard in either direction. Although Weinberger had ready access to argue Britain's cause, it would have been so easy for Reagan to go the other way. Not to back Argentina, which American public opinion would have made impossible, but to avoid doing anything substantive at all.

He did not orchestrate the divergent tendencies within the administration into a unified, coherent policy. Because he so often listened patiently at meetings, without making a decision then and there, it could all too readily be assumed that it would have made no difference if he had not been there. That was not the case over the Falklands. The balance of power at the top of the administration was not such as to justify the invaluable material assistance that was given to Britain throughout the conflict.

McFarlane, who was Deputy National Security Adviser at that time, later assessed Reagan's role positively: 'I think it's fair to say the President was making the policy. It's true he didn't sit down and say to Cap Weinberger: "I want you to provide munitions, petroleum and other stored supplies to the British." Cap came up with that idea. But for every decision taken there was strong opposition within his Cabinet. So it isn't as if the Secretary of Defense had any autonomy in this area. He and Kirkpatrick would almost always be at odds, and then President Reagan would decide. He was not a passive creature here. He was deciding things on a daily basis, always with his Cabinet split on the issue. So I thought he was a rather assertive person.'

Weinberger must always remain, in British eyes, the special American hero of the Falklands. It was for what the Foreign Office termed 'his unfailing support and assistance during the Falklands War' that on 23 February 1988, he became the first former member of a United States administration to receive an honorary knighthood from the Queen. But, central though his role was, he and others of like mind had to know that they were operating in accordinace with the President's wishes.

Reagan knew how much the issue meant to Thatcher. He realised that her position was hanging in the balance and he delivered.

9

AT THE SUMMIT: FROM VERSAILLES TO
WILLIAMSBURG

The Reagan–Thatcher relationship in some ways resembled a collection of long-running soap operas, with the same main actors but different plots and varied settings. Just as we are wondering what will be the sequel to last night's drama, we get the next instalment of another one. But the performances of the two principal actors do not seem to be affected by what is happening to them in the other series. Like the good professionals they are, they are able just to keep on relating to each other.

It was one of the notable features of the Reagan–Thatcher partnership that it was so little disturbed by the differences that they did have from time to time. As the Falklands War moved to its climax, they were assembling along with the other heads of government for their annual economic summit, this time in Versailles. The three-day meeting began ten days before the Argentine surrender at Port Stanley, which took place on 14 June.

There was inevitably a fair amount of discussion about the Falklands at Versailles. Thatcher appeared to have sealed Reagan's support in a long personal discussion with him. The Americans were therefore all the more embarrassed by the fiasco of a confused vote at the United Nations. Kirkpatrick was obliged, much against her wish, to cast her vote in the Security Council along with Britain against a resolution calling for a ceasefire in the islands. That was because instructions from Haig, allowing her to abstain, did not reach her in time. When they did, she announced publicly that the United States would have abstained but for this failure in communication.

The episode naturally infuriated Thatcher, because it looked like a weakening of American support, and did little credit to the United

States. But it was significant for exposing the cross-currents within the administration rather than undermining the British position. It was too late for that. The Americans might keep murmuring about magnanimity, but the war was almost won and Thatcher did not have to pay attention.

Versailles was important for another reason: the return to prominence of the other alliance drama, which had been rather overshadowed recently but remained unfinished: the saga of the Siberian pipeline. On this, it will be recalled, Thatcher took something of a midatlantic position: not sharing European enthusiasm for the pipeline, but positively alarmed by the possibility of American sanctions against companies outside the United States.

In the run-up to the summit it looked as though a compromise might be in the making. The Reagan administration had indicated in mid-April that it would not press further over the pipeline itself if new ground rules could be established at Versailles for East–West trade, which meant in effect agreement to curtail subsidised credits to the Soviet Union. At the same time Mitterrand was eager for an American commitment to prop up the French franc, which had been weakened by his policy of hectic expansion in a time of recession.

So it seemed that the stage was set for a quiet understanding. The Europeans would go along with restrictions on credits; the Americans would not impose sanctions on foreign companies, provided that something was done about credits; and Mitterrand would be offered a bit of help with the franc. But instead of being remembered for the great compromise, Versailles is remembered for the great row and the great misunderstanding.

After intense and somewhat heated bargaining between Mitterrand and Reagan a loose agreement was reached on both credits and currencies that depended more on what was implied than on the words that actually appeared in the communiqué. Neither France nor the United States really got the commitment it wanted.

Throughout Reagan's first term, which meant so long as Donald Regan was at the Treasury, the Americans were reluctant to intervene in the exchange markets. They believed, as indeed does Thatcher, that the correct exchange rate is what the market determines it should be. So the furthest they were prepared to go at Versailles was to endorse an anodyne declaration on the virtues of monetary stability and an undertaking from the conference that 'we are ready, if necessary, to use intervention in exchange markets to counter disorderly conditions'.

On credits, the communiqué promised 'commercial prudence in

limiting export credits'. It also provided for a joint exercise by officials to improve the system 'for controlling exports of strategic goods'. Everything depended on what these generalisations were taken to mean; and in each case one side left the negotiating table believing that more had been decided than the other side did. The ground had been well prepared for misunderstanding, but first the Reagan camp moved on to London.

In London the main event was to be Reagan's address to members of both Houses of Parliament in the Royal Gallery at Westminster, on 8 June, a grand though not a unique occasion. But the visit was beset by mishaps. First, there was confusion and a breach of protocol in announcing that such a speech was to be delivered at all. Some months beforehand Deaver, the prince of presentation during Reagan's first term, had been over to Britain to make arrangements that would have the desired political resonance back home.

For both Ronald and Nancy Reagan, this was to be their first visit to Britain since they entered the White House, and their first meeting with the Queen. There was great concern, for both political and personal reasons, that all should go well. The President would go riding with the Queen at Windsor, a boon for the photographers and a nightmare for the security men. To Deaver's delight the suggestion was made that Reagan might address both Houses in Westminster Hall. This would have been one for the record books. An address to both Houses in that historic setting is a magnificent and formal affair. No president of the United States has done it, and the last foreign leader to be given that honour was President de Gaulle in 1960.

But Deaver spoilt it by leaking the glad tidings at home before the necessary political soundings had been taken in London. The opposition parties had not been consulted, and Labour in particular was affronted. No doubt it was partly pique; and Michael Foot, then the Party Leader, was not known for his pro-American sympathies at the best of times. But it also reflected quite a widespread disapproval of Reagan in Britain at that stage. He was still regarded as the wild man from the West, who might be a danger to the peace.

In later years, as he became himself the man of peace negotiating with Gorbachev, British opinion mellowed. But the reaction in 1982 illustrated a truth about both Reagan and Thatcher. Neither of them attracted the warmth of admiration in Britain that they drew on the other side of the Atlantic. Perhaps an exception should be made in the case of Thatcher for about a year after the Falklands. In the general election of June 1983 voters up and down England – the

Scottish electorate was different, it has never taken to her – were describing themselves on the doorstep as 'Thatcherites', a most unusual personalisation in British politics, where party normally reigns supreme. But, for most of the time, the Thatcher–Reagan story has been in a sense an all-American idyll. That is where there has been real enthusiasm for both of them.

So in the spring of 1982 the British government was in a fix. If it went ahead with Westminster Hall it risked a Labour protest and possible boycott, which would have spoilt the dignity of the occasion and not given Deaver the kind of news coverage he was dreaming of. Yet if the British government withdrew the invitation, it would be a diplomatic insult. So there was a compromise. Reagan would speak, but to a meeting of members, not to a formal joint session of both Houses; and the venue would be changed to the less glorious, but still dignified, Royal Gallery, the chamber next to the House of Lords within the Palace of Westminster.

The speech itself helped to strengthen the personal partnership. There was the appropriate sense of occasion to do honour to him. He returned the compliment by saying what was expected of him on the Falklands, without dwelling on the issue: 'Those young men aren't fighting for mere real estate. They fight for a cause, for the belief that armed aggression must not be allowed to succeed and that people must participate in the decisions of government under the rule of law.'

That last point was the theme of his address. He was launching a crusade for democracy. Most unusually for a Reagan speech, it reads better today than it sounded then. The confidence in the march of democracy, which seemed a bit like ritual rhetoric or meddling in the internal affairs of others back in 1982, seems prophetic now.

But while Reagan performed with distinction on stage, in the wings there was turmoil. The friction between Haig and the White House staff was getting out of control. When Thatcher went out to Heathrow to greet the visiting party at the airport, Haig was not allowed to go through the official receiving line – an extraordinary slight to a serving secretary of state. By now Haig and Baker were not on speaking terms. Baker and Deaver had decided that he should go, and Meese was unsympathetic to him as well.

At Windsor the Palace authorities were appalled at the hostility between Haig and the rest of the Reagan entourage. It must have been like entertaining a couple who seem liable to announce their divorce before the dinner party is over. It was, indeed, at Windsor of all places that Haig and Clark had probably their only shouting match, and conducted themselves with such vigour that the security officials felt it prudent to close the door behind them. The issue on that occasion was the Middle East. Israel had invaded Lebanon and Haig wanted to cut the Nato summit in Bonn, where the Reagan team was going next, and fly out to the Middle East immediately himself.

But Philip Habib who, on Haig's recommendation, had gone to the Middle East as the President's emissary, indicated that he would resign if Haig were to rush there at a moment of crisis. Whether for that reason, or because Reagan needed to have the Secretary of State at his elbow for the Nato summit, the President insisted that Haig should go on to Bonn with the rest of the party.

This was, however, one of the less successful Nato summits. Perhaps it was the disarray in the American delegation: all the wrangling certainly diverted time and energy from the matter in hand. Perhaps it was that Dr Joseph Luns, who had been Nato Secretary-General since 1971, had been in office too long. But between them they stage-managed the meeting with disastrous consequences.

The Americans were not required to deal with any controversial subject. That suited Reagan's personal inclination perfectly well. He is an instinctively friendly man who dislikes confrontations, and he may well have felt that he had had enough of those in Versailles. But avoiding controversy meant that nobody raised the deadly topic of the pipeline. The understanding on restricting credits for East–West trade which the Americans thought they had obtained in Versailles was not sealed in Bonn. This was a glaring omission, as economic summits are merely consultative. If Nato is to take any action, it has to be confirmed at an alliance meeting. When nothing was agreed in Bonn, nothing happened.

So the implied deal collapsed. The Americans reckoned that if the Europeans were not going to deliver on East–West trade, there was no reason for them to refrain any longer from sanctions on overseas companies for using American technology to build the pipeline. On 18 June Reagan not only declined to ease the ban on American companies, as the Europeans had expected, but extended it to foreign companies as well.

One of the extraordinary and rather mysterious features of this operation was the speed with which it was accomplished. It was all done so quickly that the allies had no opportunity to object beforehand. There were no consultations, merely a few hours' advance notice. The basic decision was taken in an afternoon, at an NSC meeting at which Haig could not be present himself. Not even the

British Embassy, which had a formidable reputation for monitoring the administration's internal movements and which had performed so brilliantly over the Falklands, was prepared for what happened.

There were all the marks of a Perle policy coup in this case, swiftly taking advantage of half an opportunity to wrong-foot his opponents. But why did Reagan agree to inflict such a blow upon Thatcher only four days after the completion of her triumph in the Falklands, and only ten days after he had been speaking as her guest at that memorable occasion in the Palace of Westminster? It may have been partly that he never gave the impression of being deeply and emotionally involved over the pipeline. He had been persuaded that it was an issue on which it was necessary to take a tough stand, but it was not really his issue. Another, no less important, factor was that the pipeline was seen in Washington at this stage as being primarily an argument with the Germans and the French. Thatcher's main concern up to then had been over what the Americans had been threatening, not what they had done. So they did not see it as an Anglo–American confrontation.

But when they did take legal action to inflict penalties on the companies of other countries and on American subsidiary companies overseas, she was appalled. The United States was seeking to make its own law operative in the territory of others. She objected to that in principle and she was all the more horrified that one of the principal victims was the Scottish company, John Brown, which was reported to have contracts for the pipeline amounting to more than £100 million. It would be especially disturbing if that company were to be put into difficulties at a time of high and rising unemployment in Scotland. So legal and political considerations were joined together in her mind.

If the administration had any hope that she would mute her criticism out of gratitude for what the United States had done over the Falklands, it was swiftly disabused. On 22 June, four days after Reagan's announcement, she was in Washington for the first time since her triumphant state visit in February 1981, when the new President gave her such a rapturous reception. This time she took the opportunity to make her views plain.

In a meeting in the White House with the President she had Bush, Haig and possibly Clark lined up on the sofa opposite her to hear what amounted to a lecture on the iniquities of extra-territoriality. On such occasions, certainly in the early days, she would hardly ever argue directly with the President. Instead, she would employ the device of turning to the Secretary of State or the National Security

Adviser, or some other official, and saying: 'Al' – or 'Bill', or 'Bud' – 'I just don't understand your logic on this matter.' She would then proceed to dissect what she saw as the fallacies of the American position without attacking Reagan at all.

Everyone knew what she was doing. She was adapting the age-old principle in monarchies of saving the sovereign from criticism by always putting the blame on his advisers. Reagan appreciated the technique, both for the humour of it and because it kept him out of the firing line. It gave him time to consider his response and enabled her to get far more than her share of the conversation without quite seeming to talk him down. His advisers over the years are divided only as to whether she would customarily take up two-thirds of a discussion with him, or rather more than that.

On this occasion she also tried to persuade them to do something about the budget deficit, but the most skilful part of the operation was the way she avoided receiving any lecture on the need for magnanimity after the end of the Falklands War. She knew that there were many in the administration who believed that this was the time for Britain to mend fences with Argentina. She suspected that the President might be about to urge this course on her, and she was having none of it.

As the conversation moved to the Falklands, she gave a dissertation on the sufferings of British troops there from trench foot, and the problems they had experienced with their boots. Did the American army have better boots? Then there were all those mines which the Argentines had laid around the Falklands. What was the best way to deal with them? Did Secretary Haig, with all his military experience, have any suggestions? And then ... there just was not time for anything more. The President was informed that the press were waiting, warm farewells were exchanged and the Prime Minister had avoided any unwelcome suggestions being put to her. For once there was brilliant calculation in her incessant talk.

She also went to discuss the pipeline sanctions with Donald Regan at the Treasury, when she was less restrained on the subject than she had been in the White House. The word harangue would not be inappropriate for what Regan received. Nor, on this issue, did she express her displeasure only in private. In the press conference at the end of her visit she declared with calculated understatement that she had 'some difficulty' with the administration's decision to block licences for John Brown's to supply parts manufactured in Europe for building the pipeline. That phrase in the mouth of such a loyal ally as Thatcher was an indication of anger.

More was to come. After her return home Thatcher was more specific in her public criticism, telling the House of Commons on 1 July: 'The question is whether one very powerful nation can prevent existing contracts being fulfilled; I think it is wrong to do so.' The verbal assault was backed up by action. A month later the British government used its legal powers to forbid four companies – John Brown's and three subsidiaries of United States corporations – from complying with the American ban. The United States embargo was an 'unacceptable extension of American extraterritorial jurisdiction in a way which is repugnant in international law', the House of Lords was told by Lord Cockfield, then Britain's Trade Secretary and subsequently a European commissioner in Brussels and father of the blueprint for 1992.

This was strong stuff, but Thatcher had not finished. 'I now feel particularly wounded by a friend,' she commented at the beginning of September. 'I feel very strongly that once you have made a deal you have got to keep it. The whole City of London was built on "my word is my bond".' Rather than being overwhelmed with appreciation for the American role in the Falklands, Thatcher seemed if anything to have been emboldened by the British success there. Her mettle having been proved in that conflict, when the risks she ran can too easily be underestimated, she was not about to bow the knee to a haughty ally.

Not for the first or the last time, her robust spirit gave quiet pleasure to her friends in Washington. In the State Department they had, just about from the moment Reagan took office, been warning their colleagues elsewhere in the administration that there was a price to pay when allies were ignored. That was not a popular message in Reagan's first term. It savoured of wimpishness. So officials at State were not altogether sorry to have their judgment confirmed. More than any other foreign leader, Thatcher made Reagan's Washington appreciate that allies could not simply be pushed around.

If the United States was to maintain its existing policies, it was on course for a major Nato crisis – with its most vociferous critic being the very leader who had just won such widespread admiration on both sides of the Atlantic for her nerve in winning the Falklands War. To have a confrontation in which the Iron Lady would have to be portrayed as selling out to the Soviets made little political sense. Reagan would never have been comfortable with that. With a direct clash between American and British law in the offing, some face-saving formula had to be found.

But Haig was no longer around to seek it. Immediately after

Thatcher's visit in June, Reagan secured his resignation – or rather accepted it before it had been given. At the beginning of the Falklands crisis, Haig is reported to have said to Clark: 'Bill, Maggie and I will rise or fall together.' If he had replaced the word 'together' with the phrase 'at the same time', he would have been right. What he did not foresee was that Thatcher would rise and he would fall.

There is an element of classical tragedy about Haig's tenure as Secretary of State. He came to office with wide knowledge of foreign affairs and impressive international experience. He knew how Washington worked from those dramatic days when, as Chief of Staff, he held the Nixon administration together in its final throes. He was welcomed as a friend in Europe. He tried to help Britain, according to his lights, as well as to save his own career over the Falklands.

Yet he left office as a storm was raging with Europe which he had been powerless to prevent, and having upset the British government as well as Argentina over the Falklands. In London he was considered tiresome and vain, a different personality from the man who had won such excellent opinions as SACEUR (Supreme Allied Commander in Europe). Perhaps he was affected by physical ill-health, or perhaps it was simply that right from the beginning of the administration he was trying to function without a political blood supply.

For any secretary of state his contact with the White House is his life-support system. Without close communication and strong backing from the president he may posture on the world stage, but what he says is not necessarily American policy. He may be wise, but he is doomed to be ineffective. That is what happened to Haig.

This was a perpetual frustration to British ministers and officials throughout his time at the State Department. They did not know who was making American foreign policy. It was not unusual for them to have to deal with a secretary of state who was not the principal influence. That was the case under Nixon when Kissinger was National Security Adviser and William Rogers the Secretary of State. When Cyrus Vance was Secretary of State under Carter, with Zbigniew Brzezinski as National Security Adviser, not many people in London considered Vance the more powerful.

But it is relatively easy for a foreign government to cope when it is clear that the national security adviser is calling the shots. That was not the case under Reagan. When Richard Allen had the job it was deliberately downgraded. Clark had more standing within the administration, but not enough experience of foreign policy. The British government's impression during Haig's stewardship was that nobody was consistently making American foreign policy. Reagan was setting the broad direction, but specific policies would depend upon who caught his ear or who won in the cockpit of debate in the NSC.

Whether or not that was a good method of government, it was not good for other governments. Thatcher had the advantage of her personal relationship with Reagan. But she could not rely on that for everything, and in the early years not so many people in the administration appreciated the political influence of the connection. As time went on, more and more officials in Washington came to recognise the impact her judgment had upon him and therefore the potential of a Thatcher intervention for swinging a policy battle.

Haig ended with too little power because he gave the impression of seeking too much. He saw himself, in a fatal phrase, as Reagan's vicar for the conduct of foreign policy. The White House staff never got over the suspicion that he also saw himself as the next president. Thatcher was not sorry to see Haig go. With his successor, George Shultz, she was to form a much closer relationship. This may be attributed in part to their shared interest in and common approach to economics. Above all, they shared a faith in the practical value of free markets.

Before entering politics in the Nixon administration, Shultz had been in academic life – first at the Massachusetts Institute of Technology and then at the Graduate School of Business in Chicago, where he had been Professor of Industrial Relations before becoming Dean. Under Nixon he was in turn Secretary of Labour, Director of the Office of Management and Budget, and Secretary of the Treasury. Then he went into business, becoming President of the Bechtel Corporation before responding to Reagan's invitation.

Just as Thatcher came to the Premiership with the conviction that the economy presented the most pressing challenge, so Shultz began his career in diplomacy with greater experience in economics, national and international. Because they were true believers in the same economics, she felt they were kindred spirits as they turned their attention to diplomatic issues.

It was ironic, when Haig had been appointed Secretary of State as the man who could reassure the Europeans, that he had not got on better with the man who was British Foreign Secretary for most of his time at the State Department, Lord Carrington. On one occasion a leaked report suggested that Haig had called Carrington a 'duplicitous bastard' – a comment that seemed more in keeping with Haig's military past than his diplomatic present. Haig was on better terms with Carrington's successor, Francis Pym, but the two of them were in harness together for only a few months before Haig's departure.

After the British general election of June 1983, Pym was replaced by Sir Geoffrey Howe. This was the long-running partnership of foreign ministers, Shultz and Howe both holding office until the end of the Reagan–Thatcher era. Both were courteous, civilised, low-key personalities, with much stronger opinions than the mildness of their manner would suggest. Above all, they were dogged.

Shultz speaks highly of their partnership nowadays: 'I developed a very close relationship with Geoffrey Howe, and had a great deal of communication back and forth.' But in the early years their staffs were concerned at what seemed a distance between them.

Robert McFarlane, who himself enjoyed a strong working relationship with Shultz, first as deputy, then as the full National Security Adviser, later seemed to share that view. 'Their exchanges were rather set piece,' he remembered. 'To be fair, Geoffrey was a more congenial, less stiff, party to the talks when they occurred, and it did warm gradually.'

For some time officials felt it necessary to do what they could to bring them closer together. On one occasion Shultz took Howe for dinner on the Potomac on the barge of the Chief of Naval Operations. Howe had arrived in Washington after an exhausting trip to South Africa and the front-line states. Unfortunately, he dozed off over dinner. Then, when he awakened, he gave the impression, in the course of a catalogue of American misdemeanours, such as the budget deficit and Middle East policy, of blaming the United States for introducing AIDS to the Western world. The evening was not rated a total success.

Yet in due course officials believed that it became one of those strange relationships where there is a deeper understanding than ever appears on the surface. Their lengthy pauses indicated more confidence than many a fulsome tribute that ministers customarily bestow on each other.

Between defence secretaries there was usually, but not invariably, a good relationship. Weinberger was such an ardent anglophile that he was probably always keen to get on well with his British counterpart, which between politicians is more than halfway to a fruitful partnership. He enjoyed one with John Nott, which was of great advantage during the Falklands War. There was one occasion during the conflict when he telephoned Nott to make sure that his own people had not driven too hard a bargain with the British, which says something for his desire to be helpful.

Between Weinberger and Nott's successor, Michael Heseltine, however, relations were not so smooth. Perhaps Heseltine seemed too much of a European and not sufficiently pro-American. Perhaps he wanted to drive too hard a bargain. Perhaps he was just too vivid a personality for the quieter Weinberger. But there is no doubt that Weinberger was relieved when Heseltine was succeeded in January 1986 by George Younger. As one administration official put it: 'George Younger lives up to Cap Weinberger's ideal of what a British minister should be, an English gentleman.' Younger, one should add, is a Scotsman.

It was not only with Weinberger that Younger established an excellent rapport. He became a popular and respected figure in Reagan's Washington as a minister who was not intellectually brilliant, but who thought clearly, knew his mind and was reliable.

Even when the people at the top get on as well as Thatcher and Reagan did, these secondary relationships matter. When they are smooth, they facilitate the practical cooperation that the leaders want. It was because of the entry of Shultz that the long saga of the pipeline sanctions, which had all the ingredients of a soap opera except romance, was finally brought to a happy conclusion.

Shultz recognised, as had Haig before him, that the sanctions were doing more damage to Nato than to the Soviet Union. The difference was that Haig had lacked the credit within his own adminstration to secure a change of policy. Shultz was able to manoeuvre carefully, as a top priority during his first few months in office, to resurrect the main elements of the Versailles deal that had fallen apart. So on 13 November 1982 Reagan announced that he was lifting the sanctions in return for substantial agreement within Nato on a more restrictive approach to economic dealings with the Soviet Union. It was not the last to be heard of the extraterritoriality issue, but it was the end of the sanctions row. The main credit must go to Shultz. It was he who secured the compromise and persuaded Reagan. But Shultz himself acknowledges that Margaret Thatcher's strong objections made an impact on the President. Although she was by no means the only allied leader to protest, she was the one whose voice was heard with most respect in Washington. This agreement cleared the way for a new start to allied cooperation at the next economic summit, which was held in Williamsburg, Virginia, at the end of May, 1983. But three months before that Reagan was host to the Queen when she visited California.

One morning, after the President and his wife had spent the night aboard the Queen's yacht, HMS *Britannia*, Michael Deaver came up to him with the text of a speech he was about to deliver. It was Reagan's first sight of the speech so Deaver explained that there was one particularly difficult foreign name – oh, and this is your thinking on Nicaragua today. 'Fine. Thanks Mike', said the President in sunny mood. One of the senior members of her entourage remarked to the Queen that they would never dare to give her a speech unseen like that. To which she responded: 'And they call *me* a constitutional monarch!'

The Williamsburg summit came right in the middle of the British general election campaign. Thatcher agonised for a bit over whether to attend. Might she jeopardise her chances of re-election by appearing to ignore the voters for the sake of prancing on the world stage? But she need not have worried. She was bound to be re-elected a year after the Falklands, with Labour in disarray, and in any case she benefited from the favourable publicity at Williamsburg.

On the first evening, dinner was served for the seven heads of government in the dining room of what had been the British colonial governor's residence. As they were seated, Reagan recalls, he was all set. He turned to Thatcher. 'I said: "Margaret, if one of your predecessors had been a little more clever . . ." She said: "I know, I would have been hosting this gathering." '

To steal the punch line of a world leader is not always a sure path to his affections. But what is particularly illuminating about this story is that years later Reagan tells it with such evident enjoyment. Not a flicker of irritation or vanity. Just laughter and admiration for a smart woman who was so quick on the draw.

In many ways Williamsburg saw Ronald Reagan at his best. First of all, he was determined, as host with the right to conduct proceedings as he saw fit, to cut through what he regarded as some of the traditional nonsense. This time there would be no communiqué prepared in advance. At previous summits, he felt, they had spent too much time haggling over a text already in draft. Now they would discuss, and the communiqué would reflect the discussions. It was an approach with which Thatcher professed herself much in agreement.

Reagan then chaired the conversations with what was regarded as impressive skill by the British as well as the American team. That did not always owe a lot to preparation. David Gergen, Reagan's Director of Communications, recalls that the afternoon before Reagan's critical bilateral meeting with Mitterrand his staff gave him two unusually heavy briefing notebooks. They were afraid at the time that they might be overburdening him because he would always read all the briefing material he was given, even if it meant staying up late. He was always conscientious about this, says Gergen; it was Mrs Reagan who kept asking the staff to cut down the material.

Sure enough, the following morning he came in 'terribly droopy' for breakfast. 'He looked as if he had been hit by a truck,' as Gergen puts it. So he sat down and said: 'I'm sorry I didn't read your briefing books last night. I sat down to read this material and it was interesting. But then I turned on the television and, you know, they had *The Sound of Music* on. I'd never seen it before.' So he stayed up to one o'clock at night. The staff were horrified; but then according to Gergen, 'the people who went swore that those were his best bilaterals. He was terrific.'

It was at Williamsburg that Thatcher made her last attempt to persuade Reagan to do something about the American budget deficit. She devoted most of her bilateral meeting with him to arguing that he ought to follow her example and raise taxes. That was what her government had done, in the teeth of a depression, in its 1981 Budget. It had been extremely unpopular at the time, but it had been necessary to squeeze out inflation and to bring the deficit under control. If Reagan failed to do the same, interest rates would remain high and investment would be squeezed out in the United States.

She came out of that meeting aware that she had failed to make any impression on him. His mind was set against raising taxes partly on economic grounds: he believed in the supply-siders' argument on the incentive effect of lower taxes, which would stimulate growth and therefore increase revenue. But he also saw lower taxes as a political commitment on which he could not afford to compromise.

Thatcher resolved then that she would not try to convert him on that issue. It was a waste of time and was likely to be counter-productive. Further pressure would be more likely to damage Anglo–American relations than to bring any change of policy.

Their disagreement on that issue did nothing to deter Reagan from using the summit to do everything he could to aid her re-election. For once Deaver, who was always sensitive to the President's wishes, appeared to be just as concerned to get good publicity for her as for him. In speaking to the press Deaver went out of his way to praise her contribution. As the master of the photo-opportunity he saw to it that she was well presented. It was noticed by the *Washington Post* that she almost invariably walked beside the President when entering or leaving buildings, and therefore benefited from better television coverage than the other leaders. She was probably able to campaign more effectively in Williamsburg than she ever could have done by staying at home.

But the summit was not confined to such pleasantries. On one issue, Reagan recalls, 'it really became downright bitter'. Thatcher, Chancellor Helmut Kohl and Reagan himself led the battle on one side against Mitterrand and Pierre Trudeau as the principal opponents on the other. It was a familiar line-up and, as Reagan puts it, 'we fought it down to the wire'.

The cause of this bitter struggle was a statement on security which Reagan decided they should put out. This was the time when the public-relations battle over the deployment of cruise and Pershing Two missiles was rising to a frenzy in a number of Western European countries. It was a season of mass demonstrations and fierce protests. Some governments were wondering if they would be able to resist the pressure and honour their commitments. So it was hardly surprising that the seven leaders should dwell on this topic at their dinner on that first evening.

The discussion went so well from his point of view that Reagan afterwards asked Shultz to draft a statement, and handed him a set of full and careful notes which the President had taken during the conversation. Shultz showed that he too had mastered the art of delegation by passing the initial task on to Richard Burt, the Assistant Secretary of State for European Affairs.

It was the following day that the difficulties began. Meeting in the House of Burgesses, the heads of government were supposed to have approved the declaration in time for a press conference at noon. That plan had to be abandoned. The leaders went for lunch, the argument dragged on for much of the day and Thatcher had to postpone her return to Britain to resume her election campaign.

There were two points at issue. How tough a stand should the conference take on the missiles? And should a specifically economic summit take a collective position on security questions? The statement that was finally agreed included the historic declaration that: 'The security of our countries is indivisible and must be approached on a global basis.' This was the first time that Japan had been brought explicitly into the fold of the Western security system as a whole. The Western powers wanted this. It was also important to Japan because it feared – with good reason, as would become evident at the summit meeting between Reagan and Gorbachev at Reykjavik in 1986 – that a deal might be done to eliminate INF in Europe while leaving Soviet SS-20s in Asia.

But the French initially objected to a statement on arms control being published before one on economic matters, as that was supposed to be the main work of the conference. They were also wary of being lumped together with the rest of Nato, as they are not part of the alliance's military structure. The Japanese, who might have been hesitant, raised no objections.

This was the first high-profile statement on security issues that Japan had made jointly with the leading Nato countries. Before Yasuhiro Nakasone, who was Prime Minister from 1982 to 1987, the Japanese representative at these meetings had generally kept his head down, concerned above all to avoid criticism for Japanese trading practices. Nakasone, who speaks better English than his predecessors, and whose English improved further after he left office, was the first Japanese Prime Minister to make an impact on his fellow heads of government. He was strong on East–West relations and developed a particularly friendly relationship with Reagan. Subsequently Noboru Takeshita, Prime Minister from 1987 to 1989, was listened to with respect because he was known to be an effective operator in Japanese politics. His successor, Toshiki Kaifu, has begun to make his mark; but while Japanese prime ministers now speak more at these meetings, they still confine themselves to formal contributions rather than taking part in the cut and thrust of debate.

The Williamsburg statement on security was immediately controversial in Japan, but it was a breakthrough in the country's foreign policy. Before it could be made, however, the French had somehow to be brought into line.

How French resistance was finally broken down has never previously been revealed. It was a remarkable example of diplomatic arm-twisting.

Since the early 1970s the French had received invaluable assistance for their nuclear deterrent from the United States, as Richard Ullman disclosed in a notable article in *Foreign Policy* in the summer of 1989. A system known as 'negative guidance' was begun under Nixon and Kissinger. As Ullman described the arrangement: 'French experts would describe what they were thinking of doing and then their American interlocutors would let them know, in general terms, whether they were on the right track.' It was an ingenious means of giving the French the benefit of American nuclear research without specifically passing on the data.

The French were threatened with the loss of this helpful arrangement if they persisted in resisting the security statement at Williamsburg. During one of the breaks in the proceedings Reagan's National Security Adviser, Judge Clark, approached Jacques Attali, Mitterrand's chief of staff, as he sat at a table in a corner. Unless the French would explain in an hour why they were blocking this statement,

Clark told Attali, he would recommend to Reagan cancelling all nuclear agreements between the two countries. Faced with such an ultimatum, the French had no alternative but to concede. To have done otherwise would have been like breaking one's own arm to stop the other man from twisting it further.

There was an ironic postscript. Shultz and Thatcher were standing in a corner of the room, arguing with Mitterrand, when the French President suddenly came up with a new suggestion for the contentious sentence. Having been forced to give way, Mitterrand was doing so in style. The new wording was in fact stronger than the old. It was sufficiently positive to suit the Americans, while still not associating the French with the Nato bargaining position. Shultz and Thatcher looked at each other, and Shultz remarked that he thought he could say on behalf of the President that this would be fine.

The episode has wider implications. That the United States should use its leverage in such a way suited Thatcher well enough at that time. She believed that it was in the interest of the West to issue this statement, and the French were clearly being obstructive. It might not be so reassuring in the long run that the United States was able to use this kind of nuclear pressure. What might be done to the French deterrent in a good cause on one day might be done to the British deterrent in perhaps a more doubtful cause on another day.

There were other questions on which Thatcher was displeased with some of her European colleagues at Williamsburg. David Gergen remarked that his clearest recollection of that summit was when 'they were considering a political resolution for the missile deployment. It was during a break and some European ministers were coming up with a really weasel-worded statement about the representative group that was there. They took it to the Americans, who by this time said "Well, this is probably the best we can do." They took it to her. She was on the other side of the room and I remember when she took one look at this thing, stalked across the room, threw down the piece of paper and said to one of the German ministers and the Italian: "This is impossible. I will not sign this," and forced them to change it.' Gergen acknowledges that he was 'terribly impressed. A lot of the Americans just held her in awe.'

So Reagan and Thatcher could look back on Williamsburg with much satisfaction. They had got what they wanted in the statement. He had given her a helping hand towards what would be an electoral triumph, and the habit of fighting successfully side by side had been taken a stage farther.

10

TESTING THE BEAR

A heavy snowfall in Washington and everything slithers to a standstill. This occasional paralysis has its compensations. In a city where the normal pace of life is so frenzied that everyone is always rushing on to the next appointment, if not to the one after that, suddenly there is time to relax. Nobody can go anywhere. The snow creates its own atmosphere of timelessness.

So it was, one evening in February 1983, when George Shultz went over to the White House. He had just come back from a foreign trip and the President had invited him for supper. The mood would have been informal anyway, and the snow made it the ideal occasion for a reflective chat. Shultz had been Secretary of State for little more than half a year and he wanted to probe the President's thinking on the most critical question of all for any holder of their offices. What kind of relationship should the United States be seeking with the Soviet Union?

Shultz knew what others in the administration thought. He knew where Weinberger and Casey stood. But in what direction did the President himself want to go? Shultz felt he needed to know if Reagan was happy just to maintain the deadlock of antagonism, building up the defences of the West, but not seriously trying to find new openings to the East. Or did the President want him to explore, to see if there might be opportunities to forge a more constructive relationship with the Soviets? Until he knew the answer Shultz did not really know how to go about his own job.

When he left the White House later that evening he believed he was on the same wavelength as the President. There was no direct mandate, no precise instructions on the next steps. Once again, that was not Reagan's way. But Shultz was confident that Reagan believed it was important to develop a more stable relationship with the

Soviets if this could be done on reasonable terms. It was up to the Secretary of State to find out if such terms were available.

So began a process of gentle enquiry. There were quiet conversations with Anatoly Dobrynin, the long-serving Soviet Ambassador in Washington. At that stage there were two test cases. Would the Soviet authorities permit the emigration of the six Siberian Pentecostalists who had spent nearly five years in the sanctuary of the United States Embassy in Moscow? And could agreement be reached to open an American consulate in Kiev and a Soviet consulate in New York?

Shultz appreciated that he could not go far down that road without becoming involved in some bruising bureaucratic in-fighting at home. Others in the administration would want their say on such a decision as the exchange of consulates, which could hardly be accomplished simply on the nod of the President without anybody else noticing. He could emerge victorious from such combat only if he had the considered blessing of the President.

Shultz soon had cause to wonder what Reagan really wanted. Only a few weeks after that apparently reassuring talk in the White House, the President made probably the most controversial speech of his incumbency. What became known as the 'Evil Empire' speech, castigating the Soviet Union as the 'focus of evil in the modern world', did not sound like a man patiently feeling his way towards a more constructive relationship. This was probably an example of Reagan the politician giving his immediate audience what they wanted to hear without much thought for the wider consequences: the speech was delivered to a group of fundamentalist preachers at the National Association of Evangelicals in Orlando, Florida on 8 March.

It was also in that month, in a television broadcast, that Reagan first revealed his hopes for a Strategic Defence Initiative (SDI), popularly known as Star Wars, that would render nuclear weapons 'impotent and obsolete'. Thatcher had not been consulted in advance, but then neither had many senior people in his own administration.

Weinberger had been in a particularly embarrassing position. He was attending a Nato Nuclear Planning Group meeting in Portugal where he briefed his fellow defence ministers about the speech that the President was about to deliver, but without mentioning SDI. Although Weinberger was later to become one of SDI's most ardent advocates, he was at that time still trying to secure the removal or modification of that section of the speech. It was a fruitless attempt. Reagan was clearly determined not to be thwarted by analytical objections to which he could not find a ready answer.

Thatcher maintains that 'when he came out with the Strategic Defence Initiative, it was not a surprise'. That was because she had been reading in the scientific journals that the Soviet Union was well ahead of the West in the work it had been doing on lasers, and she did not want the Nato countries to be left behind. What worried her were the exaggerated expectations that Reagan aroused in that speech. She could not see any way in which anyone could stop 100 per cent of the missiles coming in. 'Life is not like that.' Yet 'that does not stop you, if you have a terrible weapon, from having a bounden duty to try to get the best defence'. Other European allies were less charitable. Reagan's speech left them in confusion. Trying to find the right balance on this issue was to be one of the major features of the Thatcher–Reagan dialogue in later years.

Although SDI was to become a cause of bitter contention with the Soviet Union, it was not a sign that the President was in a bellicose frame of mind. Quite the reverse. His attachment to SDI sprang from his hatred of nuclear weapons. He was reaching out for some means of getting rid of them without leaving the United States and its allies at the mercy of their enemies. Yet he had no clear idea as to whether the project could work. This tendency to go off at a tangent, without having adequately prepared the senior members of his administration, was not only disconcerting to his allies. It was one of the frustrations that his Secretary of State was to experience from time to time.

In the middle of June Shultz was able to give testimony to the Senate Foreign Relations Committee that indicated the administration's new thinking very clearly. The statement was worked over carefully, and had the President's full approval. It was judiciously balanced, but the signal was clear. The Reagan administration believed in negotiating from strength. Up to then Reagan's Washington had put the emphasis on building up that strength, by restoring American military power. There would be no weakening on that score, Shultz made clear, but the time had come to put more of American energies into negotiation: 'Having begun to rebuild our strength, we now seek to engage the Soviet leaders in a constructive dialogue.'

After everything that has happened since that day, some of his remarks may seem a little mild now: 'We are not so deterministic as to believe that geopolitics and ideological competition must ineluctably lead to permanent and dangerous confrontation. Nor is it permanently inevitable that contention between the United States and the Soviet Union must dominate and distort international politics.' But Shultz was reaching out 'beyond containment' well before Mikhail Gorbachev came to power, years before George Bush had made the phrase famous in a speech at Texas A & M University on 12 May 1989. Shultz even included those words in his testimony.

His statement marked a turning-point in the administration's foreign policy. It came at a time when the alliance was eager for evidence of some forward thinking in Washington. Nato governments were engaged throughout 1983 in a trial of will with the Soviet Union and with their own peace movements over the plan to deploy intermediate-range missiles in Western Europe before the end of the year. If there could be no negotiated settlement with the Soviet Union before that date, then deployment would go ahead on time. The Germans and Italians, as well as the British, had been firm on that point at Williamsburg.

But if European governments were to retain the support of their own public opinion they had to be able to show that the West was doing all it reasonably could to reach an agreement. Arms negotiations with the Soviets had begun in Geneva more than a year before, to the relief of the European allies. Yet they were getting nowhere. Nobody believed then that there was a serious chance of persuading the Soviets to remove all their SS-20s. The original zero–zero proposal had been a propaganda ploy.

It was natural that the British, who had never been in favour of the zero option in the first place, should be keen to explore the possibility of some agreement above zero. But so were other European governments. That was what Paul Nitze, the United States arms negotiator on INF, had tried unavailingly to secure in his 'walk in the woods' outside Geneva with his Soviet counterpart, Yuli Kvitsinsky, a year before.

On the afternoon of 16 July 1982 Nitze acted on his own initiative to try to break the deadlock in negotiations. He and Kvitsinsky went for a walk in the woods around St Cergue on the Swiss side of the border with France in the Jura mountains above Geneva. Their purpose was to devise a tentative agreement between the two of them on INF which they might then try to sell to their respective governments. They settled on a figure of three hundred American cruise missiles in Western Europe and two hundred and twenty-five Soviet SS-20 warheads – the difference in numbers allowing for the greater speed of the SS-20s.

Both Nitze and Kvitsinsky had been acting without the authority of their governments. Nitze never received the expected message from Kvitsinsky of a positive response in Moscow. Nor was the reaction in Washington favourable. The project died. Thatcher had not been consulted before its death, but she was more sympathetic than others towards Nitze's approach. So in the summer of 1983 all the talk was of seeking some interim solution, though without any serious expectation that the Soviets would respond.

There was nothing for it but to go ahead and prepare to deploy. But that did not prevent Shultz from continuing to feel his way, cautiously and deliberately, to see if the Soviet Union might be interested in trying to improve the relationship generally. There was all the more reason for testing the ground because there was a new leader in the Kremlin.

After some years of ill-health, Leonid Brezhnev had finally died in November 1982 and been succeeded by the former head of the KGB, Yuri Andropov. Given that background, it was not suprising that Andropov was regarded as a somewhat sinister figure in the West. It was under him, however, that the first signs became evident of fresh thinking at the top of the Soviet Union. They were cut short by Andropov's own ill-heath and early death. Before that an ugly and dramatic incident almost put an end to Shultz's patient manoeuvring.

On 1 September 1983 a South Korean Boeing 747 airliner, KAL 007, was shot down by a Soviet fighter over the strategically sensitive Soviet island of Sakhalin to the north of Japan. The circumstances were mysterious: the airliner had clearly deviated from its planned route for no evident reason. But it was a civilian plane; two hundred and sixty-nine people lost their lives, including sixty-one Americans, one of them a Congressman; and there was a strong public reaction not only in the United States, but in Asia and Europe as well. The Soviets responded not with an instant apology, but with prevarication and lies. It was a bleak spell in American–Soviet relations.

The instinctive reaction within the administration was to break off all except basic diplomatic contact with the Soviets. In specific terms: should Nitze return to the negotiating table at Geneva, and should Shultz go ahead with a scheduled meeting in Madrid with the Soviet Foreign Minister, Andrei Gromyko?

It did not pass unnoticed in London that in both cases the Americans went ahead with the meeting. Shultz could not have taken that decision on his own. It went against much of the sentiment in the administration and in Congress. This was one of the big decisions which depended upon the President himself. As with Weinberger over the Falklands, Shultz was fashioning the policy, but he could not have done it without Reagan's backing.

Shultz is normally the most self-controlled of men, heavy in build and dour in manner. That made his encounter with Gromyko all the more memorable. Red in the face, bursting with temper, he traded charges with the Soviet Foreign Minister for a couple of hours. There is no reason to doubt that Shultz's anger was genuine, but it served a political purpose as well. The showdown with Gromyko was Shultz's justification for talking to him at all.

British ministers recognised with special approval that, for all the vigour of the American protests, the lines of communication had not been broken. The British government had begun to reassess relations with the Soviet Union about the same time. The first sign of this had come at the end of April that year when Malcolm Rifkind, then a junior minister at the Foreign Office, had visited Moscow and had a long talk with the Soviet Deputy Foreign Minister, Georgy Kornienko. But at that stage both sides were prepared to move only very tentatively.

Throughout her first term Thatcher had gloried in her reputation as the Iron Lady. Her rhetoric remained robust. She had built up Britain's defences, even if with more circumspection and more concern for the budgetary consequences than Reagan had shown in this field. She never wavered in her determination to deploy the missiles, and throughout the general-election campaign in the early summer of 1983 she concentrated on how foolish it would be to go for unilateral nuclear disarmament. She believed that passionately, and it was also a good electoral issue. But as soon as she had won a second term on 9 June she recognised that the time had come to consider the future of East–West relations more deeply.

The idea had been pressed for some time by the Foreign Office. Her new special adviser on foreign affairs, Sir Anthony Parsons, who had been so successful as Ambassador to the United Nations during the Falklands conflict, commanded her confidence and kept in close touch with the Foreign Office. He was well placed to push for the proposal. Once Thatcher was convinced, she approached the task with characteristic thoroughness. A full-day seminar was held at Chequers, and at her insistence some of the participants were experts from outside government. It is, indeed, one of her characteristics to want to go beyond the formal, official circle for advice.

The effects were soon evident. In a speech at the Winston Churchill Foundation Award Dinner in Washington on 29 September, within weeks of the shooting down of the airliner, she proclaimed the need for dialogue. The statement was intermingled with so much criticism of the Soviet Union that it was not widely noticed at the time. But it was there all right: 'We live on the same planet and we have to go

117

on sharing it. We stand ready therefore – if and when the circumstances are right – to talk to the Soviet leadership.'

Two weeks later, at the Conservative Party Conference in Blackpool, she spelt out her message again, a little more fully this time. The British government was in fact critical of its European allies for what Thatcher had earlier described as their 'totally inexplicable' and 'incomprehensible' failure to react strongly enough to the airline atrocity. She had not suddenly become soft on the Soviets, but in this speech to the party conference she went on to say:

'Whatever we think of the Soviet Union, Soviet Communism cannot be disinvented. We have to live together on the same planet and that is why, when the circumstances are right, we must be ready to talk to the Soviet leadership: that is why we should grasp every genuine opportunity for dialogue and keep that dialogue going in the interests of East and West alike.'

At this same conference her Foreign Secretary, Sir Geoffrey Howe, and Defence Secretary, Michael Heseltine, included similar passages in their speeches, so similar that it was clear they had been orchestrated. A signal was plainly being sent to other governments, and not least to the United States.

When Reagan addressed the United Nations General Assembly in New York on 26 September, he castigated the Soviets over the airliner attack and was uncompromising in his general comments about their system and record. But his main theme was the need for a disarmament agreement, especially on INF. There was not the slightest suggestion of breaking off negotiations because of the incident. By now the zero–zero option had been relegated to the status of an ideal but unlikely solution, still given pride of place in official Western statements, but no longer regarded seriously as a basis for settlement. So Reagan devoted most of his remarks to his willingness to find a compromise agreement and to the latest proposals that the United States was putting forward at Geneva.

As with every other international leader at that time, East and West, he was fighting the battle for European public opinion as the date for deployment moved ever closer. In November the missiles began to arrive in Britain and in West Germany. Neither the threats of the Soviet Union nor the protests of the peace movements had managed to stop them.

It was a victory for Nato that went far beyond the military value of the missiles. Once deployment had become such a prominent political issue, it became a test of resolve that the West could not afford to lose. Above all, this was a victory for the hard leaders of the alliance, especially for Reagan, Thatcher and Kohl. Their nerve had held and their judgment of what was politically possible had been proved correct. The Soviets acknowledged defeat by walking away from the negotiating table in Geneva.

This did not weaken the desire of American and British leaders for a new relationship with Moscow. Shultz's position on this issue had, indeed, been strengthened by the appointment of Robert McFarlane as National Security Adviser in October. Shortly after that, the practice was established of Shultz going over to the White House every Wednesday and Friday afternoon at one o'clock for private sessions with the President and McFarlane in the Oval Office.

Persistently they focused on the Soviet Union. Talking together beforehand Shultz and McFarlane had decided that the points that had to be made were, as McFarlane puts it: 'That the swing of American sentiment back towards a willingness to expend for defence and contain the Soviet Union would not last. But while it was there, with this renewal in our strength and in the strength of our economy, the President should stop and recognise that he didn't want to be remembered as someone who did no more than maintain peace in our time. That it had to last, that if he was concerned about legacy – in short a political point, just for his own place in history – then he had to leave something behind concretely: conventions, treaties, agreements, rules of the road, this kind of thing.'

With this line of argument they played upon Reagan's sensitivities. 'I believe,' McFarlane said, 'that just as a matter of self-interest, in being recorded well in later generations, Reagan began to say that it might have some merit to it.' Another point made by Shultz and McFarlane was that economic weaknesses in the Soviet Union provided an opportunity for leverage.

They still had to overcome Reagan's reluctance to believe that the Soviet Union could ever change. At one of those Oval Office sessions in November 1983, shortly after returning from Japan and Korea, McFarlane outlined a new doctrine for dealing with the Soviet Union. It was based on the principles of realism, strength and dialogue. The presentation was couched to appeal to Reagan's particular concerns: the realism to know that they disagreed with the Soviet Union, the strength to deter, but also recognising the need for dialogue. It worked.

In a televised address from the White House on 16 Jaunary the following year Reagan committed himself to seeking a new relationship with the Soviet Union in a way that he had never done before. He had come to power determined to build up American defences before negotiating. Now he was declaring that America's deterrence had been made more credible, and that the United States was 'in its strongest position in years to establish a constructive and realistic working partnership with the Soviet Union'. This was not just a throwaway line in an otherwise hawkish address. It was the theme that dominated the speech.

Just as Shultz's evidence to the Senate Foreign Relations Committee in June had marked a turning point in the administration's foreign policy, so Reagan's televised address signalled a new approach by him personally. No doubt he was influenced by the persistent arguments of Shultz and McFarlane. But they were not the only factor. Mrs Reagan was particularly upset by his reputation as a potential warmonger. She wanted him to be known as a man of peace, and as always her views carried immense weight with the President.

There were strictly political considerations as well. It was not only a matter of reassuring European opinion as the missiles went in. American opinion could do with a bit of reassuring too. Reagan was coming up for reelection the following November, and his chances would be all the better if he did not seem too threatening a figure. American voters wanted a leader who looked as if he could handle himself in a fight, but not as if he would pick one.

Reagan's change of style also reflected his long-standing anxiety about the difficulties of managing a world with nuclear weapons. It was consistent with what he had said years before that he would do. That provided a reasonable guide to his later conduct.

Reagan was not always noted for his consistency on anything but the broadest sense of direction: 'A man,' says McFarlane, 'who would listen to a persuasive argument, and be persuaded, but who would the next moment listen to Cap Weinberger give quite a contrary view and say "Well, you know, I agree with Cap too." ' That was the aspect of Reagan that was perplexing and sometimes infuriating. Yet when a man explains what he intends to do, does it and then explains what he has done, it may sometimes be reasonable to conclude that he meant to do it.

Because Reagan disliked argument it is too easy to assume that he was simply programmed by his staff. Had he been, taxes would have been raised on more than one occasion during these years and more than one deal would have been done with Congress over the budget deficit. Nobody could be more stubborn when he did not wish to take a particular course of action. He must have been impressed by the advice that he received, but it was advice that by then accorded with his instincts.

So in less than twelve months there had been a subtle but fundamental shift in the approach of both the American and British governments towards the Soviet Union. Reagan and Thatcher had come to power as hardliners, and both immediately proceeded to build up their defences. They would each have done so irrespective of the policy pursued by the other. But it has always been easier for any British government to devote more to its defences when the United States is doing so as well, and it helps an American administration that wants to get more out of Congress to be able to say that leading allies are playing their part.

Neither Reagan nor Thatcher was having second thoughts about that now. It was rather that they were adding an extra dimension to their policy. In doing so they were creating the conditions that would transform the international scene over the next few years.

They did not bring Gorbachev to power. They were not responsible for the economic failure of the Soviet Union. They did not create the yearning for freedom that brought people on to the streets of Eastern Europe in the autumn of 1989. But the military build-up which they had led demonstrated to Gorbachev more effectively than words could ever do that the Soviet Union could not afford an indefinite arms race with the West. Then – and here was where they broke totally new ground – they convinced him that it would be safe to stop it. He was persuaded that there was no threat from the Nato powers. That this was done by the most right-wing leaders in the West made the assurance all the more effective.

Without that, popular protest would have been stifled as it had been so often before in Eastern Europe. For all the economic and political decay in the Soviet Union, Gorbachev's response was not inevitable. It would have been very different if he had thought that Soviet security was at stake. The paranoia that lurked in the Kremlin had to be dispelled before freedom and democracy could flourish anywhere in the Soviet empire.

The evolution of American and British attitudes that began in 1983 was therefore of historic consequence. That this process should have been taking place in both governments at about the same time was a striking coincidence. It would be natural to assume that it was much more than that, that such a major shift in policy was orchestrated between them. But there is no evidence that one deliberately persuaded the other to follow suit. McFarlane has no recollection of such a dialogue with the British government at this time.

Shultz points out that there was a great deal of discussion back and forth between the two governments: 'There was a sharing of assessments and whenever any of us had a meeting with the Soviets we always gave the others a briefing on it, by cable and in person to the extent that it could possibly be arranged.' McFarlane doubts if Shultz and Howe had themselves developed much of a dialogue by then, but Shultz's remark indicates the most convincing explanation.

This was not one of those dramatic occasions, which were to arise later, when Thatcher flew across the Atlantic to convert the President. That she was moving in the same direction is widely considered among his entourage to have been politically and psychologically reassuring for him. But the essence of the partnership at this stage was that the two governments were basing their decisions on much the same evidence and on shared assessments at professional level.

In particular, both governments would have had the same intelligence. A critical contribution in this field was made over a period of years by Oleg Gordievski, who defected to Britain in 1985 when he was head of the KGB in London. His first contact with Western intelligence had been with the Danes when he was serving at the Soviet Embassy in Copenhagen in the 1970s, but Danish intelligence was not really in a position to run a double agent of this consequence and Britain became involved nearly a decade before his posting to London in 1982.

He was especially valuable for Britain in providing a major source of intelligence at hardly any cost and thereby helping the British to keep their end up with the Americans. This is always a serious concern for the British intelligence services. They gain enormously from the exceptional cooperation with the United States, and they are acutely aware that they do not have the resources to make anything like an equal contribution. Gordievski's information was very highly regarded and was seen by very few people anywhere. It has been particularly appreciated not just for specific facts but for the assistance it has provided in assessing Soviet attitudes. That is why he continued to see Thatcher and other Western leaders for years after his debriefing in 1985.

In his book *The Storm Birds* Gordon Brook-Shepherd tells how Gordievski drew the attention of Western leaders to the panic aroused in the Kremlin by the Nato exercise 'Able Archer' from 2 to 11 November 1983. This was simulating a crisis leading to nuclear conflict in which the allied participation was at a higher level than ever before, up to and including defence ministers. It came within a month of McFarlane taking over as National Security Adviser. He immediately realised that this high-level involvement would not be understandable to the Soviets, so he insisted that there should be some clear absences from the exercise to dispel any alarm.

He was right to be concerned. The Soviets did apparently fear that the West might be about to launch a nuclear strike upon them. This was the most dramatic and the most conclusive confirmation there has been of the Soviet need for reassurance. But was it available to Western leaders in 1983, or did Gordievski just reveal this in his debriefing after his defection in 1985?

According to McFarlane, this information was given to Reagan in 1983, and McFarlane believes it had an impact on the President. Whether it was coming from Gordievski in 1983, as he did not defect until 1985, McFarlane is not quite sure. He thinks that they had reporting as well from one of their stations in Eastern Europe, probably Prague, but this information was coming from credible sources at the time. Whether or not it was then coming from Gordievski, it would have been available at the top of both the American and British governments. That they were reacting in much the same way at much the same time is not entirely surprising.

Looking back now, McFarlane thinks that one of the reasons why such reporting of Soviet anxiety made an impression on Reagan was the President's conviction that the prophecies of Armageddon could come true in our lifetime. 'For him to see that, with this deep-seated worry about Armageddon,' McFarlane mused, 'and to see that the Russians might even think we would set it off, I'm sure generated very serious thought on his part about how he could relieve that concern.'

From early 1984 the talking-points that McFarlane would draw up for Reagan, reflecting the ideas that the President himself wished to express, began to include 'rather over-lengthy explanations to the Russians, teaching them why they should not fear us, castigating them for why we should fear them, going through his version of the postwar period.'

While Reagan was ruminating about Armageddon, Thatcher was preparing to pay her first visit behind what used to be called the Iron Curtain. One of the principles of the new British approach was to differentiate between Eastern Europe and the Soviet Union, and between the different countries of Eastern Europe. Following that line of thinking, Thatcher began the process of diplomatic exploration in Hungary in February 1984.

So Thatcher and Reagan were feeling their way cautiously along parallel lines towards a new international order. At almost any other time in their relationship they would have been in close dialogue about the process. But the normally free exchanges between them had been inhibited for a while by a fierce disagreement that blew up, apparently out of nowhere, in October 1983.

11

THE GRENADA INVASION

Sir Geoffrey Howe is usually the most patient and courteous of men, but on the afternoon of Monday 24 October 1983 even he was becoming a little irritable. As Foreign Secretary he had just made a statement to the House of Commons about the situation in the Caribbean island of Grenada, where ten days before there had been a bloody coup to replace one dictatorial left-wing regime with another, even more dictatorial and even more left-wing.

After his statement he had been questioned by one Labour MP after another about the threat of United States military intervention. He had told one that he knew of no such intention, and then another that the British government was 'keeping in the closest possible touch with the United States government' and that he had no reason to think that military intervention was likely. Finally, he was asked yet again if the presence of the United States fleet off Grenada was not a prelude to a landing by American forces. 'I have already explained twice,' responded Howe with the air of a man who was being tested to exasperation, 'that the presence of the United States naval vessels is not prompted by the consideration that the honourable gentleman has in mind.' Surely, the Foreign Secretary must have thought to himself as he resumed his seat, that should put a stop to all this anti-American nonsense.

It was therefore unfortunate for him that only a few hours later American forces began the invasion of Grenada. Their action brought a wave of euphoria to the United States, a political triumph to the Reagan administration, and the sharpest and most public dispute between Thatcher and Reagan throughout the whole of their time in politics together.

Thatcher herself was informed of the operation shortly before it began in a telephone conversation with Reagan. Howe had made his statement in the House at four o'clock in the afternoon (British time). Reagan made his first attempt to contact Thatcher some time after seven o'clock that evening, but she was out at dinner – ironically enough, in the company of the American Ambassador, John Louis. She returned the call to the White House at probably a little after eleven o'clock.

By then Reagan was briefing Congressional leaders, who had also been kept in the dark about the administration's intentions until that moment. He was talking to them in the yellow oval room upstairs in the White House residence, but left to take Thatcher's call in his study, which opened off that room and where there was a secure telephone. Deaver recalls that the two of them talked together for about fifteen minutes, which is quite a long while for a telephone conversation on the secure line at the best of times and even more so when the leaders of Congress have been left hanging about next door.

When the President returned to them he acknowledged that she did not like the idea. She had told him that she thought it would be badly received by the allies and expressed misgivings about an extended American involvement. She had even, it appears, suggested that it might damage him at home as well. 'He clearly was unhappy,' Deaver remembers, 'that she was not as excited about this whole thing as he was. Finally he said to us: "But I told her we were going to go ahead anyway." It was too late. But he was troubled by that, you know.'

Robert McFarlane, then the President's newly appointed National Security Adviser, confirms that. 'I was present when he talked to her on the phone hours before Grenada, and it was not a happy conversation. The President was very disappointed, not angry. His respect for her was too deep for him ever to become angry with her. But he was disappointed.'

When Reagan was asked about this conversation in 1989, his recollection was that it was Thatcher who put through the call because some rumour of the intended operation had been picked up in London. His memory must be at fault here, and the reason is revealing. It is true that that particular call had come from her, but only because the earlier initiative had come from his office. Officials in London remember the first call coming through from Washington and McFarlane says that he arranged for it to be made. He had said to Reagan: 'This is going to be something which may create some misgivings among allies who never want you to do anything but support Nato, and any time you get very far off that course they begin to worry. So you ought to consult.' Reagan took the point readily enough; but, according to McFarlane, it had not been second nature to him. He customarily left detailed decisions of that sort to his staff.

They would know that he always wanted to keep in touch with Thatcher. On that broad principle the initiative would come from him. His staff were fully aware how much store he set by the relationship, and that conditioned their actions. They knew he wanted to keep in step with the British government whenever possible. But he would nearly always leave it to his aides to suggest when a particular call should be put through. He would not think much about it, and the sequence of calls would not lodge in his mind.

Why was she not informed until the last minute? Any idea that it was a mere oversight can be dismissed immediately. The British government had been trying to discover American intentions for some days and had been deliberately excluded.

It was natural for Britain to be interested. Grenada had achieved full independence as a member of the Commonwealth in 1974. Five years later power was seized by the revolutionary Marxist Maurice Bishop, who was in turn overthrown on 13 October 1983 and then murdered six days later. The new regime was a group of extreme left-wing murderous thugs under a military ruler, General Hudson Austin, who had been in command of Grenada's modest army under the Bishop regime. But the Queen's representative, the Governor-General, Sir Paul Scoon, was still there. He was, indeed, the only constitutional authority on the island, and the invasion was subsequently to be justified on the basis of an appeal for help which Scoon was alleged to have made verbally before the operation began. A number of British nationals were also still on the island, so Britain could claim a right to be involved on both constitutional and humanitarian grounds.

The position was obviously unstable and United States anxieties about the Caribbean have been well known ever since Castro came to power in Cuba. Rumours developed that some Caribbean governments were seeking outside military help to install a more reasonable regime in Grenada. Formal requests were made to Washington by the Prime Minister of Barbados, Tom Adams, and by the Organisation of Eastern Caribbean States, with the highly articulate Miss Eugenia Charles, the Prime Minister of Dominica, as its spokesman. Whether those requests were spontaneous or were stimulated by the United States has remained in dispute. Even at the time the position appeared so confusing that on Friday 21 October the British Foreign Office asked its embassy in Washington to find out what was happening.

So began a few days of intense British diplomatic activity. On the Friday Robin Renwick (subsequently the British Ambassador to South Africa) saw the Deputy Director for Politico-Military Affairs at the State Department, who told him that at a meeting of the NSC it had been agreed to proceed cautiously. Britain would be forewarned if the United States decided to take more active steps.

The next day Renwick saw Admiral Jonathan Howe, the Director for Politico-Military Affairs. So too did Derek Thomas, the British Minister in Washington (later Ambassador in Rome), who was also assured that Britain would be consulted before the Americans took action. On the Sunday Thomas saw Howe again and Lawrence Eagleburger, though much of their discussion this time was taken up by the Middle East. Over the weekend the British Ambassador, Sir Oliver Wright, was in touch with Eagleburger. All to no avail.

Only on the Monday afternoon did Eagleburger tell the Ambassador that the President would be sending the Prime Minister a message informing her of the invasion. This was, it is true, some hours before the leaders of Congress were put in the picture. But it was also some hours after Geoffrey Howe had so cavalierly swept aside such rumours in the House of Commons. It was therefore too late to save the British government from humiliation at home. The invasion was launched in the early hours of Tuesday 24 October. British ministers and diplomats felt let down and led astray.

Not all the American officials who gave assurances may have known the true position. But some of them did, and those that did not must have been aware that they were giving assurances without the necessary knowledge and authority. They were acting under strict instructions not even to allow any suspicion to get out, which may go some of the way to explain why normally reliable and helpful officials were on this occasion not only uninformative but positively misleading.

Why should there have been such paranoia about letting even so reliable an ally as Britain know what they had in mind? After all, the two countries share so many intelligence secrets and the President had so often indicated his trust in the Prime Minister. One answer is that there was genuine dread of allowing the secret to break in Washington for fear of putting the lives of American troops at risk. Reagan is able to claim quite justifiably that not only were the Congressional leaders not told until the last moment, but neither was his own press office. That was a measure of the concern to preserve confidentiality in a city not renowned for its capacity to keep confidences.

He recalls that he had been alerted at four o'clock on that Saturday morning: 'I was down in a cottage at the Augusta golf course when the call came that the other Caribbean states, those island nations, had phoned in an appeal.' They would provide a military contribution themselves, 'but they didn't have anywhere near what was necessary and couldn't do without us'. His response was not going to be long delayed: 'I felt immediately there was no way, if our country said no to that, that we could show our faces any place in the world.' Face must have been of some concern to him and the rest of the administration that weekend, because early on the Sunday morning news arrived of the massacre of American marines in Beirut.

American troops had gone to Lebanon the year before as the heart of a peacekeeping mission in which British troops were also engaged. Haig's last act as Secretary of State had been to plan the operation, but it was not put into effect as he had envisaged. He had wanted the peacekeeping force to go in as the guarantors of an agreement that was already in place for the departure of all foreign troops from the country. The President announced the mission, however, before the agreement had been confirmed. It collapsed, and the troops who went in to Lebanon ostensibly as impartial peacekeepers found themselves in effect supporting the Christian-dominated Lebanese government.

The Pentagon was, not surprisingly, unhappy about such a use of American troops, and on Sunday 23 October their anxiety was justified. A Muslim on a suicide mission drove a truck loaded with explosives into the United States marine barracks in Beirut, killing two hundred and forty-one American servicemen. The President, who had gone to Augusta, Georgia, for what was supposed to be a quiet weekend of golf with George Shultz, was under pressure to a greater extent than ever before.

When Reagan and Thatcher did talk at last, he explained to her that his fear was not that there would be a leak on her side but on his. Even the making of a telephone call, he told her, might have allowed something to get out in Washington at an earlier stage. Reagan believes, somewhat erroneously, that once she was given that explanation it calmed a great many of her concerns.

There was another consideration in the mind of Reagan's staff, even if not in his own. Rather than Thatcher's anxieties being set at rest if she had been informed earlier, they had a shrewd idea that she would have objected to the operation. In that case, she would not just have shrugged her shoulders and let her ally get on with it. She would have been much more likely to be on the telephone to Reagan for much of the weekend trying to persuade him of his folly. He never declined to receive a call from her and was always so much influenced by her judgment that he might have had second thoughts if he had talked to her in time. At the very least, the planning would have been complicated, there might well have been delay and the operation might conceivably have been called off altogether. Whatever the outcome, it would have been a nightmare for the staff.

When he did go ahead, despite her protests, she was outraged. She appeared to have drawn the impression from her telephone conversation with him that he would think about it. There would not in fact then have been time for him to do so without causing chaos within his own administration, but an element of personal frustration seemed to be mixed with her indignation. Reagan himself believes that if they had spoken at an earlier stage he would have been able to get her agreement. Some who were close to her at that time believe he may be right.

In private, among ministers and officials, she made clear her sense of betrayal. She had a raw sense of having been let down. She believed that she had gone out of her way to support Reagan, not because she always believed that he was right, but because she felt she had an obligation to an ally and a friend. Now he had disregarded her until it was too late for her voice to count.

She had other objections as well. The Commonwealth factor weighed with her, but what seemed to worry her more was the comparison with Afghanistan. How could we in the West condemn the Soviets convincingly if we seemed to be doing much the same sort of thing ourselves? Then there were the legal considerations. It was not for nothing that she had been trained as a lawyer. She was always uncomfortable if she had difficulty in justifying any action in terms of international law. The political embarrassment for her government must also have been very much on her mind.

On the day after the invasion, on Wednesday 26 October, there was an emergency debate in the House of Commons. Geoffrey Howe can have experienced few more awkward parliamentary occasions in the course of his long career. As Foreign Secretary he had to give the principal speech explaining the government's position. He could hardly justify an action which he had loftily dismissed two days before as in effect a figment of Labour's diseased imagination. He was almost equally reluctant to undermine the Anglo–American relationship, so he declined to condemn the invasion. That left him exposed to the taunt from David Steel, the Liberal Party leader, that, while Howe was justified in saying that more than one view could be held on this issue, it was not possible for more than one view to be held by the Foreign Secretary and he had failed to say which one was his.

In the United Nations Security Council the British Ambassador, Sir John Thomson, steered a delicate course. He managed both to dissociate himself from the American action and to distance himself even more from America's critics. It was a speech that was calculated to do the least possible damage to Anglo–American relations, while not renouncing Britain's position. That faithfully reflected the line that Thatcher herself wished to take in the immediate aftermath of the invasion.

Such statesmanlike ambiguity is not a posture that she could have maintained for long. The following Sunday, when questioned during a phone-in programme on the BBC World Service, she let rip. 'We in the Western countries, the Western democracies,' she declared with passion, 'use our force to defend our way of life. We do not use it to walk into other people's countries, independent sovereign territories.'

She was clearly sceptical about the claims that the United States was responding to a call for help. 'There was no call through the British Prime Minister,' she maintained, 'the British government, nor I understand through the Head of State before invasion.' This did not mean that there was not a call, 'but there was no call through us, or that we knew about, or that was communicated to us in any way'. Her disbelief was shining through.

Even stronger stuff was to come. She told a later questioner: 'If you are pronouncing a new law that wherever Communism reigns against the will of the people, even though it's happened internally, there the United States shall enter, then we are going to have really terrible wars in the world.'

At that time, Thatcher and many British officials were so outraged because they were reading more into the special relationship than had ever existed. They were assuming that it was customary for neither side to take any decision to act on anything that touched the interest of the other without full consultation. If that was supposed to be a rule, it was not supported by precedent.

Britain and France had acted unilaterally over Suez in 1956, though they had been sorely provoked by American inconsistency and evasion. The United States had not consulted Britain before taking the critical decision in the Cuban missile crisis, as Lord Harlech made clear. He acknowledged that, even in their frequent telephone conversations after that, Kennedy had used Macmillan as a valued sounding board rather than a source of advice. Cuba was not, it is true, a member of the Commonwealth; but the Commonwealth factor was only a subsidiary cause of Thatcher's outrage over Grenada.

In the Falklands War, which was regularly paraded as a gleaming example of the special relationship in action, the British government had decided to send the task force before consulting the United States. That was a case when Britain looked to its American ally for practical assistance almost as one of the rights of friendship. Over Grenada, the United States was not looking for anything from Britain, except approval or at least the absence of public criticism.

Both over the Falklands and Grenada, the British and American governments acted on their own accord because they believed that they were responding to political necessity. Both were successful. Yet there was a difference. The Falklands War has passed into the folklore of Anglo–American cooperation. For a time Grenada had precisely the opposite image. The trouble was that the episode reinforced the worst fears that each side had of the other. To the British, Reagan came across as the bullying, trigger-happy cowboy. To the Americans, the British looked self-righteous, unreliable and feeble.

Had the operation failed, the damage to Anglo–American relations might have been severe. In the United States there was a pained reaction for a short time. A British visitor in the weeks immediately afterwards was constantly assailed by the question: 'Why did you not stand by us over Grenada as we stood by you over the Falklands?'

So the Anglo–American relationship went through a bad patch in the last few months of 1983. No doubt nerves were already taut as the trial of wills with the peace movements moved to a climax before the deployment of the missiles began in November. The two issues reacted on each other. That such a pro-American as Thatcher should be castigating the United States was bound to have an effect on British opinion, and there was anger in Washington at the rising tide of anti-American sentiment. Senior British officials in London were advised that the pot might boil over.

That was just before the appointment of Charles Price as Ambassador in London. He was the first American ambassador in Thatcher's time as Party Leader with whom she had much rapport. Although Elliott Richardson and Anne Armstrong, who were in London while she was Leader of the Opposition, are both Republicans, neither of them had established a close relationship with Thatcher. Kingman Brewster, who was appointed to London by Carter, the Democratic ambassador of a Democratic president, was even less congenial to her. John Louis was regarded as a diplomatic lightweight.

Price was also relatively inexperienced in diplomacy. A political appointee – as are all American ambassadors to Britain – he had made a fortune manufacturing candy and then in banking in Kansas City, Missouri. His diplomatic career, before taking up his post in London, had been confined to two years as Ambassador to Belgium; but he worked hard at learning the ropes. A friendly, heavily built man, with a bluff manner, he won much respect in London after a slow start. Not the least of his assets was that he and his wife were known to be personal friends of the Reagans. They also got on well with the Thatchers as a family. It was a good time to have a strong American ambassador in London to help overcome the Grenada storms.

McFarlane recalls that he had been critical of the British without realising how they had been misled. In a conversation at the British Embassy shortly afterwards, he believes with the Ambassador, he was brought up short when told of the assurances that had been given. 'It's one thing if you don't tell somebody,' McFarlane remarked, as he looked back on these events some years later. 'That's bad enough, but if you tell them the contrary and then you violate what you've told them, that's outrageous.' McFarlane acknowledges that he was astonished and told Reagan. 'It put it in a little different light for him,' according to McFarlane. 'It made it a little easier for him to go back too before long and let bygones by bygones.' Certainly, Reagan speaks of the Grenada operation now with satisfaction, and without a hint of animosity over Thatcher's attitude at the time. He had won, so it did not really matter.

Thatcher was equally convinced that she had been correct. 'I was right, wasn't I?' The question she put to an official some years afterwards may suggest a little insecurity, but not a change of heart. She was no doubt relieved that the Americans restored democracy and got their troops out of the island quickly, but she still believes that her objections were justified.

They were also shared in one particular quarter, contrary to the President's impression. In his account of his years in the Reagan administration, *The Great Universal Embrace*, Kenneth Adelman, the former Director of the Arms Control and Development Agency, tells an amusing story of Reagan returning to his advisers after his first meeting with Gorbachev at the Geneva summit of 1985. As they waited breathlessly to hear how the conversation had gone, Reagan began telling them how Thatcher and the Queen differed over

Grenada. Adelman adds privately that Reagan elaborated to say that the Queen thought that what the United States had done in Grenada was fine.

The President was mistaken. If there was any difference between them over Grenada, the Queen was even more incensed than Thatcher by the American action. She takes her role as Head of the Commonwealth extremely seriously. When she visited the island in 1985 her entourage was shown the table under which her representative, the Governor General, had been forced to take refuge during the American attack before being bundled on to an American ship.

It was fortunate for the relationship that the Grenada episode had not occurred a month or so earlier. A little while before the invasion Thatcher had phoned Reagan to seek his support for the nomination of Lord Carrington as Secretary-General of Nato. As a distinguished former Foreign Secretary, who had won wide respect for his swift and honourable resignation at the time of the Falklands invasion, Carrington had excellent credentials. He was not, however, the only possible candidate to succeed the former Dutch Foreign Minister, Joseph Luns, and there were mixed feelings about him in Washington.

He had not got on well with Haig (as exemplified by the Secretary's 'duplicitous bastard' remark). Carrington's sometimes flippant manner, which reflects an impish sense of humour, may have grated on the stern professional soldier. Carrington has a tendency to make mildly outrageous remarks in private, expecting them to be taken only half seriously. It is a pleasant characteristic, which adds to the fun of life so long as he is not misunderstood.

During his time as Foreign Secretary he was not understood well in Washington. That may have been because most of his dealings would have been with Haig, and other members of the administration knew of him only from what they heard from the Secretary of State. At any rate, when Carrington resigned there was not the sense of regret from officials in Washington that might have been expected.

The suspicion that he favoured a more conciliatory foreign policy than was then fashionable in Washington or London was strengthened in April 1983, a few months before the Nato job came up, when, in a lecture to the International Institute of Strategic Studies in London, he referred to the West's bursts of 'megaphone diplomacy'. Or, rather, he planned to use the phrase then. He omitted it from his speech for fear of giving offence, but it was in the text released to the press. As the megaphones were presumably in the hands of Reagan and Thatcher, this remark was bound to count against him in Reagan's Washington.

Although Carrington subsequently developed excellent relations with Weinberger, at that time the Pentagon was against his nomination. Other candidates had their supporters. The former Portuguese Foreign Minister, Vasco Futscher Pereira, was in the running. Leo Tindemans, the Belgian Foreign Minister and former Prime Minister, was waiting in the wings without becoming a declared candidate. It was ironic in view of his later role that Charles Price, who was still Ambassador to Belgium, was backing Tindemans. 'Charlie didn't know Carrington at that point,' Ambassador David Abshire recalls. 'Later they became very good friends.'

Thatcher's call to Reagan swept all other considerations aside. 'My understanding,' says David Abshire, who had become United States Ambassador to Nato in July that year, 'is that he was very responsive, as he always is to her, and the decision was basically made in that response. This caught the Pentagon off guard.' Instructions were given to Abshire not to get out in front but quietly to support the campaign that was developing for Carrington at Nato headquarters. 'It would have been a mistake diplomatically,' Abshire points out, 'for the Americans ever to take an open lead. It was enough for us to give quiet support behind others, for even that immediately dampened other candidates.' If Carrington's candidacy had just been pressed through the normal diplomatic channels, the Ambassador thinks he would still have got the post. But there might have been an element of doubt and Abshire believes that Carrington would not have wished to campaign for it: 'So if the Americans had seemed a little cool he might have backed off.'

Nobody, least of all the Americans, ever regretted the appointment. Carrington was exceptionally highly regarded as Nato Secretary-General, and was more widely appreciated in this post by the United States than he had been as British Foreign Secretary. 'He had the ability of an Eisenhower,' according to Abshire, 'to get diverse representatives to work together. Carrington was a master at coalition politics.' Had it not been for Thatcher's call to Reagan, it is possible that he might never have allowed his name to go forward.

It was not all sweetness and light even after Carrington's nomination had been approved. Before it was made public Luns summoned Abshire to his office and said that he had got word that Carrington wanted to take over soon after the announcement, which was planned for December. Luns was incensed and declared in no uncertain terms that unless he was caught in some dastardly sexual act he would not be leaving before the following summer. Word was passed along, and Carrington became Secretary-General of Nato on 26 June 1984.

12

THE SECOND TERM BEGINS

Thatcher and Reagan did not see each other again for some months after Grenada. She had last been in Washington at the end of September 1983, less than a month before the operation. That was shortly after the shooting down of the Korean airliner, when both the American and British governments were beginning to reassess their long-term attitude towards the Soviet Union. They were marching in step in September, with not a hint of the disagreement to come the following month.

Thatcher had been reelected in June for a second term with an enlarged majority in the House of Commons, and had every reason to be grateful for Reagan's assistance at Williamsburg in the middle of the campaign. They were facing intense protests from the peace movement, in Britain as elsewhere in Western Europe, over the deployment of cruise missiles; but that was not going to divide them. They were equally firm in resisting the pressure.

There was no reason to plan another early meeting, and after Grenada it seemed better to allow feelings to cool for a while on both sides of the Atlantic. Reagan was able blithely to disregard Thatcher's indignation over the operation, but his administration had been upset by the rise in anti-Americanism in Britain which followed it. The two leaders did not meet again until the economic summit in London in early June 1984. Now it was Reagan's turn to face reelection, though he looked as certain to win his contest in November as Thatcher had been the year before. None the less, it is one of the marks of a master politician to take nothing for granted. So it was no surprise that Reagan decided to visit Ireland before flying to London.

There are something like forty million Americans who consider themselves to be at least partly of Irish origin, and many of them have an intense sentimental attachment to the connection. What better opportunity for an Irish–American President in an election year than to go back to the family origins? It was in the village of Ballyporeen, in County Tipperary, that Reagan's great-grandfather, Michael O'Regan, was born in 1829, and from there that he later emigrated to the United States.

Ballyporeen is not renowned as one of Ireland's more picturesque villages, but it responded to the presidential homecoming with a display of commercial enterprise that was in the true spirit of Reaganism. Four years before – within hours of *Debrett's Peerage*, the authority on genealogy, determining that the Reagan family came from there – an innkeeper had renamed his hostelry the 'Ronald Reagan Lounge'. That naturally caught the eyes of the President's advance men when they were planning the visit. So Reagan had to drink a glass of local beer there, while his wife sipped an Irish liqueur: just the sort of folksy occasion that was made for the camera.

The public relations experts were also pleased to find a Ronald Reagan Gift Shop and a tea shop named The White House. They may have been less impressed by the opening of the village's first public lavatories. A ceremonial presidential entry would not have been quite the photo-opportunity they were seeking.

Reagan has the sense of style and the authentic sentiment to handle the absurdity as well as the warmth of such an expedition to discover his roots. If some of the words he was given to say more than verged upon the mawkish, his personal demeanour won friends. With the American media very much in attendance, the visit served its political purpose back home. It also had another political significance. It symbolised the importance of the Irish dimension in Anglo–American relations.

The beginning of the Reagan administration had been a time of particular tension in Northern Ireland. On 1 March 1981, little more than a month after Reagan was inaugurated, Bobby Sands, a member of the IRA who had been convicted of firearms and ammunition offences, began a hunger strike in the Maze Prison in Belfast to demand political status. The British government consistently refused to grant this to Sands or to other IRA prisoners who went on hunger strike. Sands himself and nine others died before this particular form of protest was called off in early October.

Passions were naturally aroused in the United States as elsewhere. The administration applied no pressure on Thatcher to compromise, but the episode emphasised the potential significance of Irish affairs. Haig, as the new Secretary of State, asked his deputy, William Clark, to keep abreast of the issue. Clark was interested in Irish affairs and continued to be centrally involved in this field as he moved to be National Security Adviser, then Secretary of the Interior and even after he left the administration.

When Reagan went to Ireland the British government was understandably nervous that an Irish–American President discovering his roots for the benefit of Irish–American voters might sound a little too sympathetic to the nationalist cause. There was no cause for complaint. Reagan denounced sectarian violence and the assistance that some Americans give to the IRA as firmly as Thatcher could have wished.

At the same time, he responded sympathetically to the New Ireland Forum. This was a body to which all constitutional parties in both parts of Ireland were invited to send representatives to consider in depth the future of Northern Ireland. The Unionists declined to send anyone, but the predominantly Catholic Social Democratic and Labour Party (SDLP) did attend from the north. Indeed, the idea was essentially the brainchild of John Hume, the SDLP Leader, and Garret FitzGerald, the Prime Minister of the Republic.

Hume, heavily built, rather shaggy and soft-spoken, is a moderate among nationalist politicians, with a very high reputation among most Americans who follow Irish affairs. FitzGerald, genial and loquacious, is a man of high intellect and conciliatory temperament.

Under their inspiration the Forum had produced a report, just before Reagan's arrival, that recognised the necessity to respect and reconcile the two traditions in Ireland: Catholic and nationalist, on the one hand; Protestant and Unionist, on the other. It was well-meaning and constructive in tone, but it had one fatal weakness. As the Unionist parties did not take part in the Forum, the Protestant community was not associated with its conclusions. None the less, Reagan pleased his hosts by going out of his way to endorse its work. In doing so, he encouraged hopes of a new political settlement.

From Ireland Reagan moved directly to London, where he had talks with Margaret Thatcher before they both spent a day in Normandy commemorating the fortieth anniversary of the allied landings there. That was an occasion for Anglo–American sentiment, which for both of them was entirely genuine. No flicker of resentment remained about Grenada. Then back to London for the economic summit, which opened on 7 June. Thatcher and Reagan approached the summit with different, but complementary, requirements that reflected their political circumstances.

Although she had won her reelection campaign in handsome style the previous year, Thatcher was now embroiled in the most serious domestic struggle of all her years in power. The miners' strike, which began on 6 March 1984, was for her the internal equivalent of the Falklands War.

There was a sense in which she appeared to have only a short lease on power until the miners had been defeated. Ever since the previous miners' strike had driven Edward Heath's Conservative government from office ten years before, it had seemed that any government ruled only on the sufferance of the miners. Even in the age of oil most British power stations were run on coal, and it was the lack of coal to keep electricity supplies going that had forced British industry to be restricted to a three-day working week in 1974. The miners' industrial power, it was widely assumed, could not be challenged by the elected administration. In avoiding a confrontation in 1981 Thatcher herself had seemed to confirm that belief, but if she was to be true to Thatcherism the battle had to come some time.

By the spring of 1984 the government was ready. Coal stocks had been built up to a level that could sustain a long dispute without disrupting power supplies, and there was an appropriately terrifying enemy. Arthur Scargill, the President of the National Union of Mine-workers, is a Marxist who looks and sounds like the extremist he is. His demonic style of speaking, combined with a desire to shock, qualified him well for the role of a public threat. By portraying itself as standing firm for moderation against the threat of Scargill the government went a long way to win the battle of public opinion.

The specific issue of whether uneconomic pits should be closed to provide for a commercially efficient coal industry mattered much less than the symbolism of the dispute. Two issues above all were at stake: the capacity of the elected government to run the country; and the role of the trade-union movement. One of the central objectives of Thatcherism was to curb the excessive power of the unions. Reagan had shown how that could be done in somewhat different circum-stances by his handling of the air-traffic controllers' dispute. Thatcher had moved in that direction by the series of changes in trade-union law. She had rammed the message home by refusing to consult union leaders on national economic policy in what had become the traditional fashion. Yet ultimately the issue had to be settled on the field of industrial battle.

It was a conflict with wider political implications, because the longer it went on the more it was likely to embarrass the Labour Party. As the party organically linked to the unions, Labour generally suffers electorally when there is a disruptive strike. There was the still greater danger in this instance of being associated by public opinion with an intensely unpopular union leader in Arthur Scargill. As the newly elected Labour Leader, Neil Kinnock did his best to distance the party from Scargill while demonstrating his sympathy for the miners. In the early stages he was not altogether successful in this exercise in political gymnastics. Later he was to denounce Scargill courageously and unequivocally.

Yet if her principal political opponent was embarrassed, the strike was a cause of still greater hazard for Thatcher. The success, even the life, of her government was at stake. Locked in conflict as she was at home, she needed a friendly economic summit in the summer of 1984, with general approval of her chairmanship. Above all, she had to put Grenada behind her and be fully reconciled with Reagan.

The pressures on him as he approached the summit were of a different order. It mattered to him in the run-up to his reelection campaign that he should emerge from the conference with a general aura of statesmanship. It was even more important that he should not be pilloried for his economic policies, with the budget deficit then running at more than 200 billion dollars a year and interest rates at a high level.

As chairman, Thatcher was particularly well placed to help him on both scores. So a reconciliation summit suited him politically as well as being entirely consistent with his nature. For him to have borne a grudge for Grenada would have been quite out of character, and anyway he had been able to disregard her objections with impunity.

On the whole, the summit went well for both of them. Their friendship was obviously, even ostentatiously, restored. The communiqué had a flavour of Reaganomics, pointing to the growing strain of public expenditure, the rigidities in the labour market, and the need to improve efficiency and promote growth. Above all, it referred to budget deficits and high interest rates only in general terms without pointing a finger at the United States in particular.

Reagan recalls that at one session Thatcher was attacked by one of the leaders for being undemocratic in the way that she was conducting the meeting. Reagan did not say so, but others who were there recall that the offender was Trudeau. 'I was just aghast,' the President says. 'She kept her cool fine, and the meeting went on.' After it was over he caught up with her out in the hall and expressed his indignation. ' "Margaret, he was way out of line. He had no business talking to you like that." And she said: "Women know when men are being childish," which I thought was pretty characteristic.'

*

It was at this time that Thatcher first raised seriously with Reagan a subject that was to assume dramatic proportions. A charge against British Airways of infringing American anti-trust legislation would not seem a likely candidate for stardom, but the implications were far-reaching. The Thatcher government had been eager since its early days in power to privatise British Airways. This was now being held up by two legal actions in the United States.

One was a civil action, filed in November 1982 on behalf of the creditors of Laker Airways, which alleged that it had been brought to bankruptcy by a conspiracy among other airlines to fix fares on transatlantic routes. Laker Airways' speciality had been cut-price fares on these routes. It had managed to attract large numbers of passengers for whom transatlantic travel had been no more than a distant dream. Not surprisingly, other airlines did not watch idly and benevolently. A number of them responded to the new competition by offering specially cheap fares of their own. That in itself was a perfectly legitimate business tactic. The accusation was that they had collaborated to do so, and that this collaboration had amounted to a commercial conspiracy which infringed American anti-trust laws. An action for damages against these airlines offered the best hope of Laker creditors recovering their debts. One of the most prominent of the alleged culprits was British Airways.

That was bad enough. The airline could hardly be sold off to private investors until that action had been resolved. Worse was to come in March 1983, when the United States Department of Justice launched a Grand Jury investigation into the alleged conspiracy.

This meant that the United States government was formally considering the possibility of criminal charges against British Airways, and some of its current and former employees, as well as against other airlines. It was likely to be a lengthy procedure, it might lead to serious penalties and it would give credibility to the civil action. There would be much less incentive for the plaintiffs to reach a final settlement out of court until they knew the outcome of the criminal investigation.

The British Embassy, which had been informed of the Justice Department's intentions shortly before the Grand Jury was announced, warned that this would be dynamite. It would lead to a major political row between the two governments. What followed was a classic case of transatlantic misunderstanding, not just in technical terms but in the deeper sense of exposing a gulf in thinking between the two sides.

Anti-trust legislation has a special place in the order of American values. It was implemented with particular zeal at this time by the

141

head of the Justice Department's anti-trust section, Elliott Seidon, who had the reputation with foreign officials of being something of an ogre. He struck all the more dread in their hearts because he was acknowledged to be an extremely good lawyer. Any idea that the department should not proceed with a Grand Jury for political reasons seemed to him laughable. The department's job was to apply the law without fear or favour. It was independent. Not even the President could intervene.

There followed a series of abrasive meetings in which the Americans made it clear to British officials that they expected the British to cooperate with the Grand Jury. That meant encouraging current and former employees to go to the United States to testify. If they would not testify voluntarily, then American officials implied that the United States had the power to send federal marshals to interrogate witnesses in the United Kingdom.

The British responded by invoking the Protection of Trading Interests Act (PTIA), which gave the government power to forbid a British national from cooperating with a foreign court in certain circumstances. By now the exchanges were threatening to get out of hand. Howe and Shultz began to discuss the issue quite frequently, and the message was sent down to the respective bureaucracies to 'cool it'. But on whose terms?

In British eyes the United States was once again trying to make foreign companies observe American law – the principle of extra-territoriality, which had caused so much trouble over the gas pipeline – without any regard for the political consequences. To the Americans the issue was the simple one of applying the rigour of the law, and a very special law at that. The sensitivity of anti-trust legislation inhibited Shultz and Elizabeth Dole, the Transportation Secretary, from doing much more than appeal for calm. To have intervened beyond that might have exposed them politically.

The Americans were infuriated by the British decision to invoke the Trading Interests Act. Shultz phoned Howe to protest, and a delegation of officials was suddenly assembled one Sunday afternoon in June 1983 to present the British case at urgent meetings in Washington. One member of the team had to be summoned in such haste from holiday in the Welsh mountains that he flew to Washington in his weekend clothes. The meetings were abrasive. American fury was expressed to the full, but at last the seriousness of the disagreement seemed to be appreciated.

Seidon was renowned for his refusal to socialise with diplomats. It was a mark of his incorruptibility. So it was a special moment when he phoned Roger Maynard, the official at the British Embassy principally concerned with the Laker case, to suggest that they had better go out for a drink. So concerned was Seidon to preserve his reputation that they had to find one of Washington's less reputable bars where they were not likely to meet anyone. It gave a conspiratorial touch to a deadly serious discussion. This was the first of several similar meetings between the two.

A few hours and several beers later they had worked out a compromise. This was not an agreement on the investigation itself. It was simply an understanding as to how they could manage matters during the investigation so as to prevent a diplomatic explosion.

American officials would quite informally give the British a list of those whom they wished to appear before the Grand Jury. The British would raise no objection to the questioning of British Airways employees working in the United States: they could be subpoenaed anyway. BA employees working in Britain would be permitted to testify in the United States if they wished to do so. The Trading Interests Act would not be used to stop them. Nor would it be invoked against former employees of BA, who were most at risk as individuals; but they would be told that it was not British policy to cooperate with the Grand Jury and they would not be encouraged to go. In addition, the Department of Transport in London would make its own examination of the alleged activities under scrutiny by the Grand Jury and send its report to the Justice Department in Washington. This would simply be a statement of the facts, not an assessment of the legal implications.

In return, the Americans made two promises. They would not try to question any British national without informing the British authorities first, and they would warn British officials in advance before the Grand Jury handed down any indictments.

This was a good way of allowing the Grand Jury to proceed without doing too much damage to Anglo–American relations, but it did nothing to improve the prospects for privatising BA. This was where matters stood when Thatcher and Reagan talked in London at the time of the economic summit; but there were still British hopes that, after all the diplomatic fuss, the Justice Department would find a means of avoiding indictments.

That was an illusion. The intensity of the department's determination on anti-trust legislation had been underestimated. By the autumn of 1984 it became clear to the British Embassy that the Grand Jury was considering indictments of British Airways and probably of some of its former employees as well. This provoked a sense of crisis on the British side. Possible means of retaliation were considered. One idea was to impose a ticket tax on all American passengers flying into British airports. This never reached the point of being endorsed by British ministers, but papers setting out the proposal were circulated among government departments in London and the Embassy in Washington. It was much more than a bright thought over a cup of coffee.

No retaliation was required because of the personal pressure exerted by Margaret Thatcher. As soon as Reagan won his landslide victory on 6 November she launched her offensive. Her views were made formidably plain to the American Ambassador, Charles Price, and there was the prospect of a lengthy harangue from the Prime Minister when she met the President at Camp David in December. Then, quite suddenly, Reagan agreed to call off the Grand Jury. The move, which was announced on 19 November, was both dramatic and momentous. For a president to halt a Grand Jury investigation was almost unprecedented. The British Embassy was taken quite by surprise and the Justice Department was stunned.

Justice officials were so upset that they refused to cooperate with the embassy in sending out a press statement. The embassy would have preferred to issue a simple statement that the Grand Jury had been terminated. Instead, the department leaked to the press that this was no ordinary decision, but a political intervention by the President.

He may have felt that the issue was not worth the trouble it was causing between the two governments. That was, not surprisingly, the view of the State Department and the American Embassy in London. Or Reagan may have responded more on ideological grounds to Thatcher's impassioned pleas. The argument she always used was that they both believed in reducing the role of the state in economic life, they both wanted privatisation and this fundamental objective was being impeded by this legalistic dispute.

Whatever the reason, he gave her precisely what she wanted, without ending the whole business once and for all. There was still the civil action, which continued to hold up the privatisation of BA, but Thatcher was to see Reagan at Camp David the following month. She waited until she got there before taking the Laker question further.

Reagan's reelection in November had borne a distinct similarity to Thatcher's the previous summer. Both coasted to victory without a serious challenge. Both relied heavily on their personal appeal. Both fought an essentially bland campaign that was to affect their second terms.

For Thatcher the election of June 1983 had come within a year of her Falklands triumph. That guaranteed her success unless she made an extraordinary blunder. This pointed to a cautious campaign, which gave her victory with an increased majority, but no mandate. In the early part of her second term there were many accusations that in her domestic policy she had run out of steam.

Reagan aroused the same fears at the beginning of his second term. He too had been reelected a year after a military success. The Grenada operation was as popular in the United States as the Falklands victory had been in Britain. Economists were worried about the budget and trading deficits, but most Americans were enjoying prosperity with lower inflation and increasing growth. Above all, Reagan radiated a spirit of confidence. He only had to be himself in order to win. Innovative policies were a luxury that was not necessary and might even have cost votes.

In both cases the impression of inactivity at home proved to be somewhat exaggerated. The process of tax reform – the creation of a simpler, more coherent system, with lower basic rates – is one of the principal domestic achievements of Thatcherism and Reaganism. It was begun in both countries at the same stage in the political cycle: early in the second term.

In Britain that was in the first budget of Thatcher's second administration, in March 1984. Privatisation, which had started slowly in her first year, gathered pace as the months passed; and overshadowing everything was the continuing miners' strike. The outcome of that did more to change the economic climate than any piece of legislation. In the United States, as 1984 moved towards its close, the ground was being prepared for the great battle for tax reform. But before the year was out Thatcher and Reagan had serious business to attend to in the foreign field.

13

A COUP AT CAMP DAVID

In mid-December 1984 a new, younger figure from the Kremlin paid his first visit to Britain. Mikhail Gorbachev was rumoured to be the likely successor to Konstantin Chernenko, who had succeeded Andropov in February and was known to be in very poor health; but Gorbachev had not yet taken over and there was no certainty that he would.

Up to then Thatcher had proceeded fairly cautiously in seeking a dialogue with the East. First there had been her visit to Hungary early in the year. 'We had started just to stretch out a hand,' she said, 'and then I did decide to go to Andropov's funeral. Now if it is possible to get a welcome at a funeral I did, because they realised that it was quite something for me to go.' She had not gone to Brezhnev's funeral, so this was a signal. Even so, she ruled out any early summit meeting with Chernenko, beyond the brief encounter that was appropriate on that occasion. Building a new confidence between East and West was a process, she declared at the time, that would take years not months.

The coming of Gorbachev changed that. Thatcher prides herself on making up her mind about a person within a few minutes of meeting them. It is one of her more dangerous habits, but in the case of Gorbachev it worked. The rapport between them was established in one lengthy conversation at Chequers. 'He came at about twelve-thirty,' Thatcher remembers, 'and he went shortly, I think, before six.' The speed and certainty of her assessment were astonishing. 'I like Mr Gorbachev,' she pronounced after their talk. 'We can do business together.'

It was a statement that reverberated around the world. In Washington it was heard with much interest and even greater astonishment. From anyone else it would have provoked derision within the Reagan administration. It would have been dismissed as typical wishful thinking from a wimpish European. But after the Falklands nobody on either side of the Atlantic was inclined to call Thatcher wimpish.

There were still a good many people in Washington who were dismayed by her comment. 'Thatcher's initial glowing statements about Gorbachev, tended to create a somewhat misleading impression because deep down she was quite realistic about the Soviets', in the judgment of Frank Carlucci, later Reagan's National Security Adviser and then Defense Secretary. It was because she retained her reputation for realism that some others concluded that, if Gorbachev seemed all right to her, perhaps they should take him more seriously.

The impact on Reagan was particularly notable. 'It made his acceptance of Gorbachev a great deal simpler,' according to Max Kampelman, the chief United States disarmament negotiator at Geneva from 1985 until Reagan left office. 'The fact that she indicated that she could do business with him I think strengthened the President's resolve that this was an appropriate and a proper course for him to follow. That was significant, and therefore that maybe rivals the significance of the Churchill–Roosevelt phenomenon.'

Others attest to how seriously Reagan would take her views on Soviet affairs. 'Whenever they talked about the Russians,' McFarlane says, 'he would listen rather raptly to what she had to say. I think she was a profound influence on him.'

That influence was all the greater, in terms of East–West relations, from late 1984 onwards. Her speeches in late 1983 may have made it easier for him to change rhetorical direction in his television address of January 1984. The two of them may have made their assessments on the basis of the same intelligence reports. But she had not induced him to give that address. The persuasion was exercised from within his own administration, and it was anyway in accordance with part of what Reagan had always wanted.

It was more complicated when it came to Reagan's dealings with Gorbachev. Influence was still exerted on the President by his own advisers, but Thatcher played a more central role in encouraging a dialogue with the new Soviet leader. By now her friendship with Reagan was totally restored after the Grenada spat. She was the first Western leader to meet Gorbachev and Reagan was ready to be told that this was the first Soviet leader with whom serious exchanges would be both possible and worthwhile.

Of equal, some would say even more, consequence was the impact of the meeting with Thatcher upon Gorbachev himself. From the first, they argued vigorously. Both of them are people of intellectual assurance, both have a grasp of substance and both have confidence in their ability to debate. Her closeness to Reagan was an essential element of her appeal as an interlocutor for the Russian. He, for his part, needed to be convinced that the American President was a man he could do business with.

Thatcher explained how she set out to win the confidence of the future Soviet President without losing that of the American President. First of all, she made it absolutely plain that she was not a conventional go-between. There was not a whiff of moral equivalence in her approach. 'I am an ally of the United States,' she stressed to Gorbachev. 'We believe the same things, we believe passionately in the same battle of ideas, we will defend them to the hilt. Never try to separate me from them.' She emphasised that she would be telling Reagan about their conversation.

Having said that, she indicated that she understood Soviet concerns: 'You are as much entitled to defend your way of life as we are to defend ours, and you are as much entitled to have your security within your borders as we are.' She went on to point out that the world was coming to the end of the generations that remember the last war. 'I said to him I am a little bit older than you and you probably will not remember.' But Gorbachev was not slow with the appropriate response: 'Oh, I do.'

'I reckon our generation has one great duty to the next,' she told him. 'It is so to arrange our defences that there will never again be conflict or war. And the people most likely to realise the importance of that are those who actually experienced the privations of the last war. Now let us start to talk about that.'

There was nothing startlingly original in that little homily. What was striking was that she was saying it then to a potential Soviet leader on their first meeting, probably at length and certainly with her customary intensity.

Gorbachev was careful not to behave as if he had already taken over in Moscow. He was punctilious in referring always to 'Mr Chernenko's policies'. That increased Thatcher's respect for him. She was determined to show that she was not seeking to take advantage of their conversation.

Right at the beginning she told him: 'We will agree what we are going to say to the press at the end, and if there are certain things you say to me that are absolutely confidential, that will be respected. Now you will have to learn that you can trust me and I do not expect you to take it at once.' There are few better ways for one politician to win the trust of another than by making sure that confidences are kept from the press.

As with Reagan, it was for Thatcher a fortunate combination of the person and the circumstances. She had decided as a matter of policy to break through the wall of secrecy and mistrust that surrounded the Soviet Union.

Gorbachev made clear in the course of that discussion just how disturbed the Soviets were by SDI. He got no response from Thatcher. 'Do not waste any time,' she told him, 'on trying to persuade me to say to Ron Reagan: "Do not go ahead with SDI." That will get nowhere.' She knew that there was no chance of Reagan's giving it up, and the last thing she would have done would be to act as Gorbachev's emissary in such a matter. There could have been few surer ways of jeopardising the American bond.

Thatcher did, however, have anxieties of her own about SDI. She was appalled by the extravagant claims in Reagan's speech of 23 March 1983, unfolding the project. She was convinced that there was no way known to science in which 100 per cent cover could be provided against nuclear weapons. Her other concern was how the programme related to the Anti-Ballistic Missile (ABM) Treaty of 1972. 'I just have a belief that if you enter into agreements then you have a bounden duty to keep them,' she says, 'and I wanted to see how the whole thing fitted in.'

So did quite a number of other people. The mood within the Nato alliance at that stage was one of bewilderment and disarray. Nobody really understood the nature of the project. As expressed by the President, it sounded too fanciful to be taken seriously; and yet for him it was clearly a matter of the highest priority.

Thatcher's early reactions to SDI are not easy to chart because she does not seem to have been altogether consistent. To at least some of her ministers at the time she gave the impression of being strongly in favour of Reagan's speech. To McFarlane, with whom she had a long discussion on the subject at the London economic summit in June 1984, she appeared as a critic: 'I had the impression that the Prime Minister had serious misgivings about SDI from several standpoints.'

These related not only to the technical feasibility of the project, but also to the political implications. She was concerned about the threat to allied cohesion if it seemed that the United States was downgrading the importance of arms control. Above all, she wanted to be informed. She wanted to know what the state of the technology was, and the thinking of both the President and McFarlane. The two did not coincide. McFarlane never accepted Reagan's vision of a kind of astrodome over the American people. He saw SDI as a form of leverage over the Soviet Union, forcing it to compete in the area of high technology where the United States was strongest and therefore providing a powerful inducement to disarmament negotiations.

Thatcher certainly shared his objections to the more grandiose concept of SDI. She may have changed her mind from time to time about the project, or it may have been that she deliberately varied her stance according to whom she was speaking. Rather than emphasising agreement, she would have been trying to provide a corrective to whatever excesses she was hearing.

British opinion was hostile to SDI. The Foreign Office and the Ministry of Defence were deeply sceptical. One of their concerns was that if the United States deployed a strategic defensive system, the Soviet Union would have one sooner or later. The British deterrent would then be rendered ineffective. Thatcher was never prepared to have serious discussion at ministerial level on what would happen if both the Soviet Union and the United States had such a system. Either the idea seemed to her too fanciful, or too dangerous, to be entertained.

Knowing the objections of her ministers and their advisers, she might have seemed more in favour of SDI when speaking to them, so as to prevent anti-American sentiments coming from her government; and more critical when speaking to Americans, so as to persuade them of the need to put SDI in an acceptable framework.

By late 1984 this had become her principal objective. To have argued against SDI would not have weakened Reagan's commitment. It would simply have damaged her relations with him and excluded her from influence in Washington on the issue. She was aware that the Soviets were going ahead with their research, and did not want the West to be caught at a disadvantage. She was fascinated by the scientific aspects and over the following years was to have lengthy discussions with General James Abrahamson, the director of the American programme. She knew that there could be pleasing pickings for British industry from the research programme.

With these considerations in mind Thatcher set out on a lengthy foreign journey in December. Even before Gorbachev had left Britain, she was on her way to China, where she signed the Hong Kong Agreement. This provided that when the British lease on the New Territories runs out in 1997, the whole of the British colony of Hong Kong will revert to Chinese sovereignty. China guaranteed, under the terms of the agreement, that Hong Kong's free market economy and life-style would continue for another fifty years after 1997.

Even before the massacre of Tiananmen Square, there were doubts both in Britain and Hong Kong about the value of these assurances. The anxiety in the colony was naturally particularly acute. So Hong Kong had to be the next stop on Thatcher's itinerary, where she did her best to provide reassurance. From there she flew across the Pacific to the United States. The journey was broken in the middle of the night to refuel at Hickam Air Force Base in Hawaii. Characteristically, she demanded immediately to see Pearl Harbor, waved away the offered car, grabbed a flashlight from her handbag and strode away perhaps two-thirds of a mile to the water. From there she and her party were able to see the *Arizona*, the main memorial to the events of half a century ago. Then, Pearl Harbor having been inspected to her satisfaction, on to Washington.

There was fog on the night of Friday 21 December, and her plane was diverted from Andrews Air Force Base to Dulles International Airport. The greeting party from the embassy scrambled across town to meet her. They arrived a little while after her plane had touched down, but she had put the time to good use. 'Don't worry,' she said to startled officials as she descended. 'I've worked out the rearrangements.' While waiting, she had planned how her schedule should be changed the following day if the fog made it necessary for her to leave from Dulles – which in fact it did not. It was typical of her personal thoughtfulness for individuals, but also of her instinct to manage everyone and everything.

She had been accompanied on her travels by Robin Butler, her principal private secretary, by Charles Powell, her immensely influential private secretary for foreign affairs, and by Bernard Ingham, her press officer. These three formed her praetorian guard.

With Powell in particular, Thatcher had intense discussions on SDI as they flew across the Pacific. This was to be the main topic of her talk with Reagan at Camp David.

In the autumn of 1984 joint papers were put up to the Prime Minister from the Foreign Office and the Ministry of Defence, arguing that the project was unlikely to get anywhere and if it did it would be seriously destabilising. Thatcher did not agree with these papers, nor with the briefs for her Washington visit which were written along the same lines. The British Embassy view in Washington was also critical of the papers, but for purely tactical reasons. It argued that, while the reasoning in them was right, it would be impossible to persuade the President that he was wrong to look for a better way than nuclear weapons to preserve security. In the long run Congress would not finance an ambitious programme. So the task was to prevent the doctrine of deterrence being undermined in the meantime.

151

That was essentially the course which Thatcher followed in practice. Better to support SDI in principle and apply conditions that would restore the confidence of the allies, safeguard the principle of nuclear deterrence and preserve the ABM Treaty.

Even though her plane did not touch down until about midnight, she kept her advisers up late preparing for the following day's meeting. It was then that they worked out what was likely to be the most effective approach on SDI. That was not the only subject on her mind. To the embassy's surprise she was also still very much concerned about the Laker case. When the President called off the Grand Jury the previous month he had taken the major step towards resolving the issue, but the civil action still rumbled on. Until it was settled it would be impossible to privatise British Airways. She was determined to talk about this as well as the broader international questions at Camp David.

So Roger Maynard, the embassy's expert on the issue, was summoned hastily to appear at the Prime Minister's briefing at eight o'clock the next morning. For a full hour she focused the discussion on Laker while the arms-control and political experts waited their turn. Then, at a minute to nine, she said: 'Oh well, thank you very much, Mr Maynard. I've got to go and see the Vice-President now.' – and she was off to breakfast with Vice-President George Bush, whom she made it a practice to see every time she went to Washington. That may have been partly because she suspected that he was more influential in the Reagan administration than was widely believed. It was certainly because she was looking to the future.

Then it was up to Camp David by helicopter, accompanied not only by her personal entourage but also by Sir Oliver Wright, the Ambassador, and by John Kerr and Nigel Sheinwald of the embassy staff. At Camp David she and the President first had a meeting alone, with Powell and Peter Sommer of the National Security Council staff as note-takers.

Robin Butler had been prepared for a less orthodox mission at that initial meeting. Thatcher had been invited by the President and Mrs Reagan to see them as soon as she arrived at Camp David. That sounded ominously like a social occasion, and Thatcher was determined to discuss business. So the tall, elegant and personable Butler was deputed to exercise his social charm on Mrs Reagan. He was to engage her in conversation, if that were necessary to let the two leaders discuss more serious matters. In fact Mrs Reagan left the two leaders to talk together, so Butler's services were not required in this respect.

This first talk between Reagan and Thatcher at Camp David was principally about Gorbachev, with Thatcher enthusiastically telling the President about her recent meeting in London. SDI may have been mentioned in that first talk; but, if so, only briefly.

It was the main topic at the plenary session, which followed immediately. With Thatcher were Wright, Butler, Powell and Kerr. Ingham and Sheinwald did not attend the plenary meetings. The President had with him the Vice-President, the Secretary of State, the National Security Adviser, the United States Ambassador to Britain, Charles Price, Richard Burt and Peter Sommer. There was nobody from the Pentagon. That was to prove a source of some resentment later.

The discussion was opened by Reagan in amiable mood. After he made his initial statement Thatcher responded. The President did not take up her points or questions himself. Instead, he would turn smilingly either to Shultz or to McFarlane and say: 'Well, what's our answer to that?' Thatcher appeared slightly disconcerted at first by this procedure. The President almost gave the impression of distancing himself a bit from a project which everyone knew had his fervent backing.

The Prime Minister did most of the talking, as came to be expected of her on such occasions, though Shultz and McFarlane were also called upon. The atmosphere was very friendly and the conversation seemed to be going extremely well from the British standpoint. That was hardly surprising, as those who were now the most unreserved supporters of SDI, apart from the President, were not there. He was accompanied by those who wanted to proceed with the programme but did not share his visionary concept.

So pleased were the British with the discussion that after it had been going for an hour or more Kerr suggested to Thatcher that it might be a good idea to encapsulate the understanding in an agreed statement. That seemed a wise move to her as well. So Powell, Kerr and Sheinwald were dispatched to find a typewriter in a secretary's room at the end of the corridor.

There they settled down with Sheinwald at the typewriter, while Powell and Kerr composed what became known as the Four Points of Camp David. It did not take them more than ten minutes or so to write the statement, after which Powell went back to join the group as they had drinks before lunch, while Kerr stayed behind to make some adjustments. It was then shown to Thatcher, who swiftly approved it before they went in to lunch.

There she gave it to Reagan, saying that she would have to say something to the press afterwards and it would be better if it had been agreed by both sides beforehand. The President cheerily acknowledged that and handed it on to McFarlane for detailed examination. McFarlane and Burt then left the room with Powell and Kerr to negotiate a minor change. So, swiftly and relatively painlessly, the four points were settled. They read:

1. The United States and Western aim is not to achieve superiority but to maintain balance, taking account of Soviet developments.
2. SDI-related deployments would, in view of treaty obligations, have to be a matter of negotiations.
3. The overall aim is to enhance and not to undermine deterrence.
4. East–West negotiation should aim to achieve security, with reduced levels of offensive systems on both sides.

These apparently bland and artless propositions in fact achieved a number of objectives. No. 3 restored what was for Thatcher the cardinal principle of nuclear deterrence. Reagan had begun to sound as if he was auditioning for the presidency of the peace movements, with the idea that defence could replace the need for nuclear weapons. 'Today the only defensive weapon we have is to threaten that if they kill millions of our people, we will kill millions of theirs,' he had lamented as he answered questions in front of the White House just before setting off for Camp David the previous day. 'I don't think there's any morality in that at all.'

On Saturday he promised in effect to enhance the very strategy he had castigated on Friday. The third point did not refer specifically to nuclear deterrence, but only if he ever achieved his dream of a nuclear-free world would it be possible to deter aggression through conventional weapons alone. Until that day dawns, a strategy of deterrence has to include nuclear deterrence.

The second of the four points, while not specifically mentioning the ABM Treaty as such, went quite a long way to safeguarding it. Even if the technology were available, the United States was now committed not to rush to deployment without first trying to reach an understanding with the Soviet Union.

No. 4 enshrined the objective of disarmament agreements. Although negotiations with the Soviets were soon to resume, there had been a gap of more than a year following their walk-out in Geneva and there was much suspicion in Europe at that time that the United States was not serious about disarmament.

No. 1 carried no specific commitment, but was generally regarded as an important point of principle. A touchstone of intention rather than a precise guide to policy.

The only change from the original draft was that the Americans secured the deletion of the words 'and testing' after the word 'deployments' in No. 2. They felt that that would have narrowed their freedom of action just too much. If they were able to devise a system, they might never be able to find out what it was capable of doing.

The Americans firmly believed that Thatcher had come prepared with such a document and that she had produced it from her handbag at the appropriate moment. The accusation was not correct. Thatcher did not arrive at Camp David with the four-points statement neatly prepared. It was composed on the spot in response to the diplomatic instinct to get any good agreement in writing.

At the same time, the ideas in the statement were not being dreamt up on the spur of the moment. The substance had been discussed at some length by Thatcher and Powell during their flight from Hong Kong. It had been further examined with the embassy diplomats in the early hours of Saturday morning. It had formed the essence of the case that Thatcher had presented at Camp David. The British knew what they wanted to say. Only the drafting had to be done there.

On the Monday the embassy called the Foreign Office a trifle nervously to see how well the four points had gone down there. All was well. Ideally, the Foreign Office would have preferred something stronger, as the papers put up to the Prime Minister beforehand had indicated. After her reaction to them, it was pleased to have got the four points. Had Thatcher tried to go further, she might have risked a presidential rejection. It would have been like asking Reagan to declare in public: 'I misspoke.'

The Pentagon reaction confirmed that the British had achieved their objective. That any statement on this subject should be produced without the participation of Weinberger was sufficient to arouse suspicion there. That the declaration should circumscribe its cherished SDI provoked wrath and alarm. The White House was persuaded to issue a clarifying statement that the commitment to negotiate before deployment did not mean that the Soviets were being given a veto.

The SDI enthusiasts believed that the administration had been bounced, and they were right. The meeting had not been set up specifically to discuss SDI. Had it been, it is unlikely that Weinberger would have been excluded. For the President's general discussions with foreign leaders, it was not usual to include the Defense Secretary. That was the prerogative of the Secretary of State. A meeting that was intended to focus almost entirely on a military subject was another matter.

By the time Thatcher got to the United States it was known that she wanted to discuss SDI, but it was possibly not widely appreciated just how much she intended to concentrate on it. There had not been elaborate staff preparation for discussing the issue. If it had been known what was to come out of Camp David, the Defense Secretary would have had a reasonable claim to be present.

There might well have been a suspicion of collusion between the State Department and the British. That would not have been unusual. Senior members of the department would from time to time indicate to London, often but not always through the British Embassy in Washington, that an intervention by Mrs Thatcher on such and such an issue would be well timed. The more her reputation rose in Washington, the more she was valued as a player in the game.

In this instance, most members of the State Department, with a few notable exceptions, would have shared her desire to have an agreed framework for the SDI programme. Some people, especially in the department's Politico-Military Bureau, had been suggesting that she should see the President as soon as possible after his reelection in November. Others, in the European section, for example, had been more cautious. Everything would be very busy then: better to wait until January. There was not a concerted State Department move to get her over before Christmas.

There probably did not need to be. She would have required little prompting to talk to the President very early in his second term. Shultz and Gromyko were scheduled to meet in Geneva in early January 1985, to arrange the resumption of arms-control negotiations: she would have been determined to have a word with Reagan before that. The excitement of her dialogue with Gorbachev would have made her all the more eager, but the date of her arrival in Washington must have been settled before he reached Britain.

She did not exactly wrong-foot the administration, but she did catch it in a casual posture. She knew what she wanted more than it knew what it wanted. The outcome was hardly a surprise. It has been seen ever afterwards by most people on the British side as one of Thatcher's two or three greatest accomplishments from her partnership with Reagan.

That it was a neat diplomatic coup is evident. The British saw their opportunity at Camp David, and took it. How much did they achieve? The most important practical effect was to soften the differences within the alliance over SDI. Thatcher was seen in Washington as representing the views not just of her government but of the principal European allies as well. They had, as always, conflicting anxieties. On the one hand, the United States might prevent the arms-control process getting back on to the rails. On the other, it might leave the Europeans without military protection as it neglected extended deterrence and concentrated on a strategy of Fortress America.

The Camp David agreement was designed to satisfy those concerns without challenging the American determination to go ahead with the programme. Research was not restricted by the ABM Treaty anyway. Deployment, which would not be an option for years, if ever, would be a subject for negotiation. Development and testing, the grey areas of the treaty, were not covered by the four points in their final form. The statement did not make everything crystal clear, but that was deliberate.

Was it more than a public relations success? Did it affect American policy? 'The Prime Minister on that day circumscribed an initiative that Reagan intended then and now to be perhaps the most important part of his legacy in public life,' said McFarlane in October 1988. 'The President quickly appropriated what the Prime Minister of Britain wanted him to do.'

Reagan always had a tendency to sign up without scrutinising the small print too carefully. His actions might therefore deviate from the implications of his promises without his being aware of any deception, or even inconsistency. The four points loomed much larger in the British and European diplomatic vocabulary than in the American.

Reagan had not renounced his bolder ambitions for SDI and this was to cause recurring difficulty between him and Thatcher in the years ahead. Yet the Camp David agreement may have had greater consequences than many Americans appreciated. There is nothing like a piece of paper that can be used in the political machinations of Washington and the diplomatic manoeuvres of the alliance.

One official in his administration concedes ruefully that 'she had a very material role with the Camp David agreement'. It strengthened those forces in the United States who wanted to slow down the SDI programme. It strengthened Shultz's hand at a critical time in his bid to get negotiations going with the Soviets again: this was just before his all-important meeting with Gromyko. It reinforced, perhaps it even created, the President's reluctance to break the ABM Treaty. The bitter arguments over what the treaty really meant – the broad versus narrow interpretation – lay ahead. Thatcher herself stayed well clear of that dispute, but before the issue had even been presented she had dinned into Reagan the general principle that SDI must not infringe the sanctity of treaty obligations.

The Camp David accord was an implicit deal whereby the United States would agree to conduct the SDI programme within specified limits and Britain would support the programme so long as those limits were accepted. The value of the deal depended on its spirit being observed. If it was to be taken seriously, it imposed restraints on the critics within the British government as well as on the United States.

That was why Thatcher was particularly affronted by the speech that her Foreign Secretary delivered on 15 March 1985. Less than three months before, she had laboured to construct a framework within which the American programme could proceed without tearing Nato apart. Now Geoffrey Howe seemed intent on dismantling it with the hatchet of sweet reason.

In his address to a distinguished audience at the Royal United Services Institution in London he reaffirmed his faith in the principle of deterrence and paid lip service to SDI. 'United States research should go ahead,' he declared. He then proceeded to ask a series of searching questions that undermined, if they did not make nonsense of, that declaration.

The least damaging question was whether 'the supposed technology' would actually work. The way in which it was couched did not betray ardent enthusiasm, but the purpose of a research programme would be to find out. To pose the question was not contrary to the letter or spirit of any of the four points. None of them expressed an opinion on the feasibility of the project.

It was different with some of his other questions. Could the process of moving towards a greater emphasis on active defences be managed without generating dangerous uncertainty? Might we be better advised to employ other methods of protecting key military installations, such as more mobile and undersea forces? Would the prospect of new defences being deployed inexorably crank up the levels of offensive nuclear systems designed to overwhelm them?

The trouble with these questions was not that they were analytically unsound, but that they were politically embarrassing. They related not to whether SDI could be made to work, but to whether it would be wise to have it even if it did work. If that would be unwise, did it really make sense to have an ambitious research programme? The tone and implications of the speech were hostile to the whole project, even if the attack was wrapped in the protective armour of a question mark.

Howe was raising issues which had to be left untouched if the Camp David compromise was to have its effect. The speech had been originally drafted the previous October. Had it been delivered then, it would have been expressing anxieties which needed to be resolved. In March it seemed to be challenging an understanding which had been reached.

The Americans were outraged. Perle, who was in London for a conference that week, launched a public attack upon Howe that was extraordinary coming from the member of a friendly government. Perle is no desiccated bureaucrat, and his language was robust. Howe's speech 'proved an old axiom of geometry that length is no substitute for depth'. The Foreign Secretary had misrepresented the development of the strategic relationship between the United States and the Soviet Union over the previous decade.

Perle's reaction removed some of the embarrassment that Howe's speech had caused on the British side. Diplomatic decorum had now been infringed on the American side. The President sent no phone call or message of protest at the Foreign Secretary's speech. A message was drafted by the NSC staff, but it never even reached the President's desk. Had it done so, it is hard to believe that he would ever have agreed to send it.

Thatcher had a double cause for anguish over Howe's speech. She was furious when she read it, and she was furious that she had not read it earlier. It had been sent to her in Downing Street some days before Howe delivered it, and she took it with her to Moscow when she attended Chernenko's funeral. She had more important things on her mind than an apparently routine speech by her Foreign Secretary. Gorbachev was taking over power in Moscow and she had another substantial conversation with him, this time for about an hour. That was on 13 March, two days before Howe gave the speech. On the flight home, no doubt exhilarated but exhausted, she had it on her lap. But she fell asleep. It remained unread. For once Thatcher had failed to do her homework.

Howe had followed the proper procedures. He had given her a reasonable opportunity to raise objections. So there was a limit to how far she could press complaints. That was presumably all the more galling as Americans began to protest that she must have approved the speech if she did not do anything about it.

The episode none the less served to illustrate one basic truth about SDI. No matter how great Thatcher's achievement at Camp David, this was not an issue which could be settled in a single meeting. She had chosen to walk a fine line. She was both justifying the programme and trying to restrict it. That meant appearing hawkish one moment, and doveish the next. It would put her reputation for consistency to the test and require many further hours of argument.

14

IN CHURCHILL'S FOOTSTEPS

As Winston Churchill paced rapidly up and down the small room in which he was waiting to address a joint meeting of both Houses of Congress on 26 December 1941, he turned to his personal doctor and confidant, Lord Moran: 'Do you realise we are making history?'

To address both Houses of Congress is no longer such a rare honour as it was then. Churchill himself was to do so on two other occasions. Only one foreign head of government had ever been given that opportunity before, David Kalakaua, King of the Hawaiian Islands, in December 1874.

When Margaret Thatcher spoke to both Houses on 20 February 1985 she was one of five heads of government from overseas to do so that year. She was still the first British prime minister to have the opportunity since Churchill had spoken to Congress for the last time in 1952. So, barely two months after her successful meeting with Reagan at Camp David, Thatcher was back in the United States for another, very different, but equally memorable occasion.

She received an enthusiastic reception before, during and after her speech. Observers noted, in the fashion of the political statistician, that she was interrupted by applause twenty-four times. At the end, a number of members were on their feet chanting: 'Maggie, Maggie, Maggie.' The response in Britain was not altogether so rapturous, and for exactly the reason that had contributed so much to the pleasure of her American audience. She had been warm, even fulsome, in her praise of the United States.

'No one of my generation can forget,' she declared, 'that America has been the principal architect of a peace in Europe which has lasted forty years.' She went on to express her appreciation in even more glowing terms: 'For our deliverance from what might have befallen us, I would not have us leave our gratitude to the tributes of history.

The debt the free peoples of Europe owe to this nation, generous with its bounty, willing to share its strength, seeking to protect the weak, is incalculable. We thank and salute you.'

This recognition of America's role was described in the *Christian Science Monitor* as 'a moment of heartfelt history'. In a later passage she focused her praise more directly on the Reagan administration: 'There is a new mood in the United States. A visitor feels it at once. The resurgence of your self-confidence and your national pride is almost tangible. Now the sun is rising in the West.'

At home, all this was too much for some critics. 'She lay on her back,' wrote Alan Watkins in his column in the *Observer*, 'put her paws in the air and asked to be tickled.' Professor Emeritus Keith Buchanan wrote more sternly in a letter to *The Times*: 'The "special relationship" of which so much is made always seemed to imply a measure of partnership between equals; it has been Mrs Thatcher's achievement to reduce the status of Britain from that of a partner to that of a US satellite.'

These were not lone voices. Nor was this an isolated occasion. Throughout the eight years when they held power together, Thatcher was often accused in Britain of sycophancy towards Reagan. In its way, her speech was as typical as the criticism it provoked. It demonstrated the style that she customarily deployed towards him, and indeed towards the United States in general.

Praise when you can in public, so that you can persuade when you need in private. That was the principle she almost invariably followed. There was nothing unique in it. British prime ministers from Churchill onwards have usually proceeded along the same lines. What has been striking about Thatcher's approach has been how wholeheartedly she has observed both parts of the dictum. She has praised without restraint, but she has also tried to persuade with considerable vigour.

There was in fact quite a bit of persuasion between the lines of that speech. She delighted the administration by declaring her support for SDI, but she did so in terms that reinforced the compromise that she had pressed on the President at Camp David. She enthused about the research programme, endorsed the ABM Treaty and warned that deployment would be a matter for negotiation under the treaty.

She reasserted the doctrine of nuclear deterrence, from which he was always liable to stray, and reminded her listeners that the task was not only to prevent nuclear war, but conventional war as well. She was, in effect, congratulating the President on pursuing what was rather more her strategy than his.

In the economic field she gave her full backing to the administration for the policy she wanted it to follow, but which it was not in fact pursuing. That was to bring down the budget deficit.

A substantial section of her speech was devoted to the problems of Northern Ireland. The previous October she had narrowly escaped assassination at the hands of the IRA. During the Conservative Party Conference at Brighton a bomb wrecked the hotel in which she and many of her Cabinet ministers were staying. Two of them were seriously injured; a number of people were killed; and Thatcher herself was lucky to escape unhurt. When she reminded Congress of IRA terrorism, she was speaking with the authority of personal experience.

In that sense it was a good time for her to speak in Washington about the troubles of Northern Ireland. Something else that happened a month after the Brighton bombing made it essential for her to do so. Dr Garret FitzGerald, the Prime Minister of the Irish Republic, spent a day with her at Chequers discussing the way ahead in the light of the New Ireland Forum report. Their conversation went quite well, but the same could not be said of the press conference she gave afterwards.

Referring in turn to the three specific proposals examined in the report, she declared that a unified Ireland was out, so was a confederation, so was joint authority. It became notorious as the 'out, out, out' press conference. Not for the first or the last time, it was the style rather than the substance of what she said that caused so much offence. She paid no tribute to the report's constructive tone. FitzGerald was humiliated, Irish Catholics were incensed, an influential section of American opinion was disenchanted and British officials were embarrassed. It was not just that she seemed to have set back the chances of a political agreement. She had made the British government appear responsible for any failure in negotiations.

Thatcher knew when she went to Washington that for the sake of Anglo–American relations she needed to offer reassurance on this score to two people in particular. Reagan had behaved impeccably on his visit to Ireland the previous summer, but he had the natural sentiment of an Irish–American. He was also a naturally friendly man, who becomes uncomfortable when his associates quarrel.

On at least two occasions, once in the Oval Office and once in a telephone conversation, he expressed the hope that she would get on better with FitzGerald. In doing so, he was acting on a suggestion from Clark, who remained highly influential on Irish affairs even after he ceased to be National Security Adviser. Reminding Thatcher of the importance of the Irish issue in American politics, the President

indicated that it would make the conduct of Anglo–American relations easier for him if she were to treat the Irish Prime Minister
more as an equal partner.

It is inconceivable that Reagan delivered this message bluntly. Part
of his charm is that he likes to be charming. One of the frustrations
for his staff was that even when he had agreed to deliver a stern rebuke
he would often soften the blow. He would never have reprimanded
Thatcher, but she was capable of taking the point without that. She
indicated that she had done so and FitzGerald subsequently told
colleagues in Dublin that for the first time for a long while she was
according him equal respect.

The other person in Washington whom she especially needed to
reassure was Speaker Tip O'Neill, who often appeared to British eyes
as a caricature of an Irish–American politician, with his thick white
hair, heavy build and Boston brogue. He had particularly asked
Thatcher to say something of consequence on Northern Ireland in
her speech. O'Neill's wishes were not to be taken lightly. Not only was
he Speaker of the House of Representatives, but he was exceptionally
influential on America's Irish policy. Much more restrained than
some other American politicians, and more responsible than he
was often given credit for by British opinion, in his heart he was
unquestionably with the nationalists, as was natural for a staunch
Catholic. No British government could ever take it for granted that
he would be sympathetic to its endeavours in Northern Ireland.

So Thatcher deliberately, almost ostentatiously, presented herself
as standing shoulder to shoulder with the Irish Prime Minister. 'Garret
FitzGerald and I, and our respective governments,' she declared, 'are
united in condemning terrorism.' She went on to point out that the
two of them were united on a good many other things as well. They
recognised the differing traditions of the nationalist and Unionist
communities in Northern Ireland and wanted to find a political way
forward acceptable to both. They agreed that the wishes of the
majority in Northern Ireland should be respected, whether they
wanted to remain in the United Kingdom or to be united with the
Republic. She saluted FitzGerald for passing a special law the day
before to see that money did not get to the IRA.

There was relief in the British camp that O'Neill approved of
Thatcher's comments. So too did Reagan. Once again the President
and his wife paid Thatcher the rare compliment of attending a dinner
at the British Embassy.

The following month Thatcher had further cause to be grateful to
Reagan. The long saga of the Laker case was finally brought to what

was for her a satisfactory conclusion. The President had terminated the criminal case against British Airways when he called off the Grand Jury the previous November. But it would be impossible to proceed with the privatisation of British Airways so long as there was the threat of a civil action against the airline by Laker's creditors. Heavy, but unpredictable, damages might be imposed upon it if a United States court concluded that the Laker bankruptcy had been brought about by a conspiracy among British Airways and other airlines. So potential purchasers could not be sure what British Airways was worth until the case was out of the way.

The largest creditor was the Export-Import Bank (Exim) of the United States. Its agreement would be the key to an out-of-court settlement with all the creditors. Without that, the possibility of a civil action might be hanging over the airline for years. Unfortunately for the British government, Exim was fully aware of its strong bargaining position. It was in no hurry to settle.

When Thatcher had raised the matter again with Reagan at Camp David in December she could not have expected any immediate decision, but she had kept up the pressure. Exim is an independent agency of the Federal government, but pressure can always be brought to bear by the President if he is sufficiently determined. By March Reagan was. He was receptive to Thatcher's argument that the case was blocking the privatisation policy that was a cornerstone of their joint beliefs, and he was probably responsive to her sheer persistence. Word was passed down to Exim to settle.

So at last the threat of damages in the American courts no longer presented a bar to the privatisation of British Airways. It was a remarkable episode which could not have ended so soon and so favourably for Britain without the quite exceptional intervention of the President himself on two separate occasions. Allen Wallis, the former Under-Secretary of State for Economic Affairs, has recorded that 'in any dispute with the United Kingdom it had to be kept in the back of our minds that if things got to the point where the Prime Minister got sufficiently agitated she could place a Margaret-to-Ron phone call and count on a friendly hearing'. In this instance she had received a very friendly hearing indeed.

Thatcher was not always so adroit in her dealings with the administration. When she was next in Washington five months later, in July 1985, a seminar on arms control was staged for her in the East Room of the White House. The President was there with his Chief of Staff, Donald Regan; the Secretary of State, George Shultz; the Defence Secretary, Caspar Weinberger; the National Security Adviser, Robert

McFarlane; the Director of the Arms Control and Disarmament Agency, Kenneth Adelman; and a number of others.

Reagan began the proceedings with a graceful and uncontroversial reference to the importance of the arms-control debate. Then Thatcher began. She has a torrential style of conversation. It pours impartially over friend and foe alike. Agreement is no protection against the flow. On this occasion, while there would be much agreement with her in that room, she was concerned about disagreement in one quarter in particular.

Her recurring fear was that in his enthusiasm for SDI and his horror of nuclear weapons Reagan would throw away the West's nuclear deterrent, or at least render it ineffective. In her speech to Congress in February she had made her message plain: 'Let us never forget the horrors of conventional war and the hideous sacrifice of those who have suffered in them. Our task is not only to prevent nuclear war, but to prevent conventional war as well.'

Just to rub the point home, she had then quoted Churchill's words in his last speech to Congress: 'Be careful above all things not to let go of the atomic weapon until you are sure and more than sure that other means of preserving peace are in your hands.' She did not say so in so many words, but in her judgment SDI did not qualify as those 'other means'.

Now, sitting at a long table in the White House, she started by saying how Reagan's ideas had caught fire in Britain and how many British economic policies were along the lines of Reaganomics. It was the familiar, but always valuable, rhetorical device of identifying herself with her audience before getting on to more controversial ground. 'It was,' says Adelman, 'a very effective way of saying how similar we are, how much we share and how we're really two peas in the same pod.'

Then she expanded on her main theme. After she had been going for a little while, Adelman passed a note to his neighbour, Donald Regan, saying: 'Thatcher Loves the Bomb.' Adelman himself was one of the more hardline members of that gathering on nuclear weapons. He agreed with the substance of most of what Thatcher had to say. He is an enthusiast for SDI, but not as a replacement for nuclear weapons. As he puts it, 'she said it many, many different ways. Her point was that all this talk surrounding SDI was delegitimising nuclear weapons and basically taking away any kind of justification for the presence of nuclear weapons in Europe, or anywhere around the world to protect Western Europe. She went on and on in that vein.'

She added what to Adelman was a new point: that there was a

tremendous imbalance in chemical weapons in Europe and one of the purposes of the West's nuclear armoury was to compensate for this imbalance. The British did not want to go into the chemical weapons business, which they had been in years ago; but at one point she warned that, if Western Europe were to lose its nuclear shield, it might be necessary for Britain to start manufacturing chemical weapons again.

'Several of us,' Adelman recalls, 'tried to get into the act. She said "Let me make one more point" when we held up our fingers or did whatever one does in a situation like that. At one stage her Defence Secretary, Heseltine, who was sitting on her left, said "Well, let me say . . ." and she says "One minute, Michael," or whatever, and just proceeded on and on.'

It was a somewhat rueful group that left what was supposed to have been a discussion after about an hour. Adelman walked out with the President and Shultz: 'the Secretary just kind of shook his head and said something like "Boy, she's not a very good listener, is she?" '

So ended the only seminar of its kind in the White House, but it was not the only occasion, even on that visit, on which Thatcher tried to guard the President against the perils of nuclear heresy. McFarlane recalls a tense occasion over lunch in the White House. There was another very thorough exchange on the implications of SDI for allied strategy. She went with great care and deliberation through the various lines of argument, the purpose of SDI and the danger of devaluing nuclear weapons.

It was not the SDI programme itself that alarmed her, but the illusion that because of SDI it would become possible to dispense with nuclear weapons. 'If you follow that logic to its implied conclusion,' she put it to the President, 'and do get rid of nuclear weapons, you expose a dramatic conventional imbalance do you not? And would we not have to restore that balance at considerable expense?'

Years later McFarlane has a vivid recollection of the response: 'The President looked her square in the eye and said "Yes, that's exactly what I imagined." It was a rather awkward silence there while both sides absorbed the weight of just what had been exchanged. I think the staffs of both sides agreed that this had better never get out.'

Reagan never liked personal confrontations, but when the Prime Minister spelled out the implications of getting rid of nuclear weapons, what this would mean for stability in Western Europe and for military spending, he had simply replied that he understood all that. The exchange revealed the extent of the gulf between them on this issue, well before the difference was exposed to public view at the Reykjavik summit. It was not just a little misunderstanding. 'It was alarming to a lot of us,' says McFarlane, 'and I am sure a rather cold splash of water to this side from the UK.'

Thatcher now describes the disagreement over nuclear arms as 'the only real divergence we had'. It was certainly by far the most serious. Her response to Reagan's desire for a world without nuclear weapons was to say: 'That is not the objective. The objective is to have a world without war and at present it is necessary to have nuclear weapons because they are the greatest deterrent to war.' That in a sentence was the basic principle to which she returned time and again during these years.

On the issue itself Thatcher is grimly realistic. Where she is less realistic is in believing that the difference between them did not emerge until he had been President for quite a time. That can mean either that they did not discuss such fundamentals in the earlier years or, more probably, that she thought she had persuaded him when he simply no longer wished to continue the argument. She would not have been the first person to have mistaken a benign smile from Reagan for acquiescence.

The disagreement in July 1985 revealed the one weakness in the Camp David accord the previous December. It was valuable for the Nato alliance and for political manoeuvres in Washington. The one thing it did not do was to convert the President. She may have got him to accept then that their overall aim was to enhance not to undermine deterrence, but in his second inaugural address a month after their Camp David meeting he was proclaiming once again: 'We seek the total elimination, one day, of nuclear weapons from the face of the earth.'

He agreed to the Camp David statement because Thatcher wanted it. He left the examination of the small print to aides who did not share his ambitious concept of SDI or his vision of a nuclear-free world. He moved on, glad they could agree on a statement, but personally untouched by the process.

In the circumstances, what is remarkable is not that they had to keep on returning to the same basic issue, but that it did not cause more difficulty between them. That was essentially because he was preoccupied with his vision, while she was concerned above all by what should be done here and now. They could generally agree on the practical steps – he had no more desire than she had just to be soft on the Soviets – provided that he was not required to renounce his dream.

*

The practical question in the summer of 1985 had been decided in Thatcher's favour the month before she arrived in Washington. That was whether the United States should continue to abide voluntarily by the limits of the SALT Two Treaty. This had been signed by President Carter back in 1979, but never ratified. The Senate had always been unlikely to give its consent, but after the Soviet invasion of Afghanistan Carter withdrew the treaty from consideration and it was never resubmitted to the Senate.

During their days in opposition both Reagan and Thatcher had been strong opponents of the treaty. Even Paul Nitze, who later came to be regarded as the outstanding voice of moderation on disarmament in the Reagan administration, had been a vociferous critic of SALT Two in the late 1970s. It might have been expected that both the British and American governments in the 1980s would have had no hesitation in renouncing it altogether, but office brings new considerations.

Thatcher was the first to change on SALT because she was the first to get power. A variety of pressures were brought to bear upon her. A succession of emissaries from the Carter administration flew to London. Although unable to secure its ratification, Carter had decided to abide by the treaty's provisions. It was the diplomatic equivalent of keeping a promise without making it. Thatcher's official advisers did not think it was worth a battle over an agreement that did not affect British security directly, only what the United States could do with its own weapons.

That was also the view of one of the political associates who carried weight with her on this issue at that time. Sir Geoffrey Pattie had been one of the small group of Conservative MPs who had regularly helped her prepare for Prime Minister's Question Time when she was Leader of the Opposition. When the Conservatives came to power he was given the relatively modest post of Parliamentary Under-Secretary of State for Defence, but for a year or so he had Thatcher's ear on such matters. This was at a time when she was much less interested in strategic questions than she later became. It was the political implications that had most impact on her then, and she was persuaded that relations with the United States mattered more for Britain than the treaty.

When he came to office Reagan also decided to accept the treaty's restrictions in practice without saying a good word for it in principle. Although there was quite a struggle over this within the new administration, the Chiefs of Staff pointed out that the Soviets stood to gain more by casting the treaty aside. They were in a position to increase the number of warheads on their ballistic missiles quickly, whereas there was nothing of consequence that the United States was being prevented from doing by the SALT limitations. Haig also argued powerfully along these lines and carried the weight of a former senior military man, even if he did have his enemies in the White House.

So the position remained until 1985. Then the administration was faced with a hard choice. A new Trident submarine, the *Alaska*, would be ready for service before the end of the year, but if the SALT limits were still to be observed an older, Poseidon submarine would have to be retired at the same time. This was the first of two occasions when a critical debate developed within the administration on continuing to accept the treaty.

In favour of doing so were the Joint Chiefs of Staff, who were more than happy to exchange a new boat for an old one, Shultz and McFarlane. Against were Weinberger and Perle in the Pentagon, as well as Adelman at the Arms Control and Disarmament Agency (ACDA). Thatcher intervened on the side of observing the limits. The matter was not raised in her bilateral meeting with Reagan during the Bonn economic summit in May. She sent him a personal message on the subject before the final decision was taken in June, almost certainly prompted delicately and indirectly by those of like mind in the State Department.

By then the principal considerations for her were public opinion in Europe and the need to avoid disrupting the arms-control negotiations, which had been resumed in Geneva in March after more than a year's interruption. Gorbachev had taken over in Moscow that month. There was the prospect of a new dialogue with the Soviet Union. Why jeopardise that for no military advantage?

The two arguments that were decisive in Washington were that to break the SALT limits would benefit the Soviets militarily more than the United States, and that it would be a gratuitous affront to the allies. Thatcher's intervention gave powerful reinforcement to the second argument. The decision would almost certainly have gone that way anyway. What she did was to strengthen the existing balance of power in Washington and to make the President more comfortable in going in that direction.

It was to be different when the issue came up again a year later, but in the meantime another struggle developed over a treaty that had been ratified and was the focus of so much attention over these years: the ABM Treaty. Thatcher's purpose at Camp David had been to ensure that the SDI programme should be conducted within the

boundaries permitted by the treaty. In October 1985 the administration shifted those frontiers, or at least announced that they were
not where everybody had previously thought they were.

The treaty, which was signed in 1972, banned not only the deployment but also the development and testing of anti-ballistic missile
systems based on technologies existing at the time. It had always been
assumed that the ban also covered newer technologies discovered
since then. That assumption was challenged in 1985 by the State
Department's new legal adviser, Abraham Sofaer, a former federal
judge from New York. His judgment was accepted by the administration and promulgated by McFarlane on the television programme
Meet the Press on 6 October. The treaty, he pronounced, 'does indeed
sanction research, testing and development of these new systems'.
This substantially changed the treaty's nature and implications. A
commitment to keep to it would no longer give the allies the reassurance that it did.

Thatcher reacted swiftly. Towards the end of that month two
emissaries from the Ministry of Defence in London went to see
McFarlane to express anxiety on behalf of the Prime Minister about
this broadened interpretation. 'While terribly kind and courteous,'
he says, 'they were in a considerable state of alarm.' When the staff
of both sides were present, 'I gave kind of a party line about it,'
McFarlane recalls. They got up and everybody left except the senior
of the two visitors. 'I took him aside over to the window and I said:
"Look, you must assure the Prime Minister it is not the intention of
the President to execute or carry out this authority that he believes is
there. My own position in pushing it to that limit is purely orientated
towards next month's summit." '

He was referring to the first meeting between Reagan and Gorbachev that was to be held in Geneva in November 1985. As always,
McFarlane was concerned to give the President the greatest possible
leverage in dealing with the Soviet Union. The broad interpretation
would give him more room for bargaining. It was on that basis that
Shultz and McFarlane had recommended the idea to the President,
and on that basis that he agreed.

This explanation was enough to reassure the British official that
day. He told McFarlane that he was quite relieved and would explain
to the Prime Minister.

Thatcher herself never became directly involved in the long-running
battle of the broad versus narrow interpretation of the ABM Treaty.
She always declared that it was for the signatories of the treaty to
determine what it meant. She never wavered from that position in

public or quasi-public discussion. When she was talking to a group of visiting senators in the Cabinet Room in Downing Street more than two years later, in February 1988, she made a point of saying that she was not taking a position on that issue – directing her remark very deliberately towards Senator Sam Nunn, the Chairman of the Armed Services Committee, who was later to come out strongly in favour of the narrow interpretation.

She based herself instead on the twin principles of feasibility and predictability. It must be right, she told the senators, to pursue the SDI programme to a point where it would be possible to determine whether it would work. She used two analogies. If the necessary testing was not done it would be like taking all the components that are required to build a plane and then not flying it.

Then she reminded her visitors that during the Second World War we had devoted time, expense and lives to destroying the heavy-water facilities in Norway and northern Germany. What kind of situation would we be in today, she asked, if we had negotiated some kind of deal that prohibited us from making the atomic bomb when we knew well enough that the Germans were doing so?

She used a similar argument on at least two occasions with the President and on more than one with Shultz. Radar saved the United Kingdom in the Battle of Britain, and it would be foolish now not to do the work that would provide the democracies with a similar advantage. Hence feasibility.

At the same time, both the Soviet Union and the West had to be assured that the other would not spring a surprise on it. Each side should therefore keep the other informed of what it was doing in its anti-missile programme. So predictability.

Her stance was politically shrewd. It avoided becoming entangled in the bitter machinations of Washington. But it ducked the issue. What assurances should the United States give to its allies and the Soviet Union about the SDI programme? Should it promise to abide by the narrow definition of the ABM Treaty or not?

The logic of her position pointed towards the broad interpretation. She seemed to favour doing everything necessary to find out if the system could be deployed, without deploying it; but she must have been more concerned about American intentions, even after Camp David, than she ever allowed to appear. That is evident from the deliberate sounding out of McFarlane so soon after the administration changed its public position in October 1985.

She was particularly anxious then that nothing should be done to upset the Geneva summit between Reagan and Gorbachev the following month. 'I was saying to Ron Reagan,' Thatcher remembered: 'This is a man that I can do business with and, because I believe the same things as you do, this is a man you can do business with without compromising any of your beliefs.' Max Kampelman, who had begun his task as chief American arms negotiator in Geneva earlier in the year, explained how Thatcher's influence was important in encouraging the dialogue with Gorbachev. 'Reagan had lots of trouble with this approach. He had problems with his own White House staff, he had problems with his friends and he had problems with the right wing of the Republican Party.'

At the same time as Thatcher was offering this advice, Reagan was being persuaded by Shultz and McFarlane that it was the right policy. According to McFarlane, Reagan has 'a rather romantic view of the hero, the heroic notion of how individuals can change the course of history. He viewed himself as someone who simply by power of persuasion and force and energy (certainly not of intellect) could persuade people who were wrong-headed to change their minds. We began to play upon that, quite honestly.'

They suggested that when the President engaged with the Soviet leadership, then a change in Soviet behaviour might occur. 'It would be largely dependent upon his charismatic power to influence change in the mind of his opposite number.' Just as Shultz and McFarlane emphasised the personal element in persuading Reagan, so did Reagan himself when he met Gorbachev. The Geneva summit is remembered for the atmospherics. It was a public-relations success. It was the fireside summit, where the two men chatted together. In fact it was more than that.

They talked together for about five hours. There was simultaneous translation, and a degree of passion came into the discussion. No significant agreements could be reached. SDI prevented that: Gorbachev was not prepared to move on disarmament unless Reagan would budge on SDI. None the less, they had really engaged with each other.

That was what Thatcher had wanted above all. She was one of a number of forces encouraging Reagan towards Geneva. His two most senior foreign-policy advisers were pressing him. His vision of a nuclear-free world and his fear of Armageddon were guiding him in the same direction. Before Geneva he was certainly reading carefully the warnings of the Soviet double agent, Gordievski, that Soviet leaders were genuinely afraid of the West and needed reassurance.

All these influences mattered. Reagan was not simply responding to Thatcher's prompting when he opened the dialogue, but she offered something that none of the others could: personal and political reassurance. 'Reagan is a highly political animal,' Kampelman reflects. 'He has very strong instincts, and values, and feelings; but as a political animal he is a man who likes to be liked. If people who are your friends question what you're doing, you are naturally inclined to question yourself what you're doing.'

Many of Reagan's friends are rich members of the Republican Right. They did indeed question what he was doing as they saw him cosying up to the Soviet leader. Mention of Shultz or McFarlane would not have impressed them. Thatcher was a different matter. Many strong right-wingers in the United States came to regard her as politically sounder than Reagan himself. He knew how much his Republican friends respected her. To know that he was in line with her would have helped to counter their misgivings. 'It is essential to get reaffirmation of your instincts,' Kampelman points out, 'for any human being, particularly a political human being, and I think that's what Margaret Thatcher provided.'

Before the end of the year Thatcher's influence was felt directly on two very different issues of less importance, though both aroused strong feelings. The first involved a significant change in the Western negotiating position in the long and tedious talks with the Soviet Union in Vienna on conventional arms. Ever since the Mutual and Balanced Force Reduction (MBFR) negotiations began twelve years earlier it had been a Nato principle that both sides had to agree what the current level of forces was before making cuts. Otherwise it would be impossible to know whether the reductions had really been made.

This stipulation had been a cause of deadlock throughout the negotiations. The two sides could not agree where they were, never mind where they should get to. Finally, the head of the British delegation, Sir Michael Alexander, suggested they should break out of this impasse. By the latter part of July 1985 the British and Germans had put together a new negotiating package, which dropped the contentious requirement. Howe sent a message advocating it to Shultz, and then followed this up in discussion with the Secretary of State at the anniversary meeting of the Helsinki Conference at the beginning of August. The German Foreign Minister, Hans-Dietrich Genscher, took part in the conversation as well, though he can hardly have been at his most persuasive. His remarks were apparently so confused that he then had to send a message to Washington, making clear what he really meant.

Anglo–German–American meetings of officials then took place in

September in Brussels and at about the same time in Washington, with the British making much of Thatcher's support for the proposal. Before the month was out Shultz became converted, but that did not settle the issue. As so often happened in Washington in those years, what the Secretary of State strongly favoured was vehemently opposed by the Pentagon, who saw it as a critical weakening of the Western position. Without an accepted data base, they maintained, it would be impossible to have adequate verification.

Pentagon officials, Perle in particular, suspected that this was an idea that had come up through the British and German foreign-ministry bureaucracies without Thatcher and Kohl having given it much personal attention. So the President was persuaded to initiate a second round of consultations in which the two leaders were specifically asked for their judgment. If they were to study it carefully, they would surely not take the same position again. Or at least Thatcher would not, so Perle and others reasoned.

To their dismay, she did. Perhaps they thought that, as Alexander had previously been her private secretary for foreign affairs, she had simply endorsed his idea without thinking much about it. That would have been out of character. Back came strongly-worded confirming messages from her and from Kohl.

They were enough to win the day. It mattered that the British and the Germans were taking the same position, but it was her influence that particularly counted. The Pentagon's argument would normally have appealed to the President's fear of being trapped in an unrealistic treaty, which could not be verified. It was a mark of Reagan's confidence in her judgment that he allowed himself to be persuaded in an unexpected direction. The decision was taken early in December at an NSC meeting in which he was very involved personally, and in which he referred repeatedly to her message.

The British and Germans did not get all that they wanted. The Pentagon, having lost on this issue, managed to more than halve the proposed troop reduction. The debate on conventional arms in Europe moved on the following April when the Soviets announced unilateral cuts, but it was still significant that on a military issue that aroused strong feelings the President took the advice of Thatcher and Kohl rather than the Pentagon. Some of the Americans principally involved believed that it was the judgment of Thatcher and Kohl that swayed him more than any other consideration.

The other issue was a purely bilateral one. On 6 December 1985 Britain became the first ally to sign an agreement to participate in the American SDI research program. The symbolism of the agreement was what mattered to the United States. The prospect of lush contracts was what attracted Britain.

It was not in fact as alluring a deal as the British had hoped for. There was no guarantee of business being directed to Britain, no assurance of a minimum figure for contracts. Michael Heseltine, who a month later was to storm out of Thatcher's Cabinet during the Westland crisis, had aroused expectations of a million or even a million and a half dollars. That was never realistic, and is far more than has been obtained. Many people suspect that he deliberately pitched the figure too high in order to put on the pressure.

Thatcher had obtained a share for British industry, but she was not easily satisfied. Behind the lofty strategist there lurks a politician with an eye to the main chance. When it was mentioned to her later by the Americans that there was only so much money available, and a number of countries were participating in the programme, her retort was swift and direct: 'The devil with that. We have a special relationship.'

15

CHANGING THE GUARD

Reagan began his second term in January 1985 as Thatcher had begun hers eighteen months before: he made a major change in his circle of closest advisers. The manner in which he gave his blessing to Donald Regan, the Treasury Secretary, swapping jobs with the Chief of Staff, James Baker, remains one of the curiosities of Reagan's Presidency.

With a President as uninterested as Reagan was in the mechanics of government, the whole tone of the administration was affected by the choice of Chief of Staff. When Baker held the job it was a more politically sensitive Presidency, especially in dealing with Congress. Regan put the emphasis on internal efficiency. The administration became more streamlined and less political. It was a change of substance as well as of style. Yet Reagan allowed it to take place with his customary nonchalant good humour, without appearing to take account of the implications. It was almost as a by-product of this arrangement that he found himself with a new Treasury Secretary.

Thatcher too can defy expectations in appointing her personal staff. In June 1984, a year after the general election, Charles Powell became her private secretary for foreign affairs. Many heads of government have a love-hate relationship with their foreign ministries. There is the old jibe that just as a ministry of agriculture is a ministry to look after the interests of farmers, so a foreign ministry is a ministry to look after the interests of foreigners. Thatcher has this prejudice to an advanced degree. She has always been deeply suspicious of the Foreign Office, whom she considers too emollient and too soft to stand up for British interests. Powell was not only seconded from the Diplomatic Service to Downing Street, but still looks and sounds like a Foreign Office mandarin. With thick, greying, wavy hair, he has the confident manner and assured charm.

Rather in the way that a national security adviser in Washington who is really close to the president can have more clout than the secretary of state, so Powell has carried more weight with the Prime Minister than any foreign secretary during his time in Downing Street. He is in direct, secure teleprinter communication with the National Security Adviser, and this is the means of transmitting the most confidential messages between the Prime Minister and the President. Others would be sent through their respective embassies. Most of Thatcher's messages would be drafted by Powell in the first instance, but she would almost invariably make some amendment to any communication to a foreign leader just to make sure that it expressed her meaning precisely.

Except in moments of crisis, written messages were a more frequent and more important means of communication between Reagan and Thatcher than telephone calls. Thatcher has no particular love of the telephone, and Reagan always hesitated to take up anyone else's time without a specific purpose. Sometimes the purpose in calling Thatcher was essentially social – birthdays and other anniversaries. His office was good at remembering those occasions, and sometimes what began as a social conversation would become more substantive. But it was not their custom to have general chats on how the world was getting along. Apart from their meetings, most of the substantive business between them was done through the written word.

It was no small advantage, therefore, that Powell himself got on well with the senior figures in the Reagan administration. An adviser who is known to speak for his leader always has great merit in the eyes of other advisers. They know where they are. No doubt that helped them to appreciate Powell, but he played no small part himself in making sure that goodwill at the top brought cooperation lower down.

Another especially close adviser has been her press secretary, Bernard Ingham, who has been with her almost throughout her Premiership. Ingham is a totally different personality: a bluff Yorkshireman who specialises in being a bluff Yorkshireman. Proud of his modest social background and of having begun his working life as a junior reporter on a local newspaper, he epitomises the rugged, down-to-earth qualities of the north of England. That is how he likes to portray himself. Nobody has spent more time in public polishing his own caricature. He is a controversial character, which is hardly surprising for such a combative personality; but it was for his professionalism that he was chosen to be Thatcher's chief press secretary in 1979. She had hardly met him before he began to work for her.

To her he was then an unknown who had once been a local Labour Party candidate. But he was recommended as the most accomplished information officer in the Civil Service, and she has something of a taste for converts if they bring sufficient ardour to her cause. Ingham has. He has been her personal adviser more than a civil servant. His influence has become far greater than his title would suggest. One of the tests of a person's standing in any government is how many confidential papers they receive. 'I have long gone on the assumption,' one former minister remarked, 'that Bernard gets everything.'

The appointment of Bernard Ingham without knowing him was not an isolated example. Thatcher takes a great interest in the details of government, but not so much in its organisation. She has shown no inclination to tinker with the structure of departments, and has surrounded herself with a surprising number of ministers who do not share her deepest political beliefs. A chancellor of the exchequer, however, is special. In selecting Nigel Lawson in 1983 she was making a very personal choice. He had been close to her in opposition and had proved himself in government. During her first term he had been an exceptionally influential junior minister at the Treasury, and then had distinguished himself as Energy Secretary by making sure that coal stocks were built up to a level to withstand the miners' strike.

One only has to watch Lawson's plump figure walk a few yards to know that this is a man with no lack of assurance. He has, indeed, an abundance of intellectual confidence and a notably forthright manner. Some of his colleagues have been known to put the point less politely. He has the rare gift for a speaker of quite often looking more bored with his audience than they are with him. Yet nobody doubts that he has a grasp of economic complexities that is seldom found among politicians.

The personalities of the finance ministers have had an impact on international economic relations as well as at home because they have had so much scope. While Reagan was adamant on certain areas of economic policy, such as tax cuts, he left most of the detail of economic management to his advisers. That applied even more to international economic affairs. Nor, for all her renowned attention to detail, did Thatcher control everything that the Treasury did in London. So the degree of Anglo–American economic cooperation depended critically upon whether the Treasury Secretary saw eye to eye with the Chancellor of the Exchequer.

During Reagan's first term there had been some policy differences. The deep disagreement over the American budget deficit was a perpetual strain, but Geoffrey Howe and Donald Regan were not in conflict over exchange-rate policy. Neither believed in a managed exchange rate. If domestic economic policy was right, the exchange rate could be left to the market, with just occasional intervention by the central bank in exceptional circumstances. Their personal relations were also not bad. On the American side they were thought to get on better than they probably did. That was because Howe's innate courtesy prevented any irritation from showing.

It was after Thatcher's second election victory in June 1983 that Howe had moved on to become Foreign Secretary and was succeeded as Chancellor by Nigel Lawson. There followed an uneasy eighteen months with Regan and Lawson. Relations improved sharply after Baker took over from Regan.

Geoffrey Howe had been a courageous and consistent Chancellor, but Lawson was more of a reformer and a gambler. In this as in other ways he was very different from Baker, who is renowned for his caution. Whereas Lawson's primary interest lies in economics, Baker is above all a political animal. As Treasury Secretary Regan had been more doctrinal. If a proposed policy did not fit with Reaganite economic principles, he was reluctant to adopt it. Baker was pragmatic. If a proposed policy seemed the best way to solve a problem, forget the theory.

Despite the differences in temperament, Baker and Lawson had a similar approach to their jobs. Baker wanted to solve problems and Lawson was ready to try something different, especially if it was ingenious. They got on well together personally, with occasional lapses of trust when one found the other not supporting him. These differences were essentially only tactical. They would phone each other frequently, and certainly before either made a serious move.

Lawson had, indeed, done something different in his first Budget in 1984, when he set out on the course of tax reform. This was to become one of the most notable common features of both Thatcher's and Reagan's economic policies. The essential aim was to simplify the system, remove the distortions, let people decide how to spend their own money without fiscal bribes in one direction or another, and use the money saved to cut the rate of tax.

In that Budget Lawson applied the principles of reform to company taxation. He began the phasing out of a range of allowances, such as for expenditure on machinery, plant and industrial buildings. In return, the main rate of corporation tax was to be progressively reduced over three years from 52 per cent to 35 per cent.

Personal taxation was changed only slightly at that time. Income-tax rates were unaltered, but the surcharge on investment income was abolished, as was the tax relief on life-assurance premiums. So there was a hint of rationalisation for the personal taxpayer as well, though it would be a few more years before it was more than a hint.

Throughout 1985 the United States was moving in the same direction, only more so. Baker presented legislation to Congress applying to individuals as well as to companies the principles of tax reform that Lawson had adopted for companies in 1984. The Tax Reform Act which the President finally signed in October 1986 reduced the maximum rate of federal income tax from 50 to 28 per cent. At the same time it abolished many allowances and closed quite a number of loopholes.

This was not all Baker's work. The drive for tax reform started while Regan was still at the Treasury. The President himself felt deeply about cutting taxes, and the issue had been invaluable for him in winning reelection. The Republicans had hounded the unfortunate Democratic candidate, Walter Mondale, for saying in his acceptance speech at the San Francisco Convention that the next President would have to raise taxes. As so often, Baker's contribution was essentially political. He brought an awareness of the potential political advantages of tax reform, and the political skills to help its long and difficult passage through Congress.

In this field the British and American governments gave the impression of playing a game of leapfrog. As soon as Thatcher came to power in 1979 income-tax rates were cut, though indirect taxes were raised correspondingly at the same time. When Reagan took office in 1981 American personal taxes were cut by much more. In the early part of Thatcher's second term, in 1984, tax reform was introduced for companies in Britain. In the early part of Reagan's second term tax-reform proposals for individuals and companies were sent to Congress and finally passed in 1986. Then in Britain income-tax rates for individuals as well came tumbling down in 1987 and 1988.

The British government was more influenced by the American example of tax-cutting than the Americans were swayed by British experience. Neither government needed to be persuaded that this was a desirable course. Both were drawing on the ideas that emanated from that right-wing transatlantic intellectual network. In Britain there was also the practical consideration that if taxes were too high the best managers would go elsewhere. It was essentially a matter of finding the right political and economic conditions for making the cuts. The decisive factor in Britain was that Thatcher was determined that there should be no tax reductions until they could be afforded without putting a strain on the budget deficit. So nothing much could be done until the revival of economic activity after the recession of the early 1980s.

Rapid growth then brought a surge of revenue to the Exchequer. So it became possible to cut taxes and move towards a budget surplus at the same time. By the time Reagan left office the basic rate of income tax in Britain had come down under Thatcher from 33 per cent to 25 per cent. The top rate had been reduced from 83 per cent to 40 per cent. That does not compare too badly with the top rate of 28 per cent for federal income tax in the United States after the Tax Reform Act, when state and municipal income taxes are taken into account.

How much international economic thinking was moving in a Reagan-ite and Thatcherite direction was evident at the first economic summit of Reagan's second term, which was held in Bonn early in May 1985. The proceedings there were largely overshadowed by the controversy surrounding the President's visit to Bitburg immediately afterwards. As a gesture of reconciliation to Germany he had agreed to visit a cemetery where the dead of the Second World War were buried, without realising until too late that it included graves of the notorious Waffen SS. Against much advice, Reagan was prepared to be held to his promise by Kohl. It was an indication of the importance the President attached to personal relations with another right-wing leader, whom he regarded as generally being on the same side, even though his relations with Kohl were never so warm as those with Thatcher.

At the summit itself there was agreement, as expressed in the communiqué, on removing the obstacles to growth and encouraging enterprise and initiative as the principal means to higher employment. Budget deficits were to be reduced by controlling public expenditure. It was a distinct change in the atmosphere from that first summit Reagan and Thatcher had attended together in Ottawa four years before.

As so often at these meetings, there was a bitter battle with Mitterrand, who at one point walked out of the conference room. This time the dispute was over international trade, with the French President wanting to delay the initiative for another round of General Agreement on Tariffs and Trade (GATT) negotiations to reduce trading barriers. These were begun in due course under the title of the Uruguay Round, but American indignation ran strongly at the summit and immediately afterwards. As on previous occasions, Reagan and Thatcher were fighting on the same side.

So were their finance ministers in September when the Group of Five (G5) leading industrial nations – the United States, Japan, West Germany, Britain and France – agreed to coordinate their policies so as to bring down the exchange rate of the dollar. This was where it became evident how Baker and Lawson differed from their predecessors.

Towards the end of his time at the Treasury Donald Regan had, it is true, become concerned at the excessively high exchange value of the dollar. One of his last acts there had been to preside over a G5 meeting in Washington to consider what might be done about it. Baker approached the issue, however, without the same inhibitions about intervention conflicting with economic doctrine. Characteristically, his concern was with political appearances. He did not want to be labelled as the man who pushed the dollar down. But he was always closely in touch with American business and was aware of the damage that the high dollar was doing to American trade.

Lawson also believed that this was a major cause of the American trading deficit, and was therefore disrupting international trade. He wanted to do something about it. Britain is not usually a principal player in G5. The ones who matter there are those with the three strongest economies: the Americans, the Japanese and the Germans. None the less, personalities are important in all negotiations and the strongest personalities at that meeting in the Plaza Hotel in New York were Baker, Lawson and the President of the German Bundesbank, Dr Karl Otto Pohl. Lawson's contribution in this, as in subsequent meetings, was that of a powerful debater with a strong grasp of the subject. He was able to play a part in bringing the Americans and the Germans closer together.

There was a sequel to the Plaza agreement when the finance ministers met again in Paris in February 1987. At the Plaza they had pledged themselves to take joint action to push the dollar down. Now they agreed that exchange rates were about right, and in the Louvre accord they undertook to intervene in the markets where necessary to preserve stability. Once again Baker and Lawson were principal participants, and once again they were on the same side.

There was a dissenting voice, but not present at the meeting. Thatcher had not seemed particularly interested in the Plaza agreement. The dollar had begun to fall earlier in 1985, and she had regarded the Plaza as simply putting a gloss on what was happening anyway. Whether that was correct is a matter of argument among financial experts, but it was how she saw it. The Louvre was a different question. Thatcher considered that a disaster because she saw it as an international commitment to a regime of managed exchange rates. Her belief, as she expressed it on another, memorable occasion, was that you 'cannot buck the market'.

This was a fundamental disagreement, which was a recurring cause of difficulty with Lawson until his resignation in October 1989. It did not stop him at the Plaza, the Louvre, or in subsequent discussions with his fellow finance ministers, from being active in the cause of managing exchange rates. He was not able to go as far as he would have liked. He was not able to take Britain into the Exchange Rate Mechanism of the European Monetary System. But neither did Thatcher get exactly the economic policy that she would have liked: British interest rates were governed more by the exchange rate than she thought appropriate. The outcome was that in those years the critical difference over international economic policy was not between the British and American governments. It was within the British government.

There was no disagreement between Thatcher and her ministers on another financial issue, which was a running sore during these years. A number of individual states in the United States, of which California is by far the most important, use a system for corporate income tax known as unitary taxation. A subsidiary company is taxed not on the proportion it has of the parent company's profits, but of the parent's total business activity. This means that if it represents, within the state, 10 per cent of the parent's sales, property and payroll, it will pay tax on 10 per cent of the parent's total earnings worldwide. This system is attractive to states, which may be able to boost tax revenues substantially, but it is particularly disadvantageous for international companies with subsidiaries which are less profitable than the core operation. It is a distinct disincentive to setting up new branches. Several British companies with branches in California and other American states were very hard hit.

Both Chancellors and both Regan and Baker as Treasury Secretary devoted a lot of time to this issue during the Reagan–Thatcher years. So did the British Embassy in Washington. It persuaded officials in the United States Treasury and Solicitor-General's Office to place an *amicus curiae* brief before the Supreme Court arguing against unitary taxation in a case involving the Container Corporation of America.

This was another example of how much influence British officials could exercise quietly with the American bureaucracy. The brief was consistent with the federal government's own policy on the unitary system, which is not used for federal taxation, but took no account of the sensitive issue of states' rights. It also failed to win the day in the Court. The verdict in June 1983 upheld California's right to use the unitary system for American parent companies, but it left a loophole. No judgment was passed on the legality of the system for foreign parent companies, and the Court suggested that it might not be legal if it could be shown to interfere with the right of the President to make foreign policy.

In response to foreign pressure, in which Britain played a leading part, the President set up a working group, under the chairmanship of Donald Regan as Treasury Secretary, to consider the question. Nothing much came of that. Federal departments did not want to become embroiled in new legislation to limit the power of the states.

Thatcher herself seems to have been more successful with a letter she wrote to Reagan that same year of 1983, asking him to use his influence. The President's wishes were almost certainly communicated to Governor George Deukmejian of California, probably by Reagan himself. As the Republican Governor of California he would have found it difficult not to respond to the Republican President from California. A new law was finally passed in California in 1986 under which a company could choose not to be taxed by the unitary method on payment of a fee. It was not an ideal arrangement from the British standpoint, but it was an improvement.

On another occasion, however, Thatcher was disastrously unsuccessful in trying to use her political clout to help Britain's commercial cause. The new battlefield telecommunications system, Ptarmigan, manufactured by the British company Plessey, had completed its trials successfully in the summer of 1984. Before the end of the year it had won the contract for use by the British Army. Plessey and the Ministry of Defence hoped that this would be just the beginning. Their eyes were set on the lucrative contract for exclusive use by the United States Army.

Ptarmigan's only rival was the Rita system designed by the French company, Thomson CSF. Just to make sure that this competitor was knocked out of the race, the British mounted an ambitious military exercise on Salisbury Plain in December to put Ptarmigan on show before a delegation of American generals. British hopes were riding high, and apparently with justification. Even Pentagon sources were reported to be saying that Ptarmigan was the clear favourite.

The plan was for it to be sold in the United States through the American company Rockwell International, who would have manufactured it under licence. Even so, 30 per cent of the system would still have been manufactured in Britain. As they were putting the bid together the companies assumed that it could be as much as

185

800 million dollars higher than the opposition and still win, because of the clear American preference for buying British. This was a tribute to British influence in the United States under Thatcher. It may also have been a trap for the British and their partners, because they may have been tempted to take victory too much for granted.

After much hard lobbying, it seemed the following September that the contract was after all about to go to the French on grounds of cost. At that point Thatcher wrote a personal letter to the President, claiming that Britain had been the more loyal ally and reminding him that it was the first European country to come out in favour of the SDI programme. It did not help her cause that this letter was immediately leaked, probably from within the Pentagon, where there were some who clearly felt that she was bringing improper political influence to bear in the attempt to persuade the United States to buy an unnecessarily expensive system.

She could not have found two more sympathetic judges for her appeal than Reagan and Weinberger, but it was no good. Both Rockwell and Thomson thought that the gap between their bids was no more than 800 million dollars. In fact it was nearly 3 billion dollars. Thatcher's intervention forced a delay in awarding the contract and a reworking of the figures within the Pentagon. There was no appreciable change. No political considerations, no personal sentiment could possibly bridge such a gap. Thatcher was left in the exposed position of having tried to exert excessive political pressure on behalf of a commercially unacceptable bid.

She had been encouraged to write to Reagan not only by her own officials, but also at senior levels in the American administration. That would have been a perfectly sensible tactic if the figures had been different. The British were simply caught unawares. Plessey did not know the final price at which Rockwell submitted the bid, which indicates that the cooperation between them had been less than perfect.

Originally, the American army specified that the system it bought must be nuclear-hardened – in other words, it must be capable of operating after a nuclear attack; must be proved and in service; and must be able to take digital information as well as voices. During the process of negotiation, the army took out these requirements. So the British were offering a more sophisticated and therefore more expensive system than the Americans were ultimately seeking. Rockwell did not appreciate the extent of the changes in the requirements.

Not being informed of the true position Thatcher grossly

overplayed her hand. The only surprise in the circumstances is that it did no lasting damage to her influence. The next year, 1986, a proposal was made in the House of Representatives Appropriations Committee that no money should be allocated for purchases from the Royal Ordnance. To which one Congressman retorted that this was a British company and they could not do this to Mrs Thatcher. It was thereupon agreed unanimously to restore the cut. It was a happy sequel to an unhappy episode.

One of the central features of Thatcherism and Reaganism was always the belief that the state should play a smaller part in economic life. In Britain this conviction was expressed most notably in the programme of privatisation. The process of selling publicly owned assets into private hands had been begun in Thatcher's first term. The oustanding example then was a form of social rather than industrial privatisation: the selling of municipal housing at preferential rates to those tenants who wished to buy. This was immensely popular and a great political success. There had also been some industrial privatisation. The sale of British Aerospace and Britoil was started in the first term. There were other examples, but nothing dramatic.

In the manifesto for the 1983 election, however, there had been specific commitments to privatise British Telecom, Rolls-Royce, British Airways and substantial parts of British Steel, British Shipbuilders and of British Leyland, the mammoth (by British standards) car and truck manufacturer. British Gas's offshore oil interests were to be sold off as well. The programme was obviously intended to have a much higher priority. The government went beyond its specific commitments to sell the whole of British Gas.

The sale of British Telecom and British Gas had an unforeseen side-effect. The advertising and other arrangements were deliberately designed to appeal to small shareholders. They did, to a greater extent than the government had ever expected. Many people who had never bought shares before did so then. A new class of small shareholder seemed to have been discovered. The creation of people's capitalism became a central tenet in the thinking of Thatcher and some of her ministers.

Lawson shared Thatcher's enthusiasm for privatisation. As Chancellor he had a special reason for doing so. It is a quirk of the British public-accounting system that income from the sale of public assets is classed in effect as revenue. So the more money came in from privatisation, the more was available for the tax cuts in which Lawson believed so strongly. It was a chancellor's dream, though in fairness to Lawson it should be said that he believed in privatisation for its own sake. His support was a powerful factor in pushing the programme forward.

There was no exactly corresponding development in the United States for the simple reason that not so much of American industry was ever under public ownership. Deregulation was the American counterpart to privatisation in Britain. The process had been begun under Carter and was taken significantly further in Reagan's first term. Fewer new moves in this direction were made in the second term, but this was still the trend and it affected the exercise of administrative power.

Airline deregulation had been begun under Carter. Trucking and rail deregulation followed in 1980. Oil prices were decontrolled the following year and most restrictions on the pricing of natural gas were removed as well. In 1982 came bus deregulation. Two years later the process was extended to telecommunications with the divestiture of the Bell operating companies from AT&T. There was also a change in attitude in favour of free markets among those administering regulations.

Privatisation under Reagan was much more modest. The most substantial sale of a federally owned industry during the Reagan years was of Conrail, the freight rail service in the north-east. Its privatisation in 1987 was the largest public stock offering in American history, but this was an exception rather than an example of a trend.

In Britain there were two distinct and contrary tendencies in this area. There was an increase in regulation among privatised companies. One of the benefits of privatisation in theory is greater competition, but that did not always occur in practice. Where the privatised corporation was in a monopoly or quasi-monopoly position, as in the case of British Telecom, British Gas and the water companies, regulatory systems were set up to prevent abuse in the absence of market forces. Elsewhere the trend has been towards deregulation. The City of London – in the Financial Services Act of 1986, which produced 'Big Bang', the most dramatic change in its working practices this century – the opticians and the lawyers have all had restrictions on their activities reduced or swept away.

Both tendencies, however, represented a move along the spectrum towards less state control. That remained the common denominator in domestic policy between the two governments. It was sufficient to provide a harmonious backdrop to the stirring dramas that were taking place in the foreign field.

16

THE LIBYAN GAMBIT

On the evening of Tuesday 8 April 1986 Margaret Thatcher was giving a formal dinner in Downing Street to the President of South Korea and Mrs Chun Doo Hwan. It was one of those elegant, sedate, diplomatic occasions that normally provide a pleasing contrast to the frantic bustle of ministerial life. In the midst of this calm a personal message from Reagan to Thatcher was delivered to her private secretary for foreign affairs, Charles Powell. He did not interrupt the proceedings then. Presumably that would have created precisely the sense of crisis it was necessary to avoid. There was time enough to deal with the message at the end of dinner when the Foreign and Defence Secretaries, Geoffrey Howe and George Younger, were asked to stay behind.

The four of them – Thatcher, Howe, Younger and Powell – then discussed into the early hours of Wednesday morning what the British response should be to Reagan's request to be given the right to use American air bases in Britain for a bombing raid upon Libya. Permission was required because these are Nato bases, and British approval has to be given before they can be used for another kind of operation.

The request cannot have come as too much of a surprise because American indignation had been building up for some time over the Libyan campaign of international terrorism. Libya and Syria were associated with the bomb explosion at Frankfurt's international airport the previous June. Libya was held responsible for a car bomb at the American air base of Rhein-Main near Frankfurt in August. It was one of the countries associated with the hijacking of the Italian cruise ship *Achille Lauro* by a militant breakaway faction of the PLO in the Mediterranean in October, when a disabled American Jewish passenger was shot dead and thrown overboard.

189

Libya was also blamed for the attacks on Rome and Vienna airports in December. Terrorists threw grenades and fired machine guns at passengers and staff at the check-in counters of El Al Israeli Airlines in both these airports, killing sixteen people, on 27 December. Three days later the State Department and the Israeli government produced evidence that the Palestinian terrorist, Abu Nidal, had been responsible for the attacks with the support of the Libyan government.

Americans were not the only victims of Libyan terrorism. A particularly horrifying tragedy had occurred in St James's Square, London on 17 April 1984, when a policewoman, Yvonne Fletcher, had been shot in the back by a gunman inside the Libyan People's Bureau while protecting it from protesters outside. The sense of outrage in Britain at her murder then had been equal to anything that subsequently developed in the United States. The Libyan Bureau staff were allowed to leave the country on grounds of diplomatic immunity, but the British government broke off diplomatic relations with Libya.

In the second half of that year an interdepartmental group on terrorism had been set up in Whitehall, composed of representatives from the Foreign Office, the Ministry of Defence, the Cabinet Office, MI5 and MI6. There were regular meetings about every four months with the National Security Adviser in Washington to discuss terrorism, and Anglo–American consultation was particularly close after the hijacking of the *Achille Lauro*. There was the possibility of its being diverted to Cyprus, and the question was what would happen then.

The ship returned to Egypt, however, where the hijackers were given safe conduct. The dramatic interception of their plane on its way to Tunisia by US Navy fighter aircraft gave the Reagan administration a political triumph at home, but American indignation remained. It was directed partly at those who were behind the hijackers, and partly at those allies who appeared to the United States to be feeble in their response.

At the beginning of 1986 the United States tried hard to persuade Western European governments to join a concerted programme of economic sanctions against Libya, but to no avail. So in the Gulf of Sirte in March United States carrier jets used missiles to destroy two Libyan patrol boats and damage an anti-aircraft missile site when the Libyans fired rockets at American planes. Colonel Gadaffi claimed the gulf as Libyan territorial waters and the United States maintained that it was international, so the presence of American forces there was clearly designed as a warning to the Libyan leader.

It was evidently a warning that went unheeded. The final outrage came with the bombing in West Berlin on Saturday 5 April 1986 of La Belle discothèque, which was much used by American servicemen. On this occasion two people, one an American soldier, were killed and more than two hundred, including over fifty Americans, were injured. By early April the air was thick with reports of an impending American attack of some kind upon Libya.

British sympathies were entirely with the Americans on the issue of terrorism itself. Both countries had suffered from Libyan atrocities. Neither had any illusions about Gadaffi. None the less, Reagan's message was not asking Thatcher what she thought ought to be done. It was seeking her help to implement a decision which had already been taken. As usual on such occasions, the question in Washington was whether or not there was sufficient agreement within the administration in favour of action.

In this instance, Weinberger, who was normally the most reluctant to use force, had been out of town when the decision was taken. The Joint Chiefs of Staff, whose judgment Weinberger normally accepted on such an issue, were more favourable than might have been expected. Even so, lining up everybody necessary in Washington had been a fairly slow process. There was no inclination to reopen the debate by consulting an ally.

The American request presented British ministers with a dilemma. Looking back nearly four years later, Thatcher recalled: 'It was a very difficult decision because we had to really work through the fundamental reason for it.' It was not enough to agree that some riposte to Libyan terrorism would be justified. It had to be one that could be justified before British and international opinion on a number of scores.

Thatcher herself had told American journalists at a news conference in Downing Street back in January: 'I do not believe in retaliatory strikes that are against international law.' That was one of the questions presented by Reagan's request. Would such a raid be in accordance with international law? The President had asked for approval to be given by midday (British time) the following day, Wednesday, which would be about breakfast time in Washington. Yet neither the precise nature of the operation nor how it would be presented to the world was by any means clear.

After much discussion Thatcher and her colleagues decided in effect to disregard the deadline and to send a series of questions back to Washington, rather than giving a straight 'yes' or 'no' at that stage. They wanted to know, first of all, how thoroughly the Americans had thought through the implications of an air strike on Libya. Why was it necessary for the bases in Britain to be used at all? Could American planes not fly either from land bases in the United States or from an aircraft carrier? How extensive a raid would it be? How many aircraft would be used? What weapons would be employed? What targets had been selected? Would they all be military targets? Were the American military capable of ensuring that only such targets would be hit? Was the administration going to be able to present the raid as an act of self-defence against terrorism?

On this last point Thatcher was particularly insistent: 'We still had to make quite clear that it was going to be a legitimate Article 51 defence' – referring to the article in the United Nations Charter which permits the use of force in self-defence – 'and therefore that the targets had to be quite clearly military targets.'

This detailed questionnaire was sent to Washington in the early hours of Wednesday morning. It was an indication of British anxiety: not wanting to turn the Americans down, but clearly not yet convinced about the wisdom of the operation. There is some evidence that by later that morning Thatcher had herself moved towards accepting the American request. She was still deeply affected by the murder of Yvonne Fletcher, as well as by her concern for the Anglo–American relationship, but further meetings lay ahead.

On Thursday morning, 10 April, there was an *ad hoc* meeting of ministers and officials which ended inconclusively. Thatcher began that meeting seeming to favour supporting the Americans. Her attitude was that every country has the right to decide what it must do for its own self-defence, that the British government should not attempt to second-guess the Americans on this and should certainly not prevent their using their own aircraft based in Britain to do what they believed to be necessary.

This stopped short of being a ringing endorsement of American judgment, but it would have been enough probably to settle the matter then and there if there had been no other considerations. There were two in particular. First, Thatcher was concerned about the possible repercussions throughout the Middle East, for Britain as well as for the United States, if it could not be shown convincingly that the Americans were acting in self-defence. Second, the lawyers could not provide reassurance at that meeting that the raid would be in accordance with international law.

Everyone was satisfied with the intelligence evidence that the Libyans had indeed been responsible for the British bombing. Two CIA officials were to come to London later on with further information. That was after the British government had given its approval. There was evidence from both American and British intelligence sources, some of it from Berlin. The conclusive information, however, came from SIGINT (signals intelligence) in Cyprus, which had picked up a radio message from Tripoli to the Libyan People's Bureau in East Berlin, not only offering congratulations for the bombing of the discothèque but also instructing their agents to carry out more operations of that sort.

All the intelligence information was examined by the British with great care, but that could settle only the factual question. That was not enough by itself to resolve the legal dilemma: would a bombing raid upon Libya be a proportionate use of force, and therefore be consistent with international law?

At the end of that meeting Sir Robert Armstrong, the Cabinet Secretary, and David Goodall, Deputy Secretary in the Cabinet Office (subsequently High Commissioner in India), were given the task of drafting a reasoned reply to Washington. Thatcher's attitude at that stage is interpreted differently by some of the participants in the meeting. Some believe that, although the second part of that discussion had focused on the legal difficulties, she did not waver in her conviction that the United States would have to be given permission. To others she gave the impression of being in a state of philosophic doubt.

That was never likely to last for very long. By the time a second meeting was held in the afternoon her mind was made up. By then she had spoken personally to Reagan, and a number of conversations and messages had been flowing to and fro across the Atlantic. A full and satisfactory response had been received from Washington to the list of British questions. Britain did not have to determine whether the proposed American action was the most appropriate. It would not try to decide that for them. It would stand by them as a good ally. The Armstrong–Goodall draft was amended accordingly and dispatched to Washington.

Thatcher's personal role was critical in determining the British decision. Her manner was intense, even somewhat emotional, in discussion. This was 'something that we just have to do', she kept on saying. Younger and, somewhat less readily, Howe went along with her, but their misgivings were evident. It was this small group of ministers, aided by officials, who decided. Lord Whitelaw, for so many years Margaret Thatcher's faithful deputy, would no doubt have joined their deliberations had he been present at the Korean dinner. His influence was invaluable on those delicate issues when the Cabinet could be kept united only with difficulty. As it was,

Thatcher kept him in touch even though he did not attend the vital meetings.

The full Cabinet was not presented with the issue until the following week, nor was the decision considered in advance by any Cabinet committee. That was not contrary to usual practice by that time. From about the end of 1981 the Prime Minister had become so fed up with leaks to the press that most decisions were taken at *ad hoc* meetings of small groups of ministers without papers. She would also have been fully aware that this is a process that enhances her own power.

The Libyan decision was not treated exceptionally, but the bypassing of the Cabinet was deliberate. Had its consent been required, it might well have been bullied into acquiescence by Thatcher, but it did not really agree. When the Cabinet did discuss the matter the only other member who spoke up firmly for supporting the United States was Lord Hailsham, the Lord Chancellor, in a somewhat discursive contribution in which his American mother featured.

In taking that course Thatcher had in mind what seemed to her the serious danger that if Britain refused there would be formidable pressure in the United States to reduce severely the number of American troops in Europe. Why should we keep them there to protect Europe, Americans might ask themselves, if we are not allowed to use those same forces to protect ourselves when we think it necessary?

She was also very much aware of the damage that would have been done more generally to Anglo–American relations. Libya was seen by many Americans as the third episode in a sequence. Over the Falklands they had backed Britain: the equivocations were forgotten, indeed most Americans had scarcely been aware of them. Over Grenada, Britain had failed to back the United States: a man of Reagan's sunny disposition might have banished that rejection from his mind, but that was not true of many of his colleagues or of a good many other Americans.

Curiously enough, Grenada does not seem to have figured in the Libyan discussions among British ministers and officials. Perhaps it seemed to them indelicate to remind the Prime Minister of that episode. Few Americans would have had such inhibitions if Britain had not supported them over Libya. There would have been bitter reminders that Britian had twice failed to repay the Falklands debt.

The United States may itself have contributed to the refusal of another ally to assist the attack on Libya. Although Thatcher was not consulted by Reagan as to whether an air strike on Libya would be a good idea, at least she received a personal message direct from the President. When she asked for further information she was given the courtesy of comprehensive answers. The administration took trouble with Britain.

France may well have felt that it was not accorded a similar courtesy. The request for flying rights over French territory reached President Mitterrand by a circuitous route. It went from the operations officer on the United States Joint Staff in Washington, a three-star general, to the Defense Attaché in the American Embassy in Paris, to the military adviser to the President and from him to the President himself. The rejection went back through the same roundabout channel within twenty-four hours. The Pentagon had begun to use this line of communication with the French military with some success, but it was hardly appropriate for a request of this nature when one president was asking a favour of another.

In such a politically sensitive operation the United States would no doubt have appreciated the company of one or two allies, but the planners wanted British and French assistance for practical, military reasons.

The Americans would have been able to carry out the raid without any allied cooperation, but the reply that Thatcher received from Washington made it clear that the operation would be affected if they could not use the bases in Britain. F-111s are land-based aircraft. They could have been flown direct from the United States, but this would have placed them at the far end of their range. The risk would inevitably have been greater. The alternative would have been to fly other aircraft from carriers, but they would have been capable of less accuracy.

Without the F-111s from Britain the Americans would not have been able to aim for so many targets and they could not have expected the necessary precision to go for one of the targets in particular. There were civilian apartments just across the street from the barracks where Gadaffi had his home. Without the F-111s that target would have been dropped. If they were going to be used, then the most direct route was obviously across France. What the planners did not know was that Gadaffi would be sleeping in his tent by that house on that particular night: it was his custom to rotate between a number of different sleeping quarters.

The operation was planned by American commanders in Europe. They drew up the initial list of targets, but it had not been finalised when Thatcher expressed her concern about limiting civilian casualties. The list was cut by Weinberger – who had also decreed that B52 bombers should not be used because of the bad publicity they had received in Vietnam – and then shortened still further by the White House. This was the cause of some confusion later.

On the evening of Monday 14 April Weinberger and Admiral Crowe, the Chairman of the Joint Chiefs of Staff, were sitting watching a news bulletin on television when the reporter from Libya suddenly announced that they were under attack. That was the first confirmation that the Pentagon had that the strike was taking place as planned. Or rather, the timing was as planned. Not all the bombs fell where they were supposed to. Despite all the assurances given to Thatcher, civilian targets were hit. The Americans may have been disappointed with the French denial of overflying rights, but they did not intend to bomb the French Embassy, nor to damage the Austrian and Finnish embassies and other diplomatic premises.

Weinberger denied on television that the French Embassy had been hit. He did so in all good faith because he had personally deleted from the list the one target in the vicinity. It was therefore impossible, he believed, that the embassy could have been struck. He did not know that one young pilot was admitting in his debriefing on his return: 'I think I used the wrong offset point.' This was later confirmed. Entirely through human error, the wrong target was attacked.

The effect on British opinion was severe. Harrowing pictures were shown on television, coupled with emotionally powerful reporting. Probably not many believed that the United States had deliberately struck civilian targets, but the evidence of their television screens made most people feel that the distinction between different kinds of target was academic. Some concluded that the Americans simply did not care. Others, more reasonably, concluded that the military were promising a degree of precision that they could not accomplish. All Thatcher's care in obtaining detailed conditions for the raid seemed wasted, at least in political terms.

There were protests on the streets of London and in Parliament. Public-opinion polls conducted immediately after the raid found massive majorities against both the American action and the British government's decision. The raid was approved by only 29 per cent in a MORI poll conducted for *The Times*, and by a mere 32 per cent in a Harris poll for ITN. MORI found 71 per cent and Harris 68 per cent opposed to the Americans being allowed to fly from Britain.

The stronger the political heat Thatcher had to take in Britain, the more credit she was given in the United States. Grenada was forgotten. Here was the one ally prepared to stand by the United States, no matter what the cost might be. The reputation for courage that she had won over the Falklands was more than confirmed over Libya. Over the Falklands she had indeed displayed nerve, but it had been from necessity in the British national interest. Over Libya, so it seemed to American eyes, she had been staunch in a broader international interest. She has never been more admired in the United States, and rarely has Britain been more popular.

The political price that Thatcher had to pay in Britain for this triumph in the United States was not so great as had been expected, or indeed as many suppose to this day. First of all, she was fortunate in the timing. Had it come a year later, the raid would have been launched in the run-up to a general election campaign and the immediate effect might have been the lasting effect. It could have cost her the election.

As it was, rather than sending her into the wilderness, it soon lost political impact. There were two parliamentary by-elections in the north of England the following month. Neither in West Derbyshire nor in Ryedale did the Conservatives do well. That was because of domestic factors. It was remarkable that in both campaigns the issue of Libya was brought up so rarely by voters themselves. It had become by then more a politicians' dispute, and a topic for journalists, than a question that swung votes.

The political outcome might well have been very different if the raid had been seen to fail in its purpose. Had Libyan terrorism continued unabated, had British targets been singled out for retaliation, had British interests manifestly suffered, then many people would have felt that their foreboding had been justified and that the British government had indeed taken leave of its senses. It is more difficult to maintain a burning sense of indignation against an act of deterrence that appears to have deterred.

Libya was the supreme occasion when Thatcher delivered for Reagan. In doing so she took a deliberate risk, but she won American gratitude at what turned out to be a lower price than she can have dared to hope.

The timing was particularly fortunate for Britain in a way that no minister would have thought of when they were agonising over the critical decision. It helped to get the one act of cooperation above all others that the British government had been asking of the United States in the endless saga of Northern Ireland. Without the sudden popularity which the raid brought Britain among Americans, it is very doubtful if Congress would ever have ratified the new extraditon treaty that was needed to get IRA terrorists back to stand trial in the United Kingdom.

Thatcher had continued to cooperate with the Irish Prime Minister, Garret FitzGerald, in the spirit of her speech to Congress in February 1985. Putting the 'out, out, out' press conference behind her, she reached a new political understanding with the government of the Republic nine months later. The Anglo–Irish Agreement was signed on 15 November 1986 at Hillsborough Castle outside Belfast, the former residence of the Governor of Northern Ireland, the Queen's representative in the province.

It provided for an intergovernmental conference that would meet regularly to consider different aspects of the government of Northern Ireland and relations with the Republic. The conference would deal with political matters, security, the administration of justice and the promotion of cross-border cooperation. It would have only a consultative role, but it would have a small secretariat. So this was the first institutionalised arrangement to involve the Republic, even if only indirectly, in the government of Northern Ireland. As such, it was an historic development.

From the first it was exceedingly controversial in the province itself, where it was never accepted by the Unionist parties. In the United States the reaction was highly favourable. Thatcher was seen to have responded to the promptings to deal constructively with FitzGerald. London and Dublin were no longer in conflict, which made it easier for Washington to cooperate with both.

The wishes of Washington were certainly a factor in inducing Thatcher to accept the agreement. By temperament and tradition she was more sympathetic to the Unionists. She would normally have been distinctly hostile to any idea of giving the government of another state a formal right to influence how part of the United Kingdom should be governed. To have rejected this arrangement, however, would have been to ignore the continued, discreet pressure from the President and the evident interest of even the most moderate Irish–American politicians.

The administration was never a party to the negotiations; but many drafts were exchanged between Clark and Sean Donlan, the Irish Ambassador to the United States. Reagan himself never showed any interest in the detail. He simply wanted agreement between two governments who were good friends of his. It was at that level that American pressure was felt by the British government. The American Embassy in London would regularly ask how things were going. Without pushing for any particular arrangement, the American desire for an agreement was made abundantly clear. Thatcher knew that relations with the United States would be hurt if Britain were judged responsible for a failure in the negotiations.

That was not the only reason for her acceptance. She wanted to do something about the Northern Ireland conflict, which was such a drain upon the United Kingdom's energy, resources and reputation. But American opinion was very much a consideration in her decision. It was a notable instance where Reagan successfully influenced Thatcher on an issue that was entirely the responsibility of the British government.

From her standpoint it was good to have won American approval, but she wanted more from the United States on Irish affairs than that. In particular, she wanted the Senate to ratify a new extradition treaty which had been under consideration for nearly a year at the time of the Libyan bombing.

The earlier treaty, signed in 1972, stipulated that extradition should not be granted where the offence was 'of a political character'. That provided the perfect escape clause for IRA terrorists, who could present themselves to the courts as freedom fighters. An especially controversial case was that of Joseph Doherty, who escaped from the Crumlin Road jail in Belfast in 1981 shortly before being convicted in his absence of murdering a British Army officer. Three years later an American Federal Court in New York refused to extradite him because his offence was political.

The British government then became determined to close this loophole, and in June 1985 a new treaty was signed that specified a range of serious crimes for which extradition would not be denied on political grounds. British officials had negotiated too well for their own good. The text that emerged was essentially the British draft, but the officials with whom they were dealing from the Department of Justice and the State Department were not sensitive to Congressional opinion. The draft treaty went too far to satisfy the British to stand much chance of being ratified by the Senate.

For months it languished in the Senate Foreign Relations Committee, whose Chairman, Richard Lugar, was sympathetic and was to play an invaluable role. The early hearings demonstrated conclusively that there was not a favourable majority in the committee. The Republicans were mostly for it, and at that time they still held a narrow majority in the Senate, which was reflected on the committee; but Senator Jesse Helms, the maverick right-wing Republican from North Carolina, was opposed. In any case, there would have been no point in getting the treaty out of the committee without some Democratic support because it would then have had no prospect of winning the necessary two-thirds majority in the full Senate.

Liberal Democrats objected that it would undermine the American tradition of providing a haven for political refugees from around the world. Some were opposed simply out of sympathy for the nationalist cause in Ireland. Not all the most vociferous sympathisers were themselves Irish–Americans. To shout loudly about the cause can seem a good way for a politician of different ancestry to appeal to the Irish vote. For years the more extreme *ad hoc* Committee on Ireland was led by the Italian–American Congressman Mario Biaggi from New York. The Friends of Ireland – led by such prominent Irish–Americans as O'Neill, Senators Edward Kennedy and Patrick Moynihan, and Congressman Tom Foley, the present Speaker of the House – have been far more restrained and responsible.

Towards the end of 1985, or early in 1986, Lugar devised a stratagem for putting pressure on the Democrats. Back in 1978 President Carter had said that, in the event of a peaceful settlement, 'the United States government would be prepared to join with others to see how additional job-creating investment could be encouraged, to the benefit of all the people of Northern Ireland'. That idea had been developed by Tip O'Neill and John Hume into a proposal for an international fund that would make annual payments for investment there.

There were mixed feelings about the fund in both the British and American governments. The British did not feel that the problem in Northern Ireland was financial; and if it was, they could find extra money. The American administration was not particularly enthusiastic about a further slice of the foreign-aid budget being committed to a particular recipient. None the less, nobody wanted to be seen to oppose the proposition, and Congressional Democrats, especially those with any kind of Irish connection, were keen on it.

Lugar now threatened that he would block approval for the fund in the committee unless the treaty was supported at the same time. Even the more moderate Friends of Ireland in Congress were furious. The Irish government, which steered clear of the battle over the treaty, tried to get the British Embassy to ask Lugar not to link the two issues. The British Embassy, who were very much in dialogue with Lugar over the treaty itself, refused to intervene over the tactics. The chairman of the Foreign Relations Committee ought to know best, and he was determined to maintain the linkage.

It was still not enough. In the spring of 1986 the deadlock remained unbroken. Then two developments occurred at much the same time. One was the British assistance over the Libyan raid, which provoked a wave of gratitude to Britain across the United States. The other was the redrafting of the treaty. The possession of firearms and conspiracy were removed from the list of crimes which could not be classified as a political offence.

It was in support of this amended treaty that Reagan swung into action himself. Lugar cannot recall any other legislation with which he was involved, with the sole exception of the INF Treaty, on which the President took a keener personal interest. Lugar himself received two phone calls from him, expressing the hope that the committee would make progress, and Reagan devoted one of his weekly radio talks entirely to the subject. 'Rejection would be an affront to British Prime Minister Margaret Thatcher,' the President told his listeners, 'one European leader who, at great political risk, stood shoulder to shoulder with us during our operations against Gadaffi's terrorists.'

'Ronald Reagan was generally first-rate on questions involving Irish affairs,' one highly respected Congressional Democrat believes. 'He was not at any time susceptible to gestures of support for extremist organisations. He said the right things at the right time; he supported the extradition treaty; he supported the Anglo–Irish Agreement enthusiastically. My sense was that all of his instincts were right.'

Others were cooperating by now. Senator Tom Eagleton, the senior Democrat who had been George McGovern's original choice as running-mate in 1972 and was in 1986 serving his last term in the Senate, was seen as the swing vote on the committee. Lobbied heavily by the British Embassy, he provided invaluable assistance not only in the committee but also in the Senate itself.

On 12 June the treaty was voted out of the committee by twelve votes to two, and the international fund was approved the same day. So Lugar stuck by his principle of linkage to the end. The full Senate ratified the treaty on 17 July and that evening the President phoned Margaret Thatcher in Downing Street with the good news. It was by no means all his own work, but he had played his part to the full.

Before the month was out he had his reward. In the first week of March 1984 the Nicaraguan port of Corinto had been mined by the Contras with United States approval. Indeed, on 4 April Reagan openly declared that his administration would take no steps to stop them doing so.

The Nicaraguan government responded by taking the case to the International Court of Justice (ICJ) at The Hague. In a swift pre-emptive move the United States formally told the Secretary-General of the United Nations that it was imposing a 'temporary and limited modification' of its acceptance of the Court's jurisdiction in any dispute associated with events in Central America for two years. This did not stop the Court hearing the case and on 27 June 1986 it found against the United States. It should 'cease and refrain' immediately from its illegal intervention in the affairs of another state and was 'under an obligation to make reparation' to Nicaragua.

British policy had consistently been to uphold the judgments of the Court as a matter of principle. This policy was reaffirmed that summer with the specific agreement of Thatcher, who customarily took a strong line on international law. So when a resolution calling for 'full compliance' with the Court's decision came before the Security Council on 31 July Britain might have been expected to support it. That was the wish of the Foreign Secretary. Geoffrey Howe argued that Britain would lose all credibility on ICJ judgments if it did not back this one. He was overruled by the Prime Minister. Once it was made known to her that the President himself felt strongly on this one, that was enough. The United States vetoed the resolution and Britain abstained.

Reagan and Thatcher also took much the same line towards South African sanctions. They did not approve of them and they conceded as little as they could to political pressure. The previous year Thatcher had reluctantly gone along with modest sanctions imposed by the EC in September and then by the Commonwealth the following month. After the Commonwealth Conference in the Bahamas she caused gratuitous offence to Commonwealth heads of government by explaining on television that she had conceded just 'a tiny little bit, a tiny little bit', as she contemptuously held finger and thumb a fraction of an inch apart.

It was not a performance designed to win an award for tact in the Third World, but as a statement of fact it was correct. In September 1985 Reagan had also introduced restricted sanctions by executive order as a means of heading off Congress from more severe ones.

Then, in October 1986, the United States passed the Comprehensive Anti-Apartheid Act to codify these executive orders and to add a few additional measures. It was not legislation of which Thatcher approved, but Reagan did not like it either. He had vetoed it, but a sufficient number of Republicans rebelled in Congress to override him.

Both Reagan and Thatcher found it easier to resist all but these minimum sanctions because the other was doing so as well. The risk of international isolation was reduced.

It was also in this year that Thatcher began a secret correspondence with President Botha of South Africa warning him that she could not hold the line on sanctions for ever and urging him to press ahead with internal reform. She wrote at least four or five substantial letters to him in 1986 and continued the correspondence in 1987 and 1988. She was more of a critic in reality than her public stance suggested.

Yet throughout 1986 a hidden drama of much greater immediate consequence, directly for Reagan and indirectly for Thatcher, was moving towards a shattering denouement. It would be a severe test both for Reagan's resilience and Thatcher's loyalty.

17

IRANGATE: WHAT THATCHER KNEW

On 20 February 1986 two emissaries from Thatcher had a meeting in Washington with John Poindexter, the National Security Adviser, on a topic that was to prove momentous for Reagan personally and for the United States. They were Sir Antony Acland, Permanent Under-Secretary of State at the Foreign Office, and Sir Percy Cradock, who had succeeded Sir Anthony Parsons as the Prime Minister's special adviser on foreign affairs.

A chat with the National Security Adviser would have seemed natural enough for officials of their standing at any time. An early exchange of views with Poindexter, who had succeeded McFarlane only two months before, required no explanation. It was even more understandable that Acland should go to Washington then because he was to take over as Ambassador from Sir Oliver Wright in August. What more sensible than to inspect the residence a few months in advance, have a glance at the curtains and decide which pictures to bring?

Even quite senior officials at the embassy did not know the full reason why they were there. At the top of the agenda with Poindexter was Syria. American anger with Syria was rising. Syria was known to be behind many of the terrorist exploits which were so alarming Washington. It was believed to have been responsible for blowing up the United States marine headquarters in Beirut just before the Grenada invasion back in 1983. A number of well-informed people considered Syria a more serious terrorist menace even than Libya, whose activities were to provoke the American bombing raid two months later. Was it true, the emissaries asked anxiously, that the United States might be about to take direct military action against Syria?

Having been reassured on that score, they then moved on to a more delicate subject. They wanted to know what truth there might be in the reports they were getting about American arms deals for hostages in the Middle East. The answers they received were opaque. Poindexter was not going to take them into his confidence. The natural conclusion was drawn.

Among ministers and officials back in London there was distress and some anger. They knew that Poindexter was not levelling with them, even if they were not yet aware of the full scale of the American involvement. British suspicions had been aroused in a most peculiar way. When McFarlane and Oliver North visited London the previous December to meet the Iranian arms dealer Manucher Ghorbanifar, their hotel suite had been bugged by MI5. In the strange games that security services play the world over, MI6 subsequently let this be known to the CIA in Washington.

Senior officers of the United States government customarily look forward to a warm reception in Britain, but not in that sense. Very close cooperation in the intelligence field is one of the strongest features of the Anglo–American special relationship. This is based partly upon history, partly upon practical arrangements, but also upon trust. It is understood that the two governments do not spy upon each other's activities. McFarlane was no longer National Security Adviser when he arrived in London. He had been succeeded by Poindexter three days before flying to England on 7 December 1985. By then he was a private citizen, but he was continuing to act unofficially on behalf of the administration. North was still on the National Security Staff, although the British authorities did not appear to appreciate at that stage the full significance of his role.

It was contrary to all normal procedures for either McFarlane or North to be bugged, especially for someone who had been in such a senior position as McFarlane. SIGINT (signals intelligence) in Cyprus probably picked up a message from Tehran to one of the Iranian embassies in the Middle East, saying that Ghorbanifar would be travelling to meet some important Americans in London. That message apparently caught the eye of GCHQ in Cheltenham. So it was not altogether surprising that the visit of McFarlane and North aroused some interest. For them to be bugged would have required the approval of a senior minister; perhaps the decision might have gone to the Prime Minister, but not necessarily so.

As National Security Adviser McFarlane had played a central role in trying to develop contacts with Iran and over the negotiations on the sale of arms. One hostage, the Reverend Benjamin Weir, had been released in September 1985, but attempts to secure the freedom of others through the sale of arms had been frustrated at that point. Although he had now relinquished office, McFarlane was asked by the President to conduct the next negotiations himself.

It was for that purpose that he went to London. Having flown overnight in an US Air Force special mission aircraft, he was met at Heathrow Airport by North on the morning of 8 December and taken immediately to the Hilton Hotel. They held their meeting with Ghorbanifar later that day, as is recorded in the Tower Report. The meeting was held in a West End apartment belonging to a private Israeli arms dealer, Yaacov Nimrodi. It was also attended by another Israeli arms dealer, Adolph Schwimmer; David Kimche, the Director General of the Israeli Foreign Ministry; and Richard Secord, the retired US Air Force general who had been arranging the transport of arms to Israel.

This was not the occasion for a further arms deal. There are conflicting interpretations of the instructions that McFarlane brought with him from the President. McFarlane himself has recorded that the purpose of his mission was to indicate continued American interest in a dialogue with moderates in Iran and in securing the release of the hostages, but to make no offer of arms. North wrote in a memorandum on his return to Washington on 9 December that the message to Ghorbanifar had been that no further deliveries would be undertaken until all the hostages had been released. That would indicate a continued readiness to trade if the terms were right, which of course turned out to be the American position.

It was not this meeting that was bugged, however, but at the hotel that morning McFarlane had talked with North and with Kimche. Secord has related that he saw McFarlane there as well before going on to the meeting in Nimrodi's home. It would have been evident from these conversations that something very strange had been happening. Even though McFarlane was not negotiating specifically for an arms deal on that trip, it would have been clear that such transactions had been on the agenda; and anyone listening to the conversations would have had the very reasonable suspicion that they would be again. What on earth was the former National Security Adviser doing, a week after resigning, in clandestine discussions with arms dealers and the head of the Israeli Foreign Ministry?

This information would have been circulated to only a very few people in London, which explains why the secret was kept so effectively. Thatcher's governments have not usually been so leak-proof. It would have gone to the Prime Minister herself, the Foreign Secretary, the Defence Secretary, perhaps the Home Secretary and almost certainly Lord Whitelaw as deputy Prime Minister. Apart from them, a few officials at Number Ten and the Foreign Office would have known. Always in such circumstances the distribution area is a little wider than this suggests because some people in most ministers' offices become informed as well, but the knowledge of what had happened was tightly restricted for obvious reasons.

The evidence seemed to those who did get it to be both incontrovertible and unbelievable. How could the Americans possibly be doing what they appeared to be doing? How could they behave in a way that was so contrary to everything they were saying? Surely, it was thought, there must be some mistake, some satisfactory explanation. Hence the Acland–Cradock mission.

This was nearly a year before Irangate became public knowledge. During the intervening months there were further arms deals and more hostages were released. The tempo of the operation quickened, and as the year went on British suspicions were left no room for doubt.

The Reagan administration, which was in public taking such a tough line on terrorism, was itself conducting negotiations for the sale of arms with the representatives of a regime that was connected to terrorists, and specifically had its links with the kidnappers of hostages in the Middle East. The very government in Washington that was pressing such a firm and unrelenting policy towards terrorism upon its allies was in private pursuing a very different course.

There were further contradictions. Less than two months after Acland and Cradock had their unsatisfactory conversation with Poindexter, Reagan was putting Thatcher under pressure to approve the use of American bases in Britain for the air strike on Libya. The President was taking a more ruthlessly tough line towards terrorism in this instance than the British government would have done of its own accord. No wonder Thatcher found it such a difficult decision to take.

Her own conduct, however, prompts some interesting questions. When Reagan asked her to take such a political risk over Libya, why did she not demand in return that at least the President should be more frank than his National Security Adviser about American negotiations with Iran? Why did she not require to be assured that the administration was being consistent in its opposition to terrorism?

British doubts on this score were not even raised among ministers as they pondered how to respond to the American request. It would be impossible to know whether any of them thought about this aspect without subjecting them all to psychoanalysis, but nobody discussed it. Thatcher and her colleagues behaved for all the world as if they had no suspicions of that sort at all.

The proceedings at the Tokyo economic summit in May were even more bizarre. Terrorism was the principal political issue at this meeting. It came less than a month after the bombing of Libya, and the United States was determined to secure the commitment of its allies to a united front in the struggle against international terrorism in general. 'I think we all know how we feel about terrorism,' Reagan said a few days before setting out for Tokyo. 'I'm hopeful we can sit down and work out what it is that we can do together to deal with this problem.' How did the administration want to deal with this problem? Was an ally to judge by what the President said or by what the United States did? Thatcher did not probe.

To get the kind of statement that he wanted from the summit Reagan made what a report in *The New York Times* on 6 May described as 'a dramatic and highly personal appeal' to his fellow heads of government. The proposal on terrorism that was drawn up was based largely on a British draft rather than a more ambitious American version. It was explicit enough, one would have thought, to leave no room for misunderstanding on the main proposition.

'We have decided to apply these measures,' it declared, 'within the framework of international law and in our own jurisdictions in respect of any state which is clearly involved in sponsoring or supporting international terrorism, and in particular Libya, until such time as the state concerned abandons its complicity in, or support for, such terrrorism.' The first of these measures was: 'Refusal to export arms to states which sponsor or support terrorism.'

Some tongues must have been in cheeks as the signatories completed this charade. In the British camp there was a certain cynicism about the way the Americans were behaving. Although the statement referred to Libya explicitly, it did not refer to Libya alone. Reagan may have convinced himself that he was exporting arms to those who were in touch with terrorists, not to those who were sponsoring or supporting them. Thatcher would not have deluded herself with such casuistry. For her to have taken that statement entirely at face value, as if she had no doubts about American conduct, was not an act of complicity. It was, however, an act of deliberate policy.

At the time of the Tokyo summit further evidence that the Americans were up to something cropped up elsewhere in London. Tiny Rowland, the British entrepreneur who is Chairman of the multinational corporation Lonrho, had been approached by Ghorbanifar accompanied by the Saudi businessman Adnan Khashoggi and Amiram Nir, an adviser on counter-terrorism to Shimon Peres, then Prime Minister of Israel. This trio had tried to interest Rowland in financing the shipment of weapons and spare parts to Iran. They indicated that the scheme had the approval of the White House, but Rowland was sceptical. He checked it out with the American Embassy in London.

The United States Ambassador, Charles Price, thereupon telephoned Michael Armacost, the Under-Secretary of State, in Washington. This much is described in the Tower Report, but there was a further irony. Price pointed out to Armacost the seriousness of what he had been told and the possible repercussions on the President. Armacost replied that he would send a report of their conversation to Shultz and asked Price to call Reagan directly. Knowing that Price was a personal friend of Reagan, Armacost must have been hoping that such a warning coming from him would have an impact on the President.

But it was the middle of the Tokyo summit, Reagan would be rushed from one engagement to the next, and exactly the same message that Price would have given the President was being sent through Shultz. So Price decided not to trouble the President personally, and instead telephoned Poindexter, of all people. He was told that there was just the slightest element of truth in the story, but for the most part there was nothing in it. Having warned that even the smallest element of truth could cause the greatest possible problem, Price was invited to have a chat about it with Poindexter next time he was in Washington.

Poindexter's answers on the telephone were opaque, as they had been to Acland and Cradock. The conclusion in the American Embassy in London was that, despite his efforts to minimise the importance of what Price was reporting to him, the story must be true in substance. Price did not take up the invitation to talk about the matter further with Poindexter.

Rowland was advised not to touch the project, which he did not. He was not on close terms with ministers, but it would not be surprising if word of his strange encounter with the middle men of the Middle East came to the ears of the British government. British suspicions had, however, already hardened into astonished certainty.

Still there was no confrontation with Washington, either Prime Minister to President, or at a lower level. The speeches delivered by Thatcher herself and by her Foreign Secretary, Geoffrey Howe, to the

Conservative Party Conference that October have a significance in retrospect that was not evident at the time. Neither mentioned hostages, even though there was much concern at the time about their captivity.

Thatcher did not refer to terrorism, not itself a glaring omission in a speech that had to range across national and international affairs as a whole. Howe confined his remarks on the subject to terrorism in general and to the misdeeds of Libya in particular: 'There is no subsitute for courage by peoples and firmness by governments. We must be firm in the face of blackmail. There must be no bargains, no deals with terrorists.' At the time that sounded like a message of support for Washington in the aftermath of the raid on Libya. With the benefit of hindsight, it looks like a coded message to the adminstration of a rather different sort.

Within weeks of the conference a public impression was created once again of Britain and the United States standing resolutely side by side in the battle against terrorism. A British court had found a Jordanian, Nezar Hindawi, guilty of a particularly repugnant crime. He had duped his pregnant girlfriend into carrying a bomb on board an El Al flight at London Heathrow airport in the attempt to murder three hundred and seventy-five people. MI5 had bugged the Syrian Embassy and discovered its complicity in the plot. So when Hindawi was convicted, the British government immediately severed diplomatic relations with Syria, whereupon the United States withdrew its ambassador from Damascus in a gesture of solidarity.

Obviously the cooperation was limited. The American administration was still not taking Britain into its confidence over Iran. Still the British kept quiet because it was a deliberate policy that the information on arms deals was not for use. It was one of those occasions when it was better not to acknowledge that one knew. To have done so would have been unlikely to change American policy, but might well have damaged relations. The special relationship with Reagan personally and with the United States mattered more, in Thatcher's judgement, than counter-terrorist strategy. Her silence was more eloquent testimony to her priorities than any speech could ever be. It was also a tacit acknowledgment of the limits of her influence.

This was one of the most notable instances where she decided that prudence required her to keep off the turf. The decision was not the product of any general discussion among ministers. The Prime Minister would have considered it with her advisers at Number Ten and with the Foreign Secretary, but that was all. The issue was never raised at any Cabinet meeting. It was not put before any Cabinet committee or one of those small groups of ministers where most of the decisions that mattered in the Thatcher years were taken.

Then, the day before the American mid-term Congressional elections took place, on Tuesday 4 November 1986, a little-known Beirut magazine, *Al Shiraa*, published the first details of the scandal that was to shake the Reagan administration to its foundations. By Thursday 6 November such leading American newspapers as the *Los Angeles Times* and the *Washington Post* were publishing substantial stories of the arms sales. That was when the tempest broke.

The effect upon Thatcher was not to free her from restraint. She did not conclude that now at last she was free to speak her mind. Whatever personal sympathy she may have felt for Reagan, it is inconceivable that she had any tolerance for the muddled and contradictory policies he had been pursuing over the hostages. The administration's conduct was absolutely contrary to what he had been saying to his allies and to the principles that she herself believed in. For a while the President became a hounded man, treated by the American media with more scorn and hostility than any occupant of the White House since Nixon at the height of Watergate. Thatcher never joined the pack, and never gave the slightest hint that she might be about to do so.

Shortly after the turmoil began in the United States Thatcher visited Reagan again at Camp David, on 15 November, for a very different purpose. When questioned in Washington immediately after their meeting, and again in the House of Commons the following week, she managed to dissociate herself from the critics without modifying her own stand on terrorism. In Washington she declared firmly and frequently that it remained British policy not to sell lethal weapons to either side in the Iran–Iraq war. When asked if this did not at least imply criticism of Reagan's actions she declared in ringing tones: 'I believe implicitly in the President's integrity on that subject.'

That was her general line: to defend the man, not the policy. In reply to the Leader of the Opposition, Neil Kinnock, in the House of Commons, she reiterated her own policy and announced: 'I do not answer yet for the United States.' Nor, even then, did she deliver to Reagan in private the criticism that she studiously avoided in public. That would have destroyed the whole purpose of the line she was taking. What is the use of a friend, she might have said, who supports you only when you are in the right?

This personal loyalty sealed the friendship between them, and the following July Reagan demonstrated his appreciation in most unusual fashion. Whenever Thatcher was in the United States it was her custom to appear on television at almost every opportunity. She would do the round of the morning talk shows before a day of intensive meetings. On this occasion she was interviewed by Lesley Stahl for the much esteemed CBS programme *Face the Nation*.

Stahl sought to press her on the Irangate issue, which was still running strongly, and Thatcher brought into play a lifetime's experience of dodging awkward questions in the House of Commons. When asked if the allies would be wary of helping the United States in future because the Iran–Contra hearings were airing so much in public, she made it appear that what was at stake was the principle of confidential exhanges between governments: 'One simply has to recognise that you can't carry on the business of government unless some things are confidential.'

Then she implied that anyone who concentrated on Irangate had no sense of perspective. 'We are dealing with leaders who understand the big issues and who are not going to be sidetracked from the big issues.' Time and again she declared her friendship for the United States. The President was fine, Stahl was 'taking far too downbeat a view'. Without ever having to pronounce on Irangate itself, without saying anything of substance, she conveyed a sense of optimism and confidence. It was, in its way, a bravura performance.

The programme went out on Sunday 19 July 1987. During the next Cabinet meeting, a day or so later, a former White House official remembers, an aide walked in from the West Wing reception area that leads into the Cabinet Room, went over to the President and whispered in his ear. A somewhat quizzical expression appeared on Reagan's face, which caused everyone in the room to wonder just what had been the news. Finally, the President turned to the aide and said: 'Well, I can take the call here or maybe I should go into my office to take it.' The aide whispered again: apparently it would take a minute or two to obtain the connection. Still nobody knew what this was all about, 'and you could read on many people's faces a certain apprehension as to what it might be.'

A moment later Reagan put everyone at ease by explaining that it was simply Margaret Thatcher returning his call. By then she was back in London. The President characteristically offered to take it in the other room so that he wouldn't bother 'you fellas'. The Cabinet naturally responded that it was they who should leave if he wanted to take the call in the Cabinet Room, but Reagan insisted that that was not necessary.

So, as the call was put through, he reached under the Cabinet table, pulled up the phone, and began thanking her for her kind defence of the administration on *Face the Nation*. After an exchange of pleasantries, he told her: 'Well, I'm here with a bunch of my Cabinet secretaries, and they'd all like to do the same and express their thanks for your support of our administration.' With that, he held up the phone 'and everyone took the cue and the Cabinet as one applauded Margaret Thatcher's performance so that she could hear the gratitude of the Reagan Cabinet for her support'.

If Thatcher had set out her political ambitions a decade before, she might have hoped to be Britain's first woman prime minister and the first to have been trained as a scientist. She could hardly have expected to be the first one to sit in Downing Street listening to the applause of the American Cabinet from across the Atlantic. It was a unique tribute, but a supreme irony: Thatcher, the conviction politician, receiving the warm gratitude of the Reagan Cabinet for not speaking her mind.

18

REYKJAVIK: 'IT WAS LIKE AN EARTHQUAKE'

Reagan was so appreciative of Thatcher's support over Irangate because by the summer of 1987 it was threatening to engulf his Presidency. His subsequent recovery, to leave the White House on a peak of popularity, was one of the marvels of American politics, aided in no small measure by the new spirit of harmony with the Soviet Union. The Gorbachev phenomenon was one of the reasons for the Reagan phenomenon. Yet in October 1986, just before the news of Irangate broke upon an astonished world, Reagan provoked anguish among his allies by his first attempt to bargain seriously with Gorbachev.

'It was like an earthquake.' Reykjavik remains for Thatcher a devastating memory. 'There was no place where you could put your political feet, where you were certain that you could stand.' What particularly shook her was that it looked for one moment as if Reagan and Gorbachev were agreeing to give up all nuclear weapons. It seemed as if her worst fears were being realised. Her closest ally was ready to act on all that talk about a non-nuclear world, which she had always regarded as 'pie in the sky', as she put it in an interview for *The Times* seven months before Reykjavik.

The hastily convened summit in the capital of Iceland on 11 and 12 October 1986 did not turn out quite so badly as Thatcher had at first feared. Reagan and Gorbachev talked about throwing away all their nuclear arms, but the idea was never put in the form of a specific, written proposal, which is what counts in such negotiations. None the less, the reality was disturbing enough. At the end of a summit with the leader of the Soviet Union, the President of the United States had lost the confidence of his European allies, and of the British Prime Minister in particular.

How did Reagan and Thatcher manage to get so badly out of step, and how did she achieve one of her greatest international successes by repairing the damage afterwards?

After the Geneva summit in November 1985 there was a hiatus in the East–West dialogue. Although the meeting had been well received in the West, there were signs that Gorbachev's senior colleagues had not been so pleased by it. In any case, in the early months of 1986 he was engaged in establishing his control over the Communist Party at home. He had begun the year with a grandiose disarmament proposal in January to get rid of all nuclear weapons by the end of the century. This brought a welcoming response from Reagan, for whom it had obvious appeal, but it was widely suspected to be no more than a propaganda ploy.

For some months no meeting took place between senior figures in the Soviet and American governments. Then, when one was arranged between Shultz and the Soviet Foreign Minister, Eduard Shevard-nadze, it was cancelled because of the American bombing of Libya in April. Little more than a week later came the disaster at the Soviet nuclear power plant in Chernobyl, so that Gorbachev had quite a few other things on his mind.

The following month a decision on whether to continue to observe the SALT Two limits came up again in Washington. Thatcher had not changed her mind since the debate of the previous summer, but this time she was on the losing side. There had been one critical change in Washington's cast of characters. McFarlane had been replaced as National Security Adviser by Poindexter, who took the opposite point of view. He agreed with Weinberger and Perle about breaking free from the restraint.

As the National Security Adviser is the person presenting the conflicting arguments to the President, this evidently tipped the scales. Shultz and the Chiefs of Staff also took the same position as the year before, but they did not fight so hard on the issue in 1986. They could see which way the President would go. Thatcher once again sent in a message right on time, which showed how closely her advisers were being kept in touch with the bureaucratic in-fighting in Washington. It was not enough, and she too did not struggle. She must have judged, like Shultz, that it was not worth the vigorous battle that would have been required to attempt to overturn a clear preference within the administration.

The SALT saga suggests that there were strict limits to Thatcher's influence. In 1985 her intervention gave an extra push to the winning side. It did not determine the result. In 1986 it was ineffective. There was, however, another consideration. Neither she nor Shultz had ever been enthusiastic for SALT. Both of them were looking for another treaty to replace it, so they may well not have been all that worried. Certainly neither of them waged a strenuous campaign, as some of their advisers would have wished.

Whether or not Reagan's decision upset Thatcher, there were fears that it might damage relations with the Soviet Union. In fact it does not seem to have had much effect. Perhaps it even inclined the Soviets to look more positively for a new agreement. A couple of months later the two sides were talking seriously to each other again.

Although the first half of 1986 was in general a difficult time for East–West relations, Reagan and Gorbachev were exchanging a succession of letters. Thatcher was sent a draft of each one of Reagan's before it was sent, but the only one in which she is known to have demanded and obtained a significant change was the most important one in the series. That was sent by Reagan on 25 July. She secured the deletion of any reference to the British and French deterrents. Nobody was going to negotiate about British nuclear weapons over her head. That was the first pointer to the difficulties ahead at Reykjavik.

The second pointer was an item in Reagan's letter to which Thatcher, strangely, did not object. The President proposed that both sides should stick to the ABM Treaty for five years. If subsequently one side wanted to deploy a strategic defensive system, it would have to offer a plan for sharing its benefits and for eliminating offensive ballistic missiles.

The idea of getting rid of all ballistic missiles, which was to cause so much trouble after Reykjavik, had been put on the table by the Americans months before. Thatcher did not fight over it, neither did the United States Chiefs of Staff raise serious objections.

Thatcher was always careful to select the issues on which she would attempt to change Reagan's mind. When Harold Macmillan was Prime Minister he used to give one piece of advice to young MPs: 'You should rebel on only one issue at a time.' Thatcher followed that prescription in dealing with Reagan. If she had overplayed her hand she would have lost influence. In any case, no firm date was attached to the ballistic-missile proposal. Although it was being pushed strongly by Weinberger and Perle, it looked like another of the President's visionary concepts, which prudent people of the world did not bother about. They would reserve their fire for what mattered immediately.

The proposition was repeated by the President in his speech to the United Nations in September, and still no furore. In August a group of seven American negotiators (unkindly labelled the Seven Dwarfs) had been in Moscow under the leadership of Paul Nitze. They concluded that the most likely area for agreement at the next summit, which it was hoped would be held in Washington before the end of the year, was INF.

Gorbachev had proposed the elimination of all INF missiles (with a range between 1000 and 5500 kilometres) from Europe as part of his January disarmament package. The United States had countered by insisting on getting rid of them throughout the world: global zero–zero, in arms-control jargon. Neither notion seemed likely to form the basis of an agreement. The negotiators in Moscow were talking about each side keeping a hundred warheads in Europe.

That was what Western governments thought everyone had in mind when Shevardnadze handed Reagan a letter from Gorbachev in the White House on 19 September. The Soviet leader was proposing that they should meet in October in Reykjavik. The assessment within the American administration was that Gorbachev could not afford, for political reasons, to have another summit that did not produce concrete results. Therefore he wanted to have this preliminary encounter to judge whether sufficient progress was possible to justify a full summit.

Reagan was eager to respond. He had confidence in his powers of persuasion with Gorbachev, and he very much wanted a summit in the United States before the end of the year. Whatever criticisms came from London later, and they were many, no objection was raised in advance to the idea of a summit that was not a summit.

No agenda was carefully prepared by officials, but it is not true that the Americans went to Reykjavik without advance work having been done. 'We went,' said one official, 'with the big fat book with everything in it.' They had prepared for everything except what Gorbachev did, which was to present them with a range of sweeping proposals to be negotiated then and there.

When it was all over, and confusion reigned, there were many reproaches for the manner in which the proceedings had been conducted. Working groups toiling through the night without adequate facilities do not convey the sense of order that many people feel should characterise international diplomacy. Many European governments felt uneasy that the two superpowers should be negotiating peace in our time without a European voice being heard. Thatcher's complaints were directed essentially at the substance.

It was the fear that the two leaders were about to give up all nuclear weapons, or at least promise to do so, that still provokes her particular anguish today. There were two other aspects that were disturbing to her as well. One was the willingness to renounce all offensive ballistic missiles at the end of ten years. The idea of giving up all ballistic missiles had, it will be recalled, been floated by Reagan in his July letter to Gorbachev and in his September speech to the United Nations. That was different. No date was attached to that proposal.

What happened at Reykjavik was that Richard Perle and Robert Linhard of the NSC staff took that proposition and made it part of a package, with specific dates. Both sides would cut their strategic nuclear weapons by half during the first five years of an agreement, while continuing to abide by the ABM Treaty. They would still observe the treaty for the next five years while phasing out their ballistic missiles. At the end of ten years all ballistic missiles would have gone and either side would be free to deploy a strategic defensive system.

This was more detailed and precise than the notion that Reagan had been putting forward. It was not accepted by the Soviets because it would have given a green light to SDI at the end of ten years. Perle and Linhard may well have been banking on a Soviet rejection. They felt confident they had attached a condition he could not meet, but Gorbachev was soon to show how dangerous it can be with him to rely on the device of the impossible condition.

To Thatcher it was appalling that the United States should be willing even to offer such a deal. Had it been accepted, it would have undermined the concept of extended deterrence on which the security of Europe had rested for nearly forty years. Throughout that time the nuclear armoury of the West had provided an insurance that the Soviet Union could never be tempted to use its superiority in conventional forces.

It is true that even if the Reykjavik formula had been accepted, there would still have been cruise missiles and planes armed with nuclear weapons. Thatcher's military advisers did not believe that these could offer similar assurance as a counter to Soviet conventional strength.

The proposal would also have made it impossible for Britain to continue indefinitely with its own nuclear deterrent. The paper put before the Soviet neogtiators made no mention of the British and French deterrents. The Americans had learnt in July how much Thatcher would object to that. But only the form was observed. Had the proposition gone through, it is inconceivable that Britain would have been able to purchase from the United States the very missiles that the Americans were phasing out. There was no indication at

Reykjavik that this dimension was appreciated by the American negotiators. They seemed to be thinking, and were certainly speaking, simply in direct American–Soviet terms.

It was also disconcerting for Thatcher that tentative agreement was reached on eliminating all INF missiles in Europe, while leaving the Soviets a hundred warheads in Asia and the Americans a hundred in Alaska. The zero–zero option had been around for a long time. Every so often it was taken out and formally confirmed as Western policy; but nobody thought that the Soviets were about to accept it, whatever they might say. In the run-up to Reykjavik, British ministers and officials had been wondering whether it would be better to settle for a hundred warheads each in Europe or for a figure closer to two hundred, which might make it easier to distribute the missiles around the deploying countries.

Thatcher had never liked zero–zero. She had long since ceased to fight against it because that seemed neither profitable nor necessary. She had certainly not expected it to be accepted. Just as with the ballistic-missile proposal, this too was blocked by disagreement over SDI. Thatcher speaks with warm admiration of Reagan's refusal to be tempted to give up his programme. She might reflect that at Reykjavik it saved him from himself.

It did not block an INF agreement for long. This looked to be the most serious part of the negotiations there, and it was the one item on which she was informed – though not consulted – before the summit ended. At the morning session on the Sunday, the second and last day of the conference, after the working groups had been negotiating through the night, Rozanne Ridgway, the Assistant Secretary of State for European Affairs, was asked by Shultz to telephone the capitals of the five European countries deploying the missiles.

Shultz himself had to be prompted by Perle to take this initiative. Even though they were negotiating about removing missiles from Europe, European reactions did not appear to be figuring largely in their thinking. Ridgway called Raymond Seitz, who had succeeded Streator as Minister at the American Embassy in London. Seitz's brief was to alert Number Ten only to the possibility of an INF agreement coming out of Reykjavik before the end of the day.

This was not to be. The meeting broke up in acrimony, without any agreements having been reached at all. It also ended in a fair measure of chaos. The United States had been prepared to make far-reaching agreements with the Soviets, if stringent restrictions on SDI had not been made an absolute condition. But precisely what agreements, on what conditions? American emissaries spread around the world to inform friendly governments what had really happened at Reykjavik. The difficulty was that the emissaries were not sure themselves.

In Washington the President and Shultz did not altogether clarify the picture when briefing Congressional leaders of both parties at the White House on what had been on the table at Reykjavik. Shultz spoke of eliminating all ballistic missiles, while Reagan referred to all nuclear weapons. Shultz was thinking of the precise, written proposal presented to the two leaders; Reagan had in mind what he and Gorbachev had talked about. 'It was a disturbing conversation,' one of the Republican Congressional leaders recalls, 'because it was clear to me that the President and the Secretary were not in agreement as to what in fact had been discussed in Iceland just a couple of days before.'

In London Thatcher had a meeting during the week after Reykjavik with her Foreign and Defence Secretaries, Geoffrey Howe and George Younger, and the Chiefs of Staff, at which none of them was happy at the prospect of giving up all INF missiles in Europe. The atmosphere was one of considerable gloom, which was aptly summed up by Admiral of the Fleet Sir John Fieldhouse, the Chief of the Defence Staff. Turning to the Prime Minister he remarked that he didn't like the idea, and he didn't suppose that she did either, but he did not see how it would be possible to recover the ground after what had been conceded at Reykjavik. Thatcher fairly swiftly concluded that it would be necessary to back Reagan's hopes on INF as the price to be paid for Trident.

She could not oppose Reagan on everything that was under nego- tiation at Reykjavik. It was much more important not to throw away all ballistic missiles, and therefore to be able to keep the British deterrent. In any case, there was not much that the European allies could do about it if the Soviets and the Americans were set on a zero–zero agreement for INF in Europe. The zero option had orig- inally been a Western proposal. It had been reaffirmed by Nato on countless occasions. Thatcher had herself paid lip service to it. To say no when Gorbachev at last said yes would not be an easy policy to explain.

On the Thursday after Reykjavik, 16 October, Mitterrand visited London for a two-hour talk with Thatcher in Downing Street, during which they found themselves in agreement over the folly of the summit. Above all, they concluded, Europe must not be denuclearised. Thatcher was making sure that her misgivings over Reykjavik were shared by other European leaders.

Similar unease was not so evident within the administration in Washington. It had launched a massive public-relations campaign to persuade American voters, in advance of the mid-term elections on 4 November, that the achievements at Reykjavik had only just been stopped from becoming a triumph. There was a determination to stick by the policies at the summit, once it could be determined what they were.

After a meeting of the NSC on 23 October, it was decided to put forward the zero-ballistic-missile proposal, which had been on the table at Reykjavik, as part of the formal American negotiating position at Geneva. Only Kenneth Adelman, the Director of the Arms Control and Disarmament Agency, expressed outright opposition. Admiral William Crowe, the Chairman of the Joint Chiefs of Staff, was also evidently unhappy. The British lobbied quietly, but unsuccessfully, against this decision. Then, on Saturday 15 November, Thatcher saw the President once again at Camp David.

She followed her usual procedure, which much impressed officials in Washington, of completing a week's work in London and then flying over on a Friday afternoon. She began by seeing Shultz and then Weinberger at the British Embassy. Then Rozanne Ridgway had a crucial but delicate discussion with three British officials: Charles Powell, Thatcher's private secretary who had flown over with her, and John Kerr and Stephen Band from the embassy.

Ridgway was highly respected, by the British no less than the Americans, but it was not for an official of her rank to accept changes in the position that the President had taken at Reykjavik. She was not empowered to negotiate. The conversation was invaluable to the British for all that, because it gave them a shrewd idea of what kind of statement might win approval at Camp David the following day.

It was no use expecting the President to confess that he had got it wrong at Reykjavik. Stanley Baldwin, for many years Prime Minister between the wars, was described by Churchill as having built his career on 'the honest avowal of mistakes'. Reagan is not like that. His instinct is to face down his critics, not to compromise with them. It was only with the greatest difficulty that he once managed to squeeze an acknowledgement of error through his lips over Irangate. A frontal assault at Camp David would have met a flat rejection.

After Ridgway left the embassy on the Friday evening, the British officials – Kerr, Band and Powell, who divided his time between draftsmanship and sitting in on Thatcher's discussions – worked late into the night to redraft completely the statement that Powell had brought from London. First thing the following morning it was shown to Thatcher, who expressed her warm approval of the 'golden pens' that had written it. The essence was that it did not specifically renounce anything that the President had been prepared to accept at Reykjavik; it simply reordered the priorities and did not get round to the most worrisome ideas.

Priority was to be given to an INF agreement, a 50 per cent cut in strategic arms over five years and a ban on chemical weapons. It declared support for SDI research, and at the same time confirmed that Nato strategy 'would continue to require effective nuclear deterrents based upon a mix of systems'. Finally, the draft statement had the President reaffirming his full support for 'the arrangements made to modernise Britain's independent nuclear deterrent with Trident'. Ballistic missiles were not mentioned.

The revised wording was shown to Ridgway before they all boarded the helicopter for Camp David on the Saturday morning. She responded favourably, and it was then discussed with Poindexter while they flew. He approved it after lengthy deliberations over the placing of a comma. It was one of those debates which seem exceedingly important to diplomats, and exceedingly amusing to everyone else.

The great question was whether there should be a comma after the word 'programme' in the sentence: 'We also agreed on the need to press ahead with the SDI research programme which is permitted by the AMB Treaty.' The Americans wanted a comma because that would imply that the whole research programme was permitted by the treaty. The British did not want a comma because they did not want to commit themselves to approving all research, even if it were done in space.

Finally, it was agreed that as this was to be a British statement, which Thatcher would give to the press as she was about to leave, they should be allowed to have the punctuation that they wanted. The comma could be left out. The statement was in due course typed and distributed by the British Embassy – with the comma put in by mistake. In such ways are momentous issues settled.

When they arrived at Camp David the President and the Prime Minister immediately went off together in a golf cart for a discussion of an hour or more before lunch. Normally when heads of government meet, even for a direct talk between the two of them, there is somebody there from each side to record what is said. Charles Powell would usually have been there for Thatcher, and Reagan would have been accompanied by Peter Sommer from the NSC or possibly by Charles Price, the Ambassador. In this instance the two leaders went off alone, leaving Powell in particular in a state of surprise and some frustration.

The American supporting team on this occasion consisted of Shultz, Poindexter, Ridgway, Price and Sommer. With Thatcher were Sir Antony Acland, the Ambassador, the three possessors of the 'golden pens' of the previous night – Powell, Kerr and Band – and her press secretary, Bernard Ingham.

As the others waited for the return of Reagan and Thatcher, the atmosphere was very different from the previous Camp David two years before. Then the mood had been relaxed and more personal. The Americans had been in good spirits after Reagan's landslide reelection. It was just before Christmas, presents were exchanged and there was a mildly festive air. Now the proceedings were conducted in more deliberate fashion.

Ridgway spent some time on the phone, checking out the statement with the Pentagon, in all probability with Weinberger himself. There were no objections. Some of the others were less productively engaged. Donald Regan sat apart from everybody for much of the time. Poindexter wore a thoughtful and preoccupied expression. Nobody talked very much to Bush. They had other things on their minds. The Republicans had lost control of the Senate in the mid-term elections in October and, much worse, Irangate had started to dominate the headlines. People were beginning to speculate about the unravelling of the administration.

When Thatcher and Reagan reappeared for drinks before lunch she was in excellent humour. She and the President had had a wonderful discussion. They were in agreement. She opened her hand-bag and took out the paper. That was what they thought, and that was what she would be saying with his approval. It was an occasion for everybody to say simply: 'Yes, Prime Minister.'

Over lunch the conversation moved on to a variety of regional issues. For some weeks there had been a series of high-level inter-agency meetings in Washington on the delicate subject of resuming arms sales to Argentina. These had been suspended at the time of the Falklands War, but Reagan's senior advisers were agreed that now it would be appropriate to sell some defensive equipment. The Argentines were known to be interested in certain aircraft, which the Americans were satisfied could not be used for reopening the Falklands conflict, and some army vehicles.

A lengthy position paper had been prepared for the President with three principal talking points. Such sales were needed: to make a gesture of friendly support for the Alfonsin regime; to strengthen the regime against possible military rebellions; and to avoid giving the Soviets any opportunity to extend their influence in the southern hemisphere. The Americans around the table waited for Reagan to raise the issue. The British Embassy had warned Thatcher that he would. The conversation flowed on.

Finally, Thatcher took a piece of paper out of her handbag and ran her eye down the list, for all the world like a housewife checking that she had not forgotten some last piece of shopping. 'Oh, arms to Argentina,' she said. 'You won't, will you?' Reagan did not let her down. 'No,' he replied. 'We won't.' So in one short sentence he killed weeks of careful preparation within his administration.

The issue kept on coming up among his most senior foreign-policy advisers. Shultz, Frank Carlucci, who took over from Poindexter as National Security Adviser at the beginning of 1987, and Colin Powell, Carlucci's deputy, who succeeded him when he moved to become Defense Secretary the following year – all were agreed that it would be the right policy to sell some arms to Argentina, and all were forced to acknowledge that there was no chance of getting the President to agree. 'You can keep fighting this if you want,' Shultz once remarked to a senior colleague, 'but you know damn well that if you go to the President you're going to get rolled.'

So, for a second time, Thatcher left Camp David on a high note to hold her press conference in Washington. It was her statement that she delivered there, to which Reagan had subscribed. She had managed, above all, to get the President to reassert the doctrine of nuclear deterrence. In that respect the statement went against what the President had been trying to achieve at Reykjavik. But not against what he had achieved. He was not going back on any agreement that he had reached.

He had talked about giving up all nuclear weapons, but not on Gorbachev's terms. As an acceptable deal was not possible at Reykjavik, Reagan wanted to preserve Western strength. So Thatcher had persuaded him to focus on immediate policy, where they could agree, leaving his aspirations for another day.

Many American, as well as British, policy-makers heaved a sigh of relief. Some, Shultz in particular, look back upon Reykjavik with satisfaction – 'it was the most productive summit we ever held' – without raising any objection to the Camp David agreement. Perle, on the other hand, was very angry about aspects of that agreement. He was critical especially of the priority given to a ban on chemical weapons. Although the formal American position was to seek such a ban, it was another of those offers which the Soviets were not expected to pick up. Other Americans share the British view that at Camp David Thatcher put Western policy back on the rails.

She did not do so by herself. The months after Reykjavik provide a notable example of how she and kindred spirits in the administration were able to work to the same end. At the NSC meeting on 23 October, when it was decided to table the Reykjavik proposal for eliminating ballistic missiles as the United States negotiating position in the Geneva disarmament talks, the Chairman of the Joint Chiefs of Staff was asked to proceed with an examination of the military implications. That study went ahead, a time bomb ticking away beneath the administration's policy.

Military misgivings about Reykjavik did not take long to build up. Immediately after the summit the major Nato commanders were asked for their judgment of the proposals by the alliance's military committee. They were worried about the effect on conventional submarine capability if a major part of the Western nuclear deterrent had to be in the form of cruise missiles on submarines.

On 14 January 1987 a secret British military mission, composed of Rear Admiral Jock Slater, Assistant Chief of the Defence Staff, Group Captain Prideaux and David Stephens, an official in the Ministry of Defence, visited Washington. Thatcher had suggested quite sharply to the MoD that it should examine the zero-ballistic-missile proposal.

Their purpose in Washington was to express British military objections. Slater addressed a somewhat strange meeting at the Pentagon, which was attended by not particularly senior military officers and by one civilian official. His speech received polite but restrained applause. Questions were called for and a prolonged silence followed, to be broken eventually by the civilian official, who asked a few questions.

The British were at first perplexed by this guarded reception. Why were there no senior officers? Why such reluctance to ask questions? Subsequently it became clear that the explanation was that the Americans were in agreement but did not wish to be heard criticising their Commander-in-Chief in a way that would inevitably become known around town.

The effect of this British intervention was not to change the minds of the American Joint Chiefs of Staff, but to reinforce their judgment. It was their report in due course which finally killed the proposal. They did not condemn it outright. They simply explained what would be involved in eliminating ballistic missiles, while preserving adequate defences. American defences would have to be restructured and the cost would be enormous. The idea was allowed a seemly death without an ostentatious burial.

Thatcher's intervention killed the more contentious Reykjavik proposals in political terms. The Joint Chiefs completed the job within the American bureaucracy. The Camp David statement became the basis of the declaration by Nato foreign ministers, again in Reykjavik, the following June. Its impact can clearly be seen in the communiqués from the Nato Planning Group.

The one issued a few days after Reykjavik from Gleneagles in Scotland was distinctly cautious. It 'fully endorsed the President's programme presented in Iceland', but then went on to express 'continued support for the efforts of the United States and the United Kingdom to maintain the effectiveness and credibility of their nuclear deterrent capabilities'. By May 1987 the doctrine of nuclear deterrence was unequivocally back in place: 'We will maintain and improve the nuclear forces necessary to carry out that strategy.'

Thatcher's mission to Camp David was seen in Washington as the expression of general European anxieties. Where she made the difference was in getting the President's ear so quickly and so effectively. 'The bureaucracy might have been able to hold off others,' one senior American official remarked. 'Those people who liked what happened at Reykjavik, those people who wanted a deployed SDI, did not like to see Mrs Thatcher coming to town. They could not keep her away.'

19

DOING BUSINESS WITH GORBACHEV

As they celebrated the New Year of 1987 Margaret Thatcher and Ronald Reagan must have been in very different moods. For Reagan it was the low point of his Presidency. Irangate was threatening to shatter his administration. His chief of staff, Donald Regan, was being hounded from office, with the President's wife leading the pack. Reagan himself had lost credibility with the press and was in danger of losing it with the public. His approval rating in the opinion polls was down to 37 per cent and there were even mutterings that he might not be able to serve out his term.

For Thatcher, on the other hand, political prospects were better than they had been for some time. A year before, she had almost been driven from office by the furore over her handling of the bitter dispute within her Cabinet over the future of the Westland helicopter company. The controversy was revealing in more ways than one.

The basic point at issue was whether the company, the last British manufacturer of helicopters, should be rescued from impending bankruptcy by a takeover from an American company or a European consortium. Michael Heseltine, then Defence Secretary and the most exciting orator in her Cabinet, favoured the European solution. Thatcher, true to her instincts, preferred the American option. It was because the struggle developed into a personality clash and an argument over how Thatcher ran her government that it became so damaging. But the international significance of the episode was that it confirmed that, whenever there was a choice, her heart lay across the Atlantic rather than across the Channel.

She handled the struggle badly, and for much of 1986 she had looked a somewhat outmoded figure. Her role in the bombing of Libya had not helped her popularity, even if it was not the principal cause of her unpopularity.

Yet, as 1987 dawned, she was recovering her strength. Inflation at 3.6 per cent was the lowest in Britain for nearly twenty years. The rate of growth was the highest in any major European economy. Even unemployment had begun to fall steadily, and Nigel Lawson was preparing to introduce the first of his dramatic cuts in taxes for individuals. In his Budget in March he reduced the basic rate of income tax from 29 to 27 per cent. The opposition parties were divided, and the opinion polls were encouraging for the Conservatives.

Thatcher received a little further assistance at this time from her American partner. Neil Kinnock evidently decided that it would help his chances as Labour leader in the forthcoming election if he could show that he was accepted in Washington as a potential British leader. No doubt he wished to erase the memory of his visit the previous December when his first public speech had been poorly attended and the press coverage had been unflattering.

The venture was probably doomed from the beginning. There was little chance of persuading American opinion in the spring of 1987 of the credibility of Labour defence policy. Nor was there the slightest prospect of the President allowing Margaret Thatcher's principal opponent to derive a little favourable publicity from a visit to the White House with a British general election in the offing.

The meeting began on a hilarious note with Reagan greeting Denis Healey, Labour's Shadow Foreign Secretary, with the words: 'Nice to see you again, Mr Ambassador.' Healey's famous shaggy eyebrows do, it is true, bear a distinct resemblance to those of Sir Oliver Wright, the previous ambassador, who retired from Washington the year before.

The record differs as to how the discussion then proceeded and how long it lasted. Kinnock's spokesmen maintained that it went on for longer than the twenty minutes officially announced and they deny that Reagan made some of the criticisms of Labour defence policy that were attributed to him by his press secretary, Marlin Fitzwater. The discrepancies hardly mattered. The White House was clearly intent on cutting the ground from under Kinnock. Whether it was done directly by Reagan or indirectly by Fitzwater did not affect the result.

The President was signalling that he would not have confidence in Kinnock as Britain's prime minister. Reagan had done one more good turn for Thatcher. So the most pressing political question for her in early 1987 was what date to choose for the general election.

Reagan's and Thatcher's political interest combined to focus their attention on foreign affairs. The President needed something spectacular to obliterate the memory of Irangate, and the best hope lay in an agreement with the Soviet Union. After Reykjavik Thatcher came increasingly to see herself, and others saw her, as the clearest head in the West. She felt she was needed to play a still more active international role, and it would do her no harm in the coming election to be seen to be doing so. For both of them the trail led to Gorbachev.

Thatcher was due to visit the Soviet Union early in 1987 and in December 1986 the British Ambassador in Moscow, Sir Bryan Cartledge, had a two-hour meeting with Gorbachev ostensibly to discuss the preparations. In fact, the main purpose was to find out if relations were still on a friendly basis after the Prime Minister's dash to Camp David to pour cold water on the Reykjavik terms. In particular, was the Soviet leader prepared to give the Prime Minister an appropriate reception? She would not have wished to risk a snub, especially with the election coming up.

The conversation developed into a general discussion on disarmament, nuclear and non-nuclear weapons, and bilateral relations. As this was the only time in those years that Gorbachev received any Western ambassador, it was an indication of the importance he attached to Thatcher's role.

Her visit at the end of March confirmed that. It was the first time that she had been in the Soviet Union and the impact was powerful in both directions. On her first full day there she was greeted warmly by crowds at the monastery of Zagorsk, some miles outside Moscow, where she made the dramatic gesture of lighting a candle to freedom, to the discomfiture of her political hosts. In the afternoon she conducted the first Western-style walkabout by a foreign leader in Moscow. To everyone's surprise, she attracted a friendly and fascinated crowd of about fifteen hundred.

Her performance on television, when she was interviewed for fifty minutes, was astonishingly robust. Soviet viewers cannot ever before have seen a political leader demolish questioners with such vigour, as she spoke without inhibition of the supposedly secret anti-missile system around Moscow; the size, history and siting of intermediate nuclear forces; and the practices of the House of Commons.

Above all, she had an unprecedented eleven hours of direct talks with Gorbachev. 'I cannot ever remember having spent so much time in discussion with another world leader,' she told reporters before flying home in exultant mood. In a BBC radio interview she added another judgment that startled many people in Europe and the United States: 'If he gave me his word, I would believe him.'

She must have relished the political advantage to be derived from such a visit in the run-up to the election, but there was more to it than that. The respect that she was given established beyond doubt her distinctive role as an interlocutor in the developing East–West dialogue. She was confirmed as a star on the world stage. That mattered to her from every standpoint.

Within two weeks of her leaving Moscow, Shultz was there for talks with Gorbachev. It was a visit which turned out to be a turning point for disarmament. Thatcher had discussed arms reductions with Gorbachev, but she had not negotiated. She had no authority to do so. She was determined not to put the British nuclear deterrent on the negotiating table, and she could hardly start bargaining about American weapons.

The Soviet leader had proposed shortly before her arrival that all the longer-range intermediate nuclear missiles (LRINF), with a capability of between 1000 and 5500 kilometres, should be removed from Europe. As he did not link this to American concessions on SDI, it was a breakthrough. Thatcher made it clear in her conversations with him that a balance would also have to be struck about those missiles in the shorter range, from 500 to 1000 kilometres (SRINF). Gorbachev responded by suggesting to Shultz that they should get rid of these as well. This was the proposal that became known as the second zero.

On his way back from Moscow Shultz stopped in Brussels on 16 April to inform the Nato ambassadors of this latest Soviet offer. It would be for their governments to decide what position to take, he said, observing the diplomatic courtesies, but he had to tell them that he saw great merit in the proposal. As nearly all the SRINF weapons belonged to the Soviets, there were only two ways to achieve parity. One was to accept Gorbachev's offer. The other was to build up Western SRINF to an agreed level to match the Soviets. If Nato adopted the second course, Shultz warned the ambassadors, then they would have to be prepared to deploy these missiles. It would be no use having an agreement on an equal number which the Soviets deployed but the West did not. That would not be a good bargain.

The logic of Shultz's remarks was simple and clear. The political force was even more compelling. It would not be easy to explain to European electorates why, as a result of a brilliant disarmament agreement, one class of missiles would have to be introduced as another class was being removed from Europe. Politics pointed to making the most of Gorbachev's proposal.

That is what happened, but not without a degree of anguish within the alliance. It was one of the most mysterious episodes in the Reagan–Thatcher years. Thatcher had been speaking in Moscow about the right to match the Soviet shorter-range systems, not about getting rid of all missiles in this category. She was expressing fears, indeed, about the denuclearisation of Europe, with the Soviets still having a preponderance of conventional arms.

So were others. On 19 April, the Sunday after Shultz's return from Moscow, an interesting meeting was held at the home outside Mons of the Deputy Supreme Nato Commander in Europe, General Sir Edward Burgess, attended by General Bernard Rogers, then the Supreme Nato Commander in Europe; Sir Michael Alexander, the British Ambassador to Nato; and Air Chief Marshal Sir Patrick Hine, Vice-Chief of the British Defence Staff.

The main purpose of the meeting was to discuss the second zero and General Rogers recalls that they were all opposed to it. The conversation then turned to how it might be prevented, and they agreed that the only person who might be able to persuade the President not to accept it was Thatcher. While there is some evidence of differing interpretations of the main thrust of the discussion, there is no question about the influence they attributed to the Prime Minister.

On the following Sunday, 26 April, the French Prime Minister, Jacques Chirac, talked to Thatcher at Chequers for nearly four hours and came away with the firm impression that she shared his objections to the second zero. Although Chirac speaks good English, some slight misunderstanding is conceivable. He might have exaggerated her strength of feeling on the issue. But Thatcher does not usually leave much uncertainty as to what she thinks, and there can be no doubt that the views she expressed to Chirac were different from the personal message she sent to Kohl four days later.

A debate was taking place within the German government at this time as to whether a new missile, which would have been the Pershing One B, should be deployed on German soil as a counter to the Soviet SRINF. Manfred Woerner, then the German Defence Minister and now the Nato Secretary-General, was arguing strongly for this. Genscher was opposed and Kohl had not declared his position. His staff were indicating to British officials that he would come down on Woerner's side, but the Chancellor himself seemed to be more equivocal.

Thatcher's message did not encourage him to back Woerner. It had been assumed that she, who had been arguing for the right to match the Soviet SRINF, would naturally give Woerner every help. But she told Kohl that, while she would support Germany if it wanted the Pershing One B to be deployed, the British government could go along with the second zero. The signal was clear: for all her earlier misgivings, she was not going to fight against the second zero.

There was corroborative evidence that this was a correct reading of Thatcher's message. Towards the end of April the Foreign Secretary, Geoffrey Howe, and the Defence Secretary, George Younger, had one of their regular twice-yearly meetings at Chevening, the Foreign Secretary's country house. On the basis of their discussions, Howe and Younger sent a joint memorandum to the Prime Minister arguing the case against the second zero.

This was rejected without any ministerial discussion. A message went back from the Prime Minister's office, probably in early May and certainly before the Nato Nuclear Planning Group meeting in Stavangar on 14 and 15 May, that she did not think that Britain could stand out against the second zero. To get rid of all intermediate-range missiles would make verification of an agreement easier; nobody was keen on deploying a new missile, apart from the American military; and it simply was not going to happen. She would hardly have responded like this to her ministers if she had intended her message to Kohl to be evenhanded in its effect.

Why then did she change her position so abruptly between speaking to Chirac and writing to Kohl? André Giraud, the French Defence Minister, wondered in private conversation early in June why the British, and indeed his own government, had given up their resistance to the second zero. He went on to say that the French government thought that Thatcher had come to accept it because of pressure from Reagan.

They were probably not very wide of the mark. Chirac received a telephone call from Thatcher, probably at about the time of her message to Kohl, telling him that she had changed her opinion. She was elliptical as to why she had done so. Only later did Chirac discover that her call to him had followed a very lengthy telephone conversation on the same subject with Shultz.

It is most likely that that conversation came between her meeting with Chirac and her message to Kohl, and that it convinced her that there was no prospect of the United States going along with the deployment of new missiles in Europe. For its own political reasons the Reagan administration wanted a dramatic disarmament agreement; and, with an election coming up, British ministers were aware of the political advantages for them too of a more sweeping settlement.

So the British government not only made the best of it, but made the most of it. Conservative leaders trumpeted the benefits of removing a whole category of nuclear weapons from Europe, which by then looked certain, in the campaign for the election on 12 June. It enabled them to gain a double political benefit from the defence issue: they offered both strong defence and effective disarmament. This was just one of the reasons why Thatcher was reelected by a large majority, the first British party leader this century to win three times in a row.

The following month she was back in Washington, for the visit on which she won the applause of Reagan and his Cabinet for her stalwart defence of him on *60 Minutes*. She was in exceptionally robust form throughout the time she was there. That was evident when she was questioned on Capitol Hill about British policy on Mozambique. This was an issue on which she was particularly influential with Reagan because she did not take the conventional right-wing line.

For a number of far-right Republicans support of the Renamo rebel movement in Mozambique had become a major cause. They believed that the United States administration should assist Renamo against the Marxist Frelimo government there. That, so they argued, would be in line with the Reagan doctrine of helping anti-Communist insurgents. It was an argument to which Reagan himself was liable to be sympathetic, though he was always persuaded to reject it – even if he did so sometimes with a regretful shake of the head.

Thatcher played no small part in that persuasion. She had been impressed with President Samora Machel when he paid his first official visit to Britain in 1983. Although he was leading a Marxist government, she thought he could be encouraged towards behaving more responsibly and that he was trying to move Mozambique into a more neutral position between the Soviet Union and the West. After Machel was killed in an air crash in 1986, she formed a similarly favourable judgment of his successor, Joaquim Chissano. The best hope for stability in the country, she believed, lay in backing the government.

Coming from such a staunch anti-Communist as Thatcher, this reasoning had a strong impact on the President. He was particularly impressed at the Camp David meeting in November 1986, after the statement on Reykjavik had been agreed, by her account of the atrocities for which Renamo had been responsible.

When the British government increased its aid to Mozambique by nearly 50 per cent the following May she sent a personal message to the President and the decision had a powerful effect in the White House. It also increased the anger on the far right. So when Thatcher was questioned in July by Senator Jesse Helms about British policy towards Mozambique it was not a friendly request for information.

She had been invited to take tea with an all-party group of Senators by Robert Byrd, the Majority Leader, in the somewhat ornate surroundings of the Old Senate Chambers. The setting was a little unusual for such an occasion because Thatcher was installed in the President's chair in the centre, with the Senators in the seats in front of her. Such an arrangement hardly encouraged an informal atmosphere, but it did lend Thatcher an additional authority which she used to the full when Helms had his turn to question her.

He began by saying that he did not know whether she would be able to understand his southern accent. To which she retorted very firmly: 'Senator Helms, I have heard you speak often enough to understand your accent.' He then proceeded to ask at some length why the British government was helping the Communists in Mozambique. Thatcher began her response relatively mildly, but she has a habit of winding herself up if someone persists with a line of attack. She did so to some effect that day.

'She was not very diplomatic,' one of the other senators recalls appreciatively. 'She almost went after him with a ball bat.' With a different senator that approach might have been counter-productive. His colleagues might have felt that the dignity of a senator was not being respected. But Helms is regarded as so tough and so aggressive that they did not mind the treatment being dished out to him. Not more than a handful of those present had much knowledge of Mozambique, but they were happy to hear it being indicated to him quite forcibly that he did not know what he was talking about.

The President's daughter, Maureen Reagan, was also regarded as a helpful influence by those in the administration struggling to prevent the United States from backing Renamo. 'She was very good,' according to Frank Carlucci, who became National Security Adviser at the beginning of 1987 and was later Defense Secretary until the end of the Reagan administration. 'She made a number of trips to Africa, and she served essentially as a goodwill ambassador. I thought she was very constructive.'

Thatcher was not therefore the only person from outside the administration having an impact on the President over Mozambique. Within the administration the State Department and the NSC staff were strongly of the same opinion. All of them were fighting to maintain existing American policy against right-wing pressure. The Africanists in the State Department several times appealed to the Prime Minister to send a message to the President. As always, she

234

was more effective on an issue where she had allies in Washington. But her influence, Carlucci believes, was critical. Without her it is very difficult to know which way the administration would have gone.

Shortly after Thatcher returned home from Washington she received another American plea for assistance which she initially rejected. The United States wanted British minesweepers to be sent to the Gulf to help keep it clear for international shipping.

As the Iran–Iraq war had intensified, so all shipping in the Gulf was becoming more vulnerable. As early as March that year when the British Defence Secretary, George Younger, visited his French opposite number, André Giraud, in Paris they discussed the problem of Iranian mines in the Gulf. Giraud took a tough line, and Younger too was worried by the threat to British shipping and to European oil supplies. They realised that a time might come when both their navies would have to become involved, and it would be easier politically if other European countries went along as well. After their meeting Younger phoned Willem van Eekelen, the Dutch Defence Minister, whose turn it was to be Chairman of WEU (Western European Union, consisting of Britain, France, West Germany, Italy, Belgium, the Netherlands and Luxembourg), to alert him that they might want to propose a joint WEU operation in the Gulf at some time in the future. Van Eekelen's response was favourable, which mattered later on.

For the moment others were taking the initiative. On 21 May the United States announced that it had agreed to reflag and rename eleven Kuwaiti tankers. Five days earlier the Soviet tanker *Marshal Chiukov* had hit a mine on its first trip under the Kuwaiti flag; Kuwait had chartered three Soviet tankers with Soviet crews. Not for another three months did a Western ship suffer similar misfortune. Then, on 24 July, the United States tanker *The Bridgeton* was severely damaged.

The formal American request for British minesweepers, delivered by the American Ambassador, Charles Price, on 30 July, cannot have come as a surprise in London. A number of private messages had passed during the summer from Admiral Crowe to Admiral of the Fleet Sir James Fieldhouse, Chief of the Defence Staff, asking him to explore the feasibility of sending some. At this stage Fieldhouse was just being sounded out. The two men were frequently in touch and on excellent terms, but Fieldhouse did not feel able to give a positive response. On one occasion he sent a message back to Crowe through an intermediary that he had sat on the request for two or three weeks because if he had to give an answer then it would be negative.

Fieldhouse himself was sounding a cautionary note in London, pointing out that it would take a month to get the minesweepers out to the Gulf. This was not so much an outright objection as a familiar example of a military commander wanting to make quite sure before any decision was taken that his political masters would not have exaggerated ideas of what could be accomplished.

This was only one of a number of anxieties when the exploratory American approach became a firm request. At the Ministry of Defence there were departmental concerns. Which ships would go? What would their precise role be? How long would they stay? Would this be an open-ended commitment? Would it have to be paid for out of the MoD budget?

At the Foreign Office the Minister of State, David Mellor, was in charge, as Geoffrey Howe was on holiday in France. Mellor is an articulate and pugnacious politician, capable and youthful – he was then only 38 – with a taste for publicity. He was not short of it in this instance, even though Howe was kept in touch with the issue on the phone several times a day and eventually cut his holiday short. It was neither the Foreign Office nor the MoD, however, which was principally responsible for the government's rejection of the American approach the day after it was made.

The decisive judgment came from Thatcher herself. This caused some surprise in Washington, as she had vigorously supported the American reflagging of Kuwaiti tankers during her visit there in July. She had even indicated that there would be no political objections to foreign ships registering to fly the British flag and thereby gaining Royal Navy protection as they sailed through the Gulf.

Throughout the 1980s the Armilla Patrol of two frigates and a destroyer had been deployed to keep an eye on British shipping passing to and from the Gulf through the Strait of Hormuz. Orignally the patrol's instructions were to stay in the Gulf of Oman to the south of the Strait unless there was a specific need for it to go into the Strait or into the Gulf itself. In January 1987 these orders were changed so that the warships accompanied British merchant shipping through the Strait, but no further north than Bahrein.

When the American request was received Thatcher did not want the Royal Navy to become further involved. She shared the anxiety about being sucked into an operation that might go on indefinitely. Behind this fear lay a lack of confidence in American purposes and American tactical judgment. There was the nagging worry that the United States might be spoiling for a fight with Iran. Even if it was not, there was the danger that something of that sort could happen because of a rash action on the spot. At any moment the Americans might do something stupid, blow somebody or something up, and the British would be linked to the deed.

The British refusal, though swift, never sounded conclusive. 'These are all matters,' Mellor declared, 'upon which my view this week may not be the same as my view next week.' It was an interesting use of the first person singular by a Minister of State on an issue where the Prime Minister herself was engaged. Mellor's views, not to speak of Thatcher's, did indeed change in little more than a week.

Perhaps she was never altogether comfortable in turning the United States down. When Frank Carlucci visited London on 3 August, four days after the British rejection, she told him that it was not necessarily permanent. The decisive event in changing the British government's mind was that the American supertanker the *Texaco Caribbean* hit a mine off the port of Fujeirah to the south of the Strait of Hormuz on 10 August. Later in the day more mines were found in the area. Thatcher's intense concern for the Navy's safety, which had earlier induced her to say that it must not become further engaged, now led her to conclude that the Armilla Patrol needed further protection. The Iranians were laying mines in waters where the patrol was operating and which had previously been considered clear.

There was also some pressure from the American administration for the British government to change its mind. In early August Younger received a direct phone call from Weinberger. The Americans were in difficulties because they had only a few outdated mine-sweepers in Florida. They have not traditionally had much capability in minesweeping, perhaps because there had been little need for it with only a small continental shelf off the American coast. Mines cannot easily be laid in the deep waters beyond the shelf or in the difficult currents of the Caribbean. The United States developed a technique for sweeping mines by helicopter, but this has always been regarded somewhat askance by British naval officers. On this occasion the United States needed British assistance as a military necessity, not as an extra convenience nor for political cover.

It did not take long for Thatcher to reverse her position. The day after the *Texaco Caribbean* incident the British government decided that four minesweepers should after all be sent to the Gulf. Washington was delighted, but the British were still imposing restrictions. They were not going to sweep the whole Gulf, as the adminstration would have liked, but simply the area covered by the Armilla Patrol.

That meant just as far north as Bahrein. They would also operate separately from the American operational command. There were still misgivings about American judgment in the area.

It was largely for this reason that the British government now set out to involve WEU. Within hours of the British decision, France announced that it would send two minesweepers, to which another was added later. If a joint WEU operation could be mounted that would increase the chances of keeping the mouth of the Gulf clear and would provide a justification for having a separate command from the United States. A WEU fleet would have its own identity without causing unnecessary offence to the Americans.

Within ten days a special WEU meeting decided in principle in favour of such an operation. The Germans have a provision in their constitution which debars them from using their forces outside the Nato area. So they assigned some of their own sweepers to Nato as cover for those that were being removed by other countries to go to the Gulf. Luxembourg does not have minesweepers, so it contributed money. All the other five would send at least some sweepers.

Everyone concerned in London – the Foreign Office, the Ministry of Defence and Number Ten – was delighted at the involvement of WEU. Until the Prime Minister heard of the arrangements. At a small meeting of ministers and officials Younger and Fieldhouse explained that all the WEU sweepers in the Gulf would operate as a single patrol under a rotating command. The Dutch, the Belgians, the French, the Italians and the British would all be happy to take it in turns to serve under each other.

There was an enormous explosion. 'Are you telling me,' Thatcher demanded in outrage, 'that the Royal Navy ships out there will be under the command of, did you say a Belgian or a Dutchman?' 'Well yes, Prime Minister, they're our Nato allies.' That was clearly no excuse. 'A foreigner? The Royal Navy under command of a foreigner?' A brief rearguard action was fought. 'Nato allies, Prime Minister. We operate together all the time.' It was no good. 'A foreigner? The Royal Navy? Quite impossible.'

One of the arts of serving under Thatcher is to know when you are beaten. Having presented this arrangement to the Prime Minister as a great feat of diplomacy, the Minister and the Chief of Staff were then required to go back to their allies and ask if they would mind changing it. Would it be all right if the Royal Navy was in command, after all? Fortunately, the allies agreed. So the WEU patrol did clear mines from around the Gulf. It did operate separately from the United States Navy. It was not drawn into any broader conflict, and the Americans were satisfied with the cooperation from their allies.

In mid-September the Americans caught an Iranian ship laying mines. That was doubly satisfying as the Iranian government had tried to make out after the Fujeirah incident in August that it had not been responsible for those mines: they were the work of irregular revolutionary guards. Once again the Iranians were not lost for an excuse: this was a food ship that the Americans had picked up. Which prompted Weinberger to reflect at the Nato NPG meeting in October, as he gazed with Younger at a photograph of a whole row of mines laid out on the deck, that this was 'the most remarkable shipment of groceries I have seen for a long time.'

Relations between British and American ministers were not always so friendly at this time. Nigel Lawson aroused fury in the United States Treasury by his speech at the Mansion House in London on 4 November. The stock markets had crashed on both sides of the Atlantic nearly three weeks before, on Black Monday, 19 October, and Lawson was now calling more bluntly than ever for the United States to cut its budget deficit. 'This has now become the touchstone,' he proclaimed, 'of whether the United States has the political will to make hard choices and to do what needs to be done.'

That was bad enough in the administration's eyes. Perhaps what was even worse for Reaganites was that he said this should be done 'preferably with at least some increase in the form of taxation'. For a British chancellor not only to cast doubt on the administration's political will, but also to challenge one of the President's most cherished beliefs provoked a wrath that was terrible to behold.

Lawson's efforts were, predictably, to no avail. There was a major effort that month to produce a deficit-cutting package in negotiations between Congressional leaders and the administration. It failed, because the President was not prepared to compromise on his tax cuts. Perhaps his heart was never in the negotiations. The administration was represented in those talks by the two Bakers: Howard, the President's Chief of Staff, and James, the Treasury Secretary. But they had no room for manoeuvre. 'If only you knew,' they remarked wearily to the Congressional team, 'how difficult it was for us to get authority to negotiate at all.'

Thatcher judged Reagan's attitude correctly. When she was in Washington in July officials had tried to persuade her to have another go at him over the deficit. She had refused then, and in November she was more circumspect than her Chancellor. None of the

Treasury's anger was directed against her. Her standing in the United States was exceptionally high at this time. 'Can you lend us Maggie?' I was asked at a New York dinner party. It was the kind of remark a British visitor became used to hearing in those days. Her reelection triumph in June and her general air of resolute authority seemed a refreshing contrast to the administration's travails.

Yet by now the President was pulling out of his difficulties. His reputation for inattention to detail was standing him in good stead. His refusal to confess to anything worse than a little loose management and a poor memory made it impossible for the critics to pin anything specific on him. Above all, the political agenda was being changed. Gorbachev was to visit Washington in December for an agreement in principle on the elimination of all intermediate nuclear forces, longer and shorter range, around the world.

On his way the Soviet leader stopped for a few hours to have lunch with Thatcher at Brize Norton airfield in Oxfordshire on 7 December. This was both a public-relations exercise for both sides and an opportunity for serious discussion. In going out of his way to see Thatcher before his first visit to the United States, Gorbachev was drawing attention to the triangular relationship between the leaders. He virtually said as much in his public remarks before flying on: 'The agreement on the elimination of two kinds of nuclear weapons was not an easy one. But we have covered this road together, for the Soviet Union, the United States, Great Britain and your allies and partners.'

The atmosphere was one of high good humour. 'Ah, just the person,' Gorbachev greeted Younger. 'You have never shown me Edinburgh Castle.' Younger had been Secretary of State for Scotland at the time of his first visit to Britain three years before. 'No,' Younger replied, 'we didn't have time' – Gorbachev had flown back to Moscow early because of the death of Marshal Ustinov, the Soviet Defence Minister – 'but why are you so keen to see it?' 'Oh,' said Gorbachev merrily, 'you told me that day that Edinburgh Castle had kept the English out for three hundred years, and I'm longing to see how that's done.'

During the meal he and Thatcher, who were sitting opposite each other, talked continually. It was a mixture of reminiscence, what they had been doing since they last met, and substantive debate. At one point Thatcher began to explain that, close as the British were to the Americans, Europeans do have a different perspective. Gorbachev interrupted her: 'You don't need to persuade me of that. We will never do anything to disturb the status quo in Europe.' Quite a bit has happened to the status quo in Europe since then, but at the time that was a reassuring remark.

As soon as Gorbachev flew on to Washington Thatcher was on the phone to Reagan, lecturing him for about fifteen minutes on the need to take the Soviet leader seriously. Thatcher was determined to impress upon the President that he should insist on having extended discussions himself with Gorbachev. There was a hint, and perhaps more than a hint, that the minders should not be allowed to take over. Reykjavik may have ended on a sour note, but Thatcher's message was that Gorbachev was still a man to do business with.

In Washington Gorbachev was received with appropriate cere-mony, as television viewers in the Soviet Union saw with fascination. The importance that Soviet leaders attached to the visit was evident from the television coverage and from the many goodwill messages for Gorbachev from around the country that were read out on Radio Moscow. It was seen there as a mission more than a mere diplomatic encounter. Gorbachev had gone to do more than agree in principle on a treaty that had been essentially negotiated already. He was out to woo the West.

He succeeded as much as he could have hoped. His confident, open manner appealed to the American public.

Gorbachev, Thatcher and Reagan were all helping each other to transform East–West relations, and they were helping each other politically as well. It was an advantage to Gorbachev to be flying to Washington straight from a friendly and successful meeting with Thatcher. For her it was a boost to be treated almost as one of the big three. The political benefit for Reagan was that the feeling of a new dawn pushed Irangate as well as the Cold War into the past. As Gorbachev wooed the American crowds with all the skill of a Western politician, he was doing Reagan a favour too.

It had been a year of recovery for Reagan as a politician and for the Reagan–Thatcher partnership after the low point of Reykjavik. That had dealt a lasting blow to her confidence in his judgment, but throughout Irangate she had won the no less lasting gratitude of him and his entourage for her performance as the staunch friend. The scene was set for a mellow final year, moving to a warm and sentimental climax.

20

INTO THE SUNSET

For all the personal warmth between Ronald Reagan and Margaret Thatcher, for all the views they were known to share, it took the British public a long time to appreciate the fortieth president of the United States.

Shortly before Gorbachev arrived in Washington in December 1987 for his third summit with Reagan, an opinion poll conducted by MORI for NBC News compared attitudes to the two leaders in Britain, France and Germany, as well as the United States. Reagan scored worse than Gorbachev with the British, and worse with them than with either the French or the Germans. In Britain 39 to 19 per cent put more trust in Gorbachev than Reagan to reduce tensions between the Soviet Union and the United States, whereas in France the margin was 23 to 16 per cent in Reagan's favour. In Germany more people backed Gorbachev, but the gap was smaller than in Britain.

Even more suprisingly, a majority of 54 to 31 per cent regarded Reagan unfavourably in Britain, whereas in both France and Germany he had a narrow favourable balance. The British figure for Reagan compared with a 68 to 14 per cent favourable rating for Gorbachev. Clearly the British still had a conception of Reagan as the blundering cowboy, without the judgment to make the world a safer place. Much of the story of his last year in office, the last year of the Reagan–Thatcher partnership, is of the replacement of that picture.

Reagan's fortunes were reviving at home. His stubborn refusal to behave like a guilty man, his personal attraction and the hopes of a new age of friendship with the Soviet Union were all combining to push Irangate to the side.

For her part, Thatcher was still riding high as 1988 dawned. It was less than a year since her smashing election victory. The opposition was still in poor shape. Although Labour was showing the first signs of moving back from the far left into the mainstream of British politics, the Alliance of Liberals and Social Democrats was fragmenting. Economic optimism was in the air and Nigel Lawson was shortly to introduce his second major tax-cutting Budget, bringing the basic rate of income tax down to 25 per cent and holding out heady hopes of 20 per cent in the future.

Yet all was not well between the Prime Minister and her Chancellor. The Budget statement was as always delivered on a Tuesday, and it was only the previous Thursday that Thatcher first heard of Lawson's intention to cut taxes so sharply. She was not pleased, fearing the inflationary effects. This Budget was preceded by her first serious and fateful public clash with Lawson. It was a clash with both a European and an American dimension. The Chancellor insisted on bringing interest rates down below the level that she thought safe for inflation because he wanted to keep the exchange rate for the pound in line with the German mark. Lawson was behaving as though Britain were a full member of the European Monetary System, without actually joining. Thatcher would not permit British entry, to the distress of Lawson, Howe and a number of other ministers as well. But, in Thatcher's eyes, her Chancellor was insisting on paying the membership subscription anyway.

She also believed that he and his fellow finance ministers were too keen to try to manage exchange rates internationally, not just in Europe. In other words, he was pursuing James Baker's policy rather than hers. It was a replay of their disagreement over the Louvre agreement. For once one of her ministers was more in line with the Reagan administration than she was. Lawson was at that time such a respected Chancellor that the dispute hurt her politically for a while; but this was a time when she was able to shrug off temporary embarrassments. Apparently secure at home, her confidence was swelling abroad. The President had aged and her trust in his judgment would never recover from Reykjavik. Yet all the signs were that the personal regard between them was strengthening.

This was evident when Reagan appeared for the last time at a meeting of Nato heads of government in Brussels in March. Before it began he quietly swapped the place names between Shultz and himself so that he would be the one sitting next to Thatcher. He had not played a large part in the proceedings when it came to his turn as the last speaker in the final session. As he got up, Shultz helpfully pointed to his cue cards; but the President disregarded them: 'I think I'll just take this one on the wing, George.'

243

Take it on the wing he did. In less than ten minutes he spoke movingly of what Nato meant and what it had done to preserve the freedom of the countries represented in that room. They had such a long history of fighting wars among themselves that each peace treaty in the past had been the cause of the next war. But after the last war they had forged this new unity, this new alliance. All they had to do to preserve the peace was to stay together and recognise their obligations to each other. That offered the greatest promise of peace the world had ever known.

This was classical deterrence doctrine: stay united and strong, and the other side will not dare to attack any of us. He added a specific commitment: the United States believed that its destiny, just as much as any of the others, lay with the Alliance. Characteristically, he slipped in an anecdote – about meeting a Soviet serviceman who had defected from Afghanistan and who explained the desire for freedom that he and his colleagues shared.

The ideas were hardly original; and the words, divorced from the speaker, were not particularly memorable. Yet he captivated his audience by the force of his conviction. His evident sincerity saved his remarks from being merely sentimental. Hardened diplomats speak of it as a memorable occasion. 'For the first time,' said one, 'I realised why he was such a great communicator to the American people.' It was a spontaneous performance that Thatcher could not have emulated, seizing even such a seasoned group in the grip of simple rhetoric.

In other respects she was the more dominant, some would say the most dominant, figure at that meeting. She was concerned above all that the West should not move from the INF Treaty to the denuclearisation of Europe. This led her to pressure the Germans to accept the replacement of the American short-range Lance nuclear missile, deployed on German territory and expected to become obsolete in a few years. She obtained no more than a fudged compromise then, and the question was to become a cause of division and embarrassment a year later. Just as Reagan was preparing to depart in a blaze of glory, Anglo–American storm clouds were appearing on the horizon.

Her continuing influence with him was demonstrated in April when the administration was considering how to retaliate after a United States Navy frigate had been damaged by an Iranian mine in the Gulf. A number of options were discussed. An air strike on the Iranian mainland? On one of the small islands? Or should an Iranian ship be sunk? As the argument raged within the administration, Thatcher's advice was in favour of a moderate response. If it was going to conform with international law, always one of her considerations, then it would have to be an exercise of force proportionate to the injury that had been inflicted.

To have attacked the mainland would have been escalating the level of violence. To have selected one of the islands would still have run the risk of hitting civilians, or of appearing to hit civilians. If there had been such a raid the Iranians might, so it was thought, have rushed civilians to the spot and claimed that they and their housing had been the targets. To have sunk one of their ships would, it was felt, have been too much an eye for an eye.

Before the decision was taken Charles Powell expressed Thatcher's views in a telephone conversation with Frank Carlucci, who had succeeded Weinberger as Defense Secretary. Thatcher herself may well have spoken directly to Reagan, but in any case her opinion would have been made known. Whether it was decisive in determining the President to opt for the destruction of two Iranian oil platforms in the southern Gulf is impossible to say. Not all those in the room with him can be sure. Perhaps not even Reagan himself could be certain how much a particular factor weighed with him.

But his conclusion was in line with Thatcher's advice. She had been given notice of the operation – though not of precisely which platforms would be hit – and as soon as it had been carried out stated that it 'was entirely justified as a proportionate response'. The platforms were used, according to the Pentagon, 'as command and control radar stations for the Iranian military'. The British government had also been assured that there were no civilians on them.

By that stage in his Presidency Reagan would at least have thought very carefully before disregarding Thatcher's judgment. 'On more than one occasion,' Carlucci recalls, 'I said to him: "Mr President, if you do that, Margaret Thatcher is going to be on the phone in an instant." And he said: "Oh, I don't want that".'

He would have been in no danger of having her on the phone protesting at his decision to visit the Soviet Union for the first time at the end of May. She saw herself as the matchmaker between him and Gorbachev. But like many a matchmaker before her she was uneasy about the behaviour of her charges once they were together.

In this instance, there was no cause for anxiety on her part. The ostensible purpose of this fourth meeting between Reagan and Gorbachev was the formal exchange of instruments of the INF Treaty, which had been signed in December and had now been ratified by Congress and the Supreme Soviet. Thatcher sent a message to both

Reagan and Gorbachev beforehand suggesting how the disarmament process might be taken further. She was not to be left out of the act. The visit was an occasion, however, for straight talking rather than hard bargaining, when the atmospherics mattered more than the detail. It was an opportunity for the two sides to send signals to each other and to the world at large.

This was the kind of politics of gesture at which Reagan was always a master. He irritated the Kremlin with the toughness of his speeches on human rights and religious freedom. He held a reception at the American Ambassador's residence for dissidents and Jewish refuse-niks, which was described by Tass as 'hardly aimed at improving understanding between the Soviet Union and the United States'. So he sent the signal that he was not going soft, but he sounded a note of hope as well as criticism. At Moscow University he gave an impassioned plea for freedom, not only on moral grounds but also as the key to progress and technological advance. 'Your generation,' he told the students, 'is living in one of the most exciting, hopeful times in Soviet history.' Referring to the 'Moscow spring', he declared: 'We do not know what will be the conclusion of this journey, but we are hopeful that the promise of reform will be fulfilled.'

How did this square with that speech of his on the 'evil empire'? That was renounced: 'We were talking about another time, another era.' Reagan and Gorbachev strolled out together in Red Square, meeting the crowds. It was pure public relations, but it marked the transformation of their relations. The hardline President was removing the last stigma from anyone doing business with the leader of the Soviet Union.

Straight from Moscow Reagan flew to London, where in the splendour of the Foreign Office courtyard he was greeted by the Band of the Welsh Guards playing the 'Star-Spangled Banner'. This visit was both a celebration and the beginning of hubris. That evening he invited Thatcher to Washington in November after the election. Just as she had been the first state visitor of his Presidency, so he wanted her to be the last. She accepted instantly. This would give her the opportunity, so it was presumed, for her to be the first to meet the new President after his election.

At that time Governor Michael Dukakis was running well ahead in the polls, but he was almost certainly not consulted about Reagan's invitation to Thatcher. This caused some anxiety among officials in London. What if Dukakis was elected and did not want Thatcher to be the first foreign leader he would meet? Might the new era begin not with an embrace but a snub? Vice-President George Bush was probably not consulted either, but then he knew Thatcher well. Surely his approval could be taken for granted.

Reagan and Thatcher seemed to be taking a little bit more than that for granted. In his speech at the dinner in Downing Street that evening the President was reported as saying that if he failed to achieve a deal on strategic arms before he left office he knew his successor could rely on her to maintain progress. He knew of nobody better to take on the job of continuity girl. That was gleefully interpreted in some British newspapers the following morning as preparing the stage for her to take the leading Western role in East–West relations after he stepped down. One can safely assume that George Bush had not been consulted about that.

Such niceties were of no concern when Reagan spoke at Guildhall the next day, 3 June. This was the moment to celebrate both Reagan's summit with Gorbachev and his partnership with Thatcher, and the tributes were lavish on both sides. 'Through all the troubles of the last decade,' he told her, one 'firm, eloquent voice, a voice that proclaimed proudly the cause of the Western alliance and human freedom, has been heard. A voice that never sacrificed its anti-Communist credentials or its realistic appraisal of change in the Soviet Union.' Yet it was her voice that had been 'one of the first to suggest that we could "do business" with Mr Gorbachev'.

The President went on to associate her with the success of the Soviet dialogue: 'Prime Minister, the achievement of the Moscow summit, as well as the Geneva and Washington summits, say much about your valour and strength.' His ommission of the Reykjavik summit from that list said much about his discretion as well.

Thatcher was equally fulsome in return: 'Your leadership has made us strong and confident again.' The President had achieved a politician's most difficult task of changing 'attitudes and perceptions about what is possible, not by bowing to the wishes and whims of others, but by standing firm in your beliefs'.

Both in their words and their spirit these exchanges went well beyond the conventional compliments expected between politicians when one of them is on the brink of retirement. On both sides the personal regard had become stronger, even though the element of calculation on Thatcher's part had not diminished. She still tried to use the personal relationship to get her way on policy.

On one critical issue she did not obtain all that she wanted on this visit. When she sought reassurance once again that the United States would not resume arms sales to Argentina, she received a slightly ambiguous answer. Argentina was no longer a dictatorship, the President pointed out, and that must influence policy on arms sales. This did not in fact presage a resumption during his Presidency, but it was an indication that the line could not be held absolutely and indefinitely.

Little more than two weeks later the two of them were in Toronto for Reagan's final economic summit. The atmosphere was very different from his first in Ottawa seven years before. Then only Margaret Thatcher had been with him, arguing shoulder to shoulder against the rest. Now Reagan and Thatcher were still together, but basking in the approval of the others as they all expressed their satisfaction at the healthy state of the international economy. Both Reagan and Thatcher exhorted their colleagues to pursue the free-market policies that had brought lower inflation, sustained economic growth and more jobs.

Two weeks later she was once again the loyal friend in time of trouble when the United States cruiser *Vincennes* mistakenly shot down an Iranian civil airbus in the Gulf on 3 July, killing all two hundred and ninety people on board. The cruiser's captain had shot at the oncoming aircraft in the belief that it was an Iranian F-14 fighter about to attack his ship.

At the administration's request a statement was swiftly issued from Downing Street saying that the disaster was a tragedy for all concerned, expressing 'profound regret for the loss of life', but fully accepting 'the right of forces engaged in such hostilities to defend themselves'. The statement put the best gloss it could on the disaster: 'We understand that in the course of an engagement, following an Iranian attack on the US force, warnings were given to an unidentified aircraft apparently closing with a US warship, but these warnings received no response.'

The *Vincennes* had indeed just beforehand been in a battle with several Iranian high-speed attack boats, but the airbus was not off course, as originally thought. It was a tragic case of human error. Crew members misinterpreted the signals they were receiving: they wrongly identified the airliner, and mistook its speed and trajectory, as well as its course.

The administration's response was to express deep regret without accepting blame. Reagan himself justified the action as self-defence. Vice-President George Bush, in a speech to the United Nations, said it was 'a tragic error' for the Iranians to allow 'a civilian aircraft loaded with passengers to proceed on a path over a warship engaged in battle'. A week after the action the United States offered compensation to the bereaved families without accepting any legal liability. Most international reaction was strongly critical. Thatcher's support for Washington was a rare exception.

The following month she permitted herself a touch of self-congratulation and more than a touch of over-confidence. Did she fear for the future of her special relationship with the next president? 'No, I don't,' she told the editor of the *Sunday Express* in an interview published on 24 July. 'One really has established a kind of relationship with the American people. I believe it will outlive any changes.' That read perilously like an assumption that any American president would have to come to terms with *her* popularity among *his* electorate.

That might not have pleased some people, but she upset a great many more two months later with possibly the most controversial single speech of her Premiership, at Bruges on 20 September. Its tone masked its substance, which can be a dangerous mistake for a politician to make. It sounded as if she was launching a general assault on the Community: 'We have not successfully rolled back the frontiers of the state in Britain, only to see them reimposed at a European level, with a European super-state exercising a new dominance from Brussels.'

Beneath the aggressive rhetoric she was outlining a way ahead for the Community. It should be a Europe of independent sovereign states cooperating closely together, in effect an updated version of de Gaulle's *Europe des patries*, rather than a federal Europe with too much power at the centre. It should not be too bureaucratic. It should be based firmly on free-market principles at home and should not be protectionist abroad. In stretching out a hand towards Eastern Europe the speech showed a breadth of vision that not everyone in the Community displayed at the time: 'We must never forget that east of the Iron Curtain peoples who once enjoyed a full share of European culture, freedom and identity have been cut off from their roots. We shall always look on Warsaw, Prague and Budapest as great European cities.'

All this passed largely unnoticed in the furore. The tone of the Bruges speech provoked anguish and outrage throughout Western Europe. The substance, on the other hand, struck Shultz in quite another light: 'So many people looked at that speech and said "She's against the Common Market." I looked at that speech and said "She's trying to have an impact on the shape of it, and a lot of the things that she's battling for have sense in them." '

The sharpness of the tone was not, however, an accident. The speech was not put together in a hurry under the pressure of a

249

deadline. The first version was produced by Charles Powell by the end of July. He sent it over to the Foreign Office with what was thought to be a somewhat defensive note, saying that the Prime Minister had some ideas on Europe which she wanted to get across, here was a tentative draft and he would be grateful for their thoughts. This first formulation was regarded as more provocative than the speech finally delivered. The Foreign Office, which has always been keener on the Community than Thatcher has, decided to provide a complete alternative text. This had the same structure as the original, but was more emollient in tone. It was cleared with the Treasury and other departments before being sent back to Number Ten about the first week in September. It was accepted by the Prime Minister as the basic draft, which was then reworked during approximately the second week of September.

At this stage the Foreign Office felt reasonably satisfied, even though this was not the kind of speech that it would have liked. Then over the weekend and the Monday, before the speech was delivered on the Tuesday, it was hardened to be given rather more the flavour of the first draft. Thatcher therefore made a deliberate decision to toughen it.

The reaction throughout most of the Community was immediately hostile. Thatcher had never been considered a 'good European' by her Community partners, but after early rows she had come to be accepted. Whatever misgivings they had tended to be smothered by reluctant admiration. The Bruges speech was a turning-point in her relations with them. She was set on a collision course in particular with Jacques Delors, the President of the European Commission, a French Socialist, who was pressing for the closer economic and political integration of the Community. The dispute did her no harm with the Reagan administration, but the growing friction with the Community damaged her in Washington later on.

For the moment the prospects looked good for the continuation of her extended honeymoon with whoever held power in the United States. Bush now seemed to be cantering comfortably to the White House. One of his devices, which was particularly effective in securing the support of Republican voters in the primaries, was to wrap himself enthusiastically in Reagan's colours. This was the Reagan–Bush team running for its third victory, or so the Vice-President presented it.

The nature of the campaign, as well as the outcome, was a tribute to Reagan's impact on American politics during his years in the White House. He had above all changed the mood and the terms of the dialogue. This was evident not just from the way in which the

Republicans used the word 'liberal' as a term of abuse – the 'L' word. More telling was the reluctance of Democrats to accept the description. His refusal to raise taxes had set the terms for everyone else. One of the reasons why Senator Robert Dole had lost the critical New Hampshire primary in February was probably his refusal to rule out higher taxes. In foreign policy Reagan was assailed from time to time only from the Republican right. As the peacemaker he commanded centre stage.

The flow of sentiment towards the President as he approached his last days in the White House was not confined to the United States. At last he managed to capture the approval of the sceptical British public. An opinion poll conducted by MORI for the *Sunday Times* at the end of the year showed that 60 per cent thought he had done a good job, with only 20 per cent saying he had done a bad job. That compared with a final approval rating in the United States of 68 per cent, the highest for a departing president since polling began.

Before that, in a mood of warm nostalgia all round, Thatcher arrived in Washington on Tuesday 15 November for an emotional farewell to the President. She had a bad cold, was exceedingly hoarse and for a few memorable minutes during her last meeting with Reagan in the Oval Office seemed to be in danger of losing her voice. There was, none the less, some substantive discussion. Partly this focused inevitably on Gorbachev, but her views were also sought on the opening of a dialogue with the PLO, which was to be one of the administration's last foreign-policy acts.

Thatcher had not previously exercised much influence with Reagan on the Middle East; nor had it figured largely in their discussions. That may have been because for much of the time her heart had not really been in her own government's policy. She had come to office with strong pro-Israeli instincts. She had needed some persuasion to accept the European Council's Venice Declaration in June 1980 that the PLO would have to be associated with negotiations on the Arab–Israeli conflict. Nothing she ever said to the Americans suggested that she had any misgivings about this. She was loyal to her colleagues, but she did give the impression in Washington for some years that she was simply going through the motions. It was always discussed in her meetings with the President, but nearly always briefly – as if she was putting in a good word for the policy rather than fighting for it.

As time went on, her ideas developed. She became convinced of the case for an international conference on the Middle East in which the Soviet Union would be included, and this was discussed at length

251

during her visit in July 1987, when it was top of the foreign-policy agenda. When the role of the PLO was raised again in November 1988 they found themselves in agreement.

On the Wednesday Thatcher was to be guest of honour at a State Department lunch. The day before Shultz had checked with Charles Price, the American Ambassador in London, as to whether she had a sense of humour. Perhaps a trifle uneasily, Price asked him to be more specific. 'What I don't have in mind,' said Shultz, 'is offering to seat her and then pulling the chair out from under her.' Having established that that would not be a good idea, but that she did have a reasonable sense of humour, Shultz proceeded to present her at the lunch with what he termed the Grand Order of the Handbag. Whenever a communiqué was required, he explained, no doubt thinking of those meetings at Camp David as well as economic summits, she would produce her handbag and pull out of it, 'almost like a rabbit out of a hat, a statement which invariably becomes the statement we adopt.'

'As I prepare to depart this office in January,' Reagan declared in proposing the toast to her at the State Dinner that evening, 'I take considerable satisfaction in knowing that Margaret Thatcher will still reside at Number 10 Downing Street and will be there to offer President Bush her friendship, cooperation and advice. She's a world leader in every meaning of the word.' As he uttered those words it is unlikely that any doubt crossed Reagan's mind as to whether Bush would listen to her advice as readily as he had done. After all, Bush had been such an amenable Vice-President and he had sold himself to the American voters on the basis of continuity. He was Reagan's political heir: surely he would continue to follow Reagan's lead. The Reagan–Bush team would just keep going under different leadership.

Two months later, on his last morning in the White House before going up to Capitol Hill to relinquish office, Reagan wrote a personal letter of appreciation and good wishes to Margaret Thatcher. It was a touching gesture. It may also have implied, like his earlier remarks, handing on the torch in international affairs. There is some evidence from newspaper reports at the time of a sense of that in Downing Street. If so, they were both taking the future and George Bush a little too much for granted.

'Presume not,' said the new King Henry V to his old drinking crony, Falstaff, 'that I am the thing I was.' George Bush waiting to be President could hardly be compared to the carousing Prince Hal waiting to be King. But just as Henry put his past behind him as he assumed the throne, so President Bush was not the same as

Vice-President Bush. Once he was in the White House, the theme of continuity was jettisoned. Having lived for so long in the shadow of Reagan, he was determined that this was to be Bush's first term, not Reagan's third term. To be a Reaganite was no recommendation in Bush's Washington – and who was the greatest Reaganite of them all?

Whoever had succeeded Reagan would have found it difficult to establish the same personal rapport with Thatcher. There could not have been the same shared experience of being in the wilderness together and then fighting their way to power together. Bush would not only have found it hard to have the same rapport; he did not want it. He would not have relished being pushed and manoeuvred on policy. The pushiness that Reagan found amusing was not to Bush's taste.

Reagan used to retell with relish a joke that he heard from Eduard Shevardnadze at a meeting in the White House after the Soviet Foreign Minister had just visited Thatcher. Gorbachev, Reagan and Thatcher all went to Heaven and the Lord said to Gorbachev: 'My son, you have done well. You are here in this place. God bless you.' Reagan came and the Lord said the same to him. Margaret Thatcher arrived and the Lord began: 'My son, you are here in this place . . .' And she interrupted him: 'I am not Your son, and this is not Your place. This is my place.'

This hardly suggests that Shevardnadze has a glittering second career awaiting him as a comedian in the Western world. But the joke is revealing. It is said to have been told by both Shevardnadze and Reagan with warmth and respect, and it is certainly true that nobody invents jokes about someone who has not been noticed. Yet there is a certain edge to it. It suggests assertiveness, irrepressibility, but also – the word was used in connection with this joke by one of Reagan's officials – 'brassiness'. Brassiness is not a Bush quality.

There is another, more fundamental, difference in their approach to policy. Reagan was essentially a strategic rather than a tactical leader. He had a strong sense of direction even when he appeared uncertain, and sometimes not even particularly interested, as to how to get there. This meant that he liked to deal above all with those he was sure were going his way, especially if they happened to have brought a map with them. Someone who cast herself as super-friend was well placed to form a strong partnership with such a leader.

Bush and his Secretary of State, James Baker, are different. They are tactical politicians, problem-solvers and, in the case of Baker, a Texas wheeler-dealer. They are less likely to ask who is their best friend than who has the problem that needs to be solved. Baker will ask who brings most chips to the table.

The signs were there at the beginning. Reagan had begun his Presidency with a visit from Thatcher. Bush began his with a visit from Kohl. It is Germany where the problems are, and the Germans who have the economic and the political power. It is what Germany does that will have most influence on the future of Europe and of East–West relations. The difference first became evident at the meeting of Nato heads of government in Brussels at the end of May 1989.

Thatcher had been pressing for German agreement to the deployment of a successor to the Lance missile on their soil. The Lance would soon become obsolete and, if it were not replaced, Nato would have no nuclear missiles in the shorter range below the intermediate nuclear forces which were being eliminated. The denuclearisation of Europe, which Thatcher had always feared, would be approaching.

This line of argument, persuasive though it may have been in military terms, took no account of what was happening politically in Germany. By the spring of 1989 it looked like yesterday's policy. The German government believed that it would be condemning itself to political suicide if it agreed to the introduction of more short-range missiles, which could hit only other Germans or Eastern Europeans.

Bush came down on the side of the Germans, and he did so without the kind of close prior consultation to which Thatcher had become accustomed. He resolved the dilemma by means of an imaginative proposal to cut conventional forces sharply to equal levels between East and West in Europe. If that were agreed, there would no longer be the conventional imbalance in Europe for which nuclear weapons on the ground had to provide redress. In the meantime, replacement of Lance would be postponed to an indefinite future that would never be reached unless the European scene were to be changed drastically for the worse.

With great skill Bush had resolved a potential Nato crisis. The alliance was reunited, but Thatcher was left on the sidelines, aquiescent but unhappy. Bush remarked graciously later that such an outcome could not have been achieved 'without an anchor to windward', but it is not much of an anchor that is left trailing after the ship.

Bush went straight from the Nato summit to Germany, where he made a major speech at Mainz, during which he described the Germans as being 'partners in leadership'. Only then did he stop, more briefly, in London. Thatcher neatly turned aside press queries as to whether Britain was still America's leading ally. 'I think it's quite wrong that because you have one friend,' she replied, 'you should exclude the possibility of other friendships as well. I'm sure the President doesn't and I don't. We both have many friends in Europe.' Bush described this as a good answer. So it was, but in the Reagan era she would not have needed to give it.

A further cause of difficulty emerged in July when Thatcher moved Geoffrey Howe from the Foreign Office. Thatcher and Howe were well known to have had their differences for years. This was fully appreciated in Washington. On one occasion Shultz asked the British Ambassador, Sir Antony Acland, if he was speaking on behalf of Sir Geoffrey Howe or the Prime Minister. That would make a difference, it was intimated. Acland responded with diplomatic aplomb that he was speaking on behalf of the British government.

One of the disagreements between the Prime Minister and her Foreign Secretary was over the European Community in general and the European Monetary System in particular. Howe, like Lawson, wanted Britain to be a full member of the system, which would mean joining the Exchange Rate Mechanism (ERM). At the EC summit in Madrid in June Howe and Lawson managed to press Thatcher to a compromise. Britain would go along with the first stage of the Delors plan for Economic and Monetary Union in the Community, and would be prepared to join the ERM when five specific conditions had been met.

This was a compromise that gave satisfaction to many people, but not to Thatcher. She was believed to have been pushed into it against her will, and when Howe was transferred the following month that was widely reported in Washington to have been retribution for his European enthusiasm. This did not commend her to an administration that was notably sympathetic to the concept of European unity. She was seen as being out of step and therefore less influential with her European partners.

At the same time, she was running into political trouble at home. A succession of domestic policies – reform of the health service, the poll tax and water privatisation – were proving unpopular. Inflation was rising, and the Conservatives did particularly badly in the elections for the European Parliament in June. Whether this really reflected the unpopularity of her European policies is doubtful. She fought the election on her attitude to Europe; the electorate took the opportunity to express its disapproval of health-service reform, the poll tax etc; and the result was considered a rejection of her European policies.

All these difficulties contributed to a growing impression in

Washington that she was becoming outdated. Yesterday's woman would not be the ideal partner for the president of today and tomorrow.

The difference in the emotional temperature of the relationship was evident in an interview that Bush gave to the television personality David Frost in early September. Who, the President was asked, was America's closest ally in Europe? 'The United States has always had a very special relationship with the United Kingdom, and of course I feel that very much. Having said that though,' Bush went on, 'I don't think we should have to choose up between friends.' Just to rub the message home, he added: 'I don't like to quantify, list them, put them on a thermometer chart to see who's up and who's down.'

Compare that with Reagan's answer when I asked him if his relationship with Thatcher was the closest with any head of government. 'There have been some close ones and all of that.' He paused. One could sense considerations of diplomatic discretion running through his mind. Then he went on: 'But yes, I would have to say that was the closest.'

Towards the end of November Thatcher paid her first visit to the United States since Bush's inauguration, flying into Washington on a bitterly cold day with bright sunshine and some inches of snow on the ground. That evening she, Charles Powell and Bernard Ingham talked late at the residence with the Ambassador and Lady Acland on the subject of German reunification. All of them agreed that it had to be accepted, and all of them were reluctant.

The following day it was up to Camp David for discussion with the President. The length of their talk, four hours, suggested the old intimacy. In reality it was not the same. On the future of Germany, which was the principal topic, they did not seem to differ, but there was a new disagreement that was to cause further trouble. Thatcher warned him that Britain would shortly start the compulsory repatriation of Vietnamese boat people from Hong Kong. The President made clear his disapproval, and when the first boat people were sent home a few weeks later there was a stinging public rebuke from the President's press secretary, Marlin Fitzwater.

The Camp David meeting was held just before the Malta summit between Bush and Gorbachev at the beginning of December. Immediately after that Bush went to Brussels to report to other Nato heads of government on his discussions with the Soviet leader. It was at a news conference there on 4 December that the President much embarrassed Thatcher by calling for a 'continued, perhaps even intensified, effort' of the Community to integrate. He seemed to be throwing the weight of the United States behind the French President of the European Commission, Jacques Delors, rather than Thatcher, in the bitter dispute as to what kind of Community it should be. Should it press on to a European central bank and a single currency, perhaps even to a federal government?

Bush made a brief phone call to Thatcher the following day, at the instigation of the American Ambassador in London, Henry Catto, to explain that he had not intended his remarks to create difficulties for her. A more extended explanation came from Baker when he flew in to London on 11 December for talks with Thatcher. The President had just meant to give his blessing to the 1992 programme: 'We do not seek to tell the European Community what they ought to do about monetary union, or what they ought to do about a social compact or charter.'

If that was really all that Bush had intended to convey he had displayed a Reaganite disregard for what is euphemistically termed the detail. The argument over whether there should be further integration beyond the 1992 programme had been at the centre of debate within the Community for some time.

At least open disagreement with the President had been averted, but Britian no longer had the specially favoured status that it had enjoyed for the past eight years. It was no more than one among a number of allies. The magic had gone. If it was to be restored under Bush, Thatcher would have her work to do all over again. Was reality reasserting itself? Were the Reagan–Thatcher years simply an aberration?

21

THE BALANCE SHEET

Ronald Reagan and Margaret Thatcher share one quality more important than differences of style or temperment. They are both politicians who paint in primary colours. There has been nothing neutral about them or the reactions they provoke. They are memorable personalities, who arouse feelings of enthusiastic admiration or of biting disapproval. Such leaders usually leave a strong imprint on the countries that they govern. How far is that true in their case? How much have they changed? What is the legacy of their association?

The lasting impact of political leaders can be judged by the effect on their opponents. Are the opposition parties forced to come to terms with the changes they have made? How far have Reagan and Thatcher had that effect?

Both of them cut income tax severely and made it hard for anyone to restore tax rates to their previous levels in either country without a very a good excuse. Reagan managed to make low taxes one of the sacred cows of American politics. Even his successor, his own Vice-President, was forced into exaggerated protests of innocence of any impure thought of raising taxes. 'Read my lips,' he demanded. After a year and a half in office his lips began to send a different message, but Reagan had still made it more embarrassing politically for any administration to raise taxes significantly.

Thatcher's programme of privatisation may well be modified by another government, but it is still an historic change in the ownership of British industry. Her programme of trade-union reform would be amended by a Labour government, but it is unlikely simply to be swept away as though it had never been.

Both Reagan and Thatcher came to office committed to reducing the power of government, and up to a point both did so. But here there was a strange contrast between them. Thatcher's privatisation

258

and Reagan's deregulation were in line with this strategy. These policies in their different ways transferred economic power from the state into private hands. Yet within government, Reagan handed power from the federal administration to the states, while Thatcher took power away from local authorities to concentrate it at the centre.

'I don't think Reagan is inherently or automatically anti-government nearly as much as he's anti-Washington,' said Congressman Newt Gingrich, the right-wing Republican from Georgia, in a BBC Radio *Analysis* programme in October 1988, just as the Reagan era was drawing to an end. 'There's a real ferment in the states,' said former Governor Tom Kean, the more liberal Republican from New Jersey in that same programme, with 'problems that people thought for a long time were insoluble being solved in states and localities.'

The trend had begun before Reagan took office, but gathered pace under him. One reason for this, according to Governor Bill Clinton, the Democrat from Arkansas, is that 'by cutting back on the federal role in so many areas' Reagan 'almost mandated the emergence of the governors as primary policy makers in so many areas'.

By contrast, Thatcher has taken powers away from local government. That has been evident in education with the establishment of a core curriculum in state schools; in the abolition of the Greater London Council in 1986, when some of its powers passed to central government; and in the introduction of the hated poll tax, which was devised as a means of making local authorities more accountable to their electorates. Nearly every voter has to pay the flat sum, in contrast to the rates which it replaces.

Neither Reagan nor Thatcher managed to curb total public spending, central and local, as much as their rhetoric would suggest. Yet they changed political attitudes towards public expenditure. No longer is it politically realistic for either the Democrats in the United States or the Labour Party in Britain to put their faith in massive public-spending programmes, trusting that economic growth will pay for everything. Labour's return to moderation is a severe political embarrassment to Thatcher. It deprives her of the greatest boon that any government can have: an unelectable alternative. But it is also a tribute to her.

Reagan and Thatcher represented and encouraged the international movement towards free markets. That both of them were such prominent champions of this policy, and were delivering rising prosperity to most of their peoples for most of the time, may have served as an example to others. They were certainly the most ardent advocates of free markets. They gave practical credibility to increasingly fashionable economic theories. Yet there were deeper forces at work than the example of Reagan and Thatcher. In international terms they symbolised an idea whose time had come.

The enterprise culture has deeper roots in the United States than in Britain. It needed less encouragement there, but in both countries it was nurtured during these years. Under the two of them there was greater respect for making money, greater thirst for wealth, greater self-reliance and greater inequality.

Above all, they brought a greater sense of confidence to their countries. Reagan did it by projecting a radiant optimism and insouciance. Away with the malaise that his predecessor, Jimmy Carter, had diagnosed as the American condition. If Reagan felt comfortable governing, then the country should feel comfortable being governed by him. Irangate undermined this achievement, but did not destroy it. The ghosts of Vietnam, Watergate and Tehran were exorcised.

Thatcher did it by an implacable determination. The impossible was not to be acknowledged. It was the Falklands spirit as a way of life. She may have exaggerated the extent of the conversion. Economic Thatcherism may have been accepted by large sections of the British people, though that varied sharply from one part of the country to another. It was when she tried to extend her doctrines to the social field that she ran into political trouble.

One limitation on the lasting influence of both Reagan and Thatcher is that, while both have had an impact on their opponents, neither has provided for a direct political inheritance. Reagan was not succeeded by a Reaganite. Thatcher is unlikely to be succeeded by a Thatcherite.

None the less, they have both made a difference to their countries. How much of a difference has it made that they ruled together?

The relationship between them was warmer personally and closer ideologically than between any previous president and prime minister. Their partnership did not have the same historical impact as the Roosevelt–Churchill connection: they did not have a world war to fight. But the range of their agreement was broader, embracing domestic as well as international affairs. It stood the test of time better. It was stronger at the end than at the beginning, which certainly could not be said of Churchill and Roosevelt.

It meant more to Reagan and Thatcher than the Kennedy–Macmillan connection, the other historic partnership, mattered to the two of them. Or, rather, the association with the British Prime Minister mattered more to Reagan than it did to Kennedy. Reagan's close advisers speak of the relationship with an unstinted warmth and without the reservations that Kennedy's feel it necessary to make. It is impossible to speak for long to many of Reagan's associates without realising just how important the Thatcher friendship was to him, and how it had developed over their years in power.

It mattered to Thatcher too, but in a different way. Quite apart from liking him personally, she recognised in him political qualities that she does not possess herself. He has the capacity to project his charm across a nation; she has had difficulties in making many of her own ministers like her. He has mastered television, where she often still appears either ill at ease or hectoring. As a public speaker he can captivate an audience in a way that she will never do. He has an acute political instinct and was comfortable in the exercise of power. He also possesses the kind of constancy and courage that she both shares and appreciates in others.

These are not small political virtues, but the unusually sharp contrast between his strengths and his weaknesses explains why he is so easily underestimated. He does not have the intellectual comprehension generally expected of a president, but neither was he simply manipulated by his advisers. He knew the broad direction in which he wished to go; he would indicate the route but leave it to others to work out how to get there. But when his mind was settled on a policy, or when he felt a proposed policy conflicted with his broad objective, he was not easily budged. So when he reached a specific agreement with Thatcher it stuck.

This approach to leadership fitted well with hers, given their respective offices. 'From the minute their eyes met,' according to Deaver, 'there was an instant enjoyment on both their parts. They were delighted to see each other. They could hardly wait to sit down and get at it.' But this comradeship did not just happen. Thatcher worked at it. Reagan was more influenced by personal consider-ations. With Thatcher there was always the element of calculation, sometimes even of manipulation. For her the pleasures of friendship would never have been enough. She wanted to use the friendship to get specific results. That is hardly surprising. For almost every British prime minister from Churchill on, it has been a major objective to influence the thinking of the president of the United States. For Britain the special relationship has meant a special opportunity to have an impact on American policy.

Because of the disparity in power between the two countries it is the attitude of the American president that ultimately counts. In the telling expression of McGeorge Bundy, the British prime minister 'always wants the meeting to last longer than announced'. When it runs over time that shows how close they are. It implies that the prime minister carries weight. As a general rule it is the prime minister who is eager to exercise influence over the president rather than the other way round, because American policy matters so much more to Britain than British policy matters to the United States.

In the case of Reagan and Thatcher, she therefore stood to gain more and was the more assertive. That is why the story of their relationship is so much one of her exercising her powers of persuasion upon him. She did so to good effect under one of three circumstances.

First, when it was an issue of much greater importance to Britain than the United States. The Falklands, Northern Ireland and the Laker case are obvious examples. In these instances Reagan decided that it was more important to help her than to avoid minor embarrassment for his administration.

Second, when the administration was itself divided. SDI and the ABM Treaty, Mozambique and disarmament policy after Reykjavik are cases in point. A Thatcher intervention with the President was always a powerful instrument in the ceaseless battle over policy in Washington, but it was all the more effective when she could be guided as to the appropriate time for its delivery and when it could be backed up by supporting evidence on its arrival. Washington departments and agencies were well aware of this and would try to bring her into play whenever they thought she was likely to take their side of the debate.

Third, when Reagan could be convinced that a particular course was necessary here and now, even though it conflicted with his long-term aspirations. This occurred most frequently when he was induced to continue the policy of nuclear deterrence because it was not possible to have a nuclear-free world just yet.

Thatcher was never able to talk him out of that dream, try as she might. She was able to get his agreement simply to preserving Western strength in the meantime. Nor did she make any impression when she tried to get him to cut the budget deficit: that required decisions which he was not prepared to make. Where his mind was fixed on a fundamental point she was no more successful than anybody else in getting him to budge. Her sway was not unlimited. She could manoeuvre him on a number of questions, but he was not to be programmed.

Reagan affected her in return, but her actions rather than her thinking. It is doubtful if she agreed with him either over Libya or over flouting the International Court on the mining of Nicaraguan ports. She repressed her misgivings on the INF agreement. She recognised that friendship has its obligations. She knew that if she were to be his most reliable friend, she would not only have to back him on some tough issues. She would also have to keep quiet on others. She said little in public on Central America. She maintained a tight-lipped silence on Irangate for nearly a year before the news broke.

Thatcher's greatest help to Reagan was not on those occasions, important though they were, when she deliberately decided to support him for the sake of the relationship. The essence of their partnership is that it was not a zero sum game. When Thatcher had her way, Reagan was not always having to change his mind. On the major issues of their time – the development of free markets at home and around the world, building up the military strength of the West and then stretching out a hand to the Soviet Union – they were together. They encouraged each other, and because they were in agreement they made it easier for the other to move. That was Thatcher's major contribution.

'It was a valuable coincidence of history,' she claims, 'that Ron Reagan and I were in power at the same time.' But what would have happened differently if they had not been? Thatcher's Premiership might have lasted no more than three years instead of breaking all records this century. If a different president had been less supportive over the Falklands – and Reagan himself was not short of contrary advice – that war might have been lost and she would have been out.

Without Reagan, Thatcher would never have been able to cut the same figure on the world stage. At meetings of EC leaders she was time and again in a minority, frequently of one. At Commonwealth Prime Ministers' conferences she was battling against the rest, most often over South African sanctions. Her lone stands won a fair amount of admiration among the British electorate: 'Battling Maggie Fights for Britain Again.' Yet if it had not been for Reagan, people might well have begun to ask: 'Does nobody outside the United Kingdom have a good word for our Prime Minister?' Certainly, she would not have been seen as a person of international influence, somebody whose word carried weight in the major centres of power on the most momentous issues of our time.

Reagan without Thatcher would have lost something less tangible. It is true that another prime minister would have been most unlikely to allow the bases in Britain to be used in the Libyan raid, but the air strike would still have been made. It would have been rather more difficult, but its success would not have been jeoparidsed. Reagan's position would not have been undermined.

What he would have missed was the sense of partnership. He would have been a beleaguered figure at economic summits during at least his first term. He would not have enjoyed that role, and he would not have been impressive in it. Although renowned as the great communicator, he was not good in tough debate on substantive issues with his peers. He had a different quality. Lester Pearson, the late Canadian Prime Minister, once said privately of the former British Prime Minister after a Commonwealth Conference: 'Harold Wilson has been superb. He has managed to convey every human emotion, except sincerity – even when he was sincere.' Reagan has the gift of projecting sincerity from a script he has barely mastered. It is the emotion and humanity of the man that come across.

That made him superbly effective on great occasions. It did not help him to deal with the specific criticisms of other heads of government who did not share his doctrinal beliefs. Without Thatcher he would have been much more inclined to think of the allies as unfriendly and the world outside the United States as hostile territory. He would still have received the advice from within his own administration to open the dialogue with the Soviet Union. He would still have hoped for a new relationship with Moscow, because he would still have dreamt of banishing nuclear weapons from the world; but he might have been less responsive to the changes there. That could have meant more than a mere difference in timing and tone.

The 1980s will be seen as the decade of three people: Reagan, Gorbachev and Thatcher. Between them they represented the spirit of the times. The policies they pursued and the interaction among them set international affairs on a new and more hopeful course. In their very different ways they combined to extend democracy and to make a market economy the mark of a successful state. Reagan and Thatcher did that by promoting market forces: Gorbachev did it by accepting the bankruptcy of the socialist system.

There were material factors that helped to dictate this course, especially the internal failures of the Soviet empire. The personal factors mattered as well. Events would not have developed in quite the way they did had it not been for the burgeoning confidence between Reagan and Gorbachev; Thatcher's role in encouraging the two men to believe that they could do business with each other; and, not least, Thatcher's understanding with Reagan.

Thatcher could not have played her role without that understanding. Her international clout was increased immeasurably by the knowledge that on most issues she and the President of the United States moved along the same lines. That knowledge helped him as well, politically and psychologically. No matter how powerful, resolute and relaxed a national leader may be, it is reassuring to find others proceeding in the same direction, especially if he particularly respects their judgment. His magnetism was matched by her determination.

So the partnership played no small part in the wider history of the decade. That may be too easily forgotten in the immediate reaction to the Reagan–Thatcher period. It provided the climax to the Anglo–American special relationship: a president who gave precedence to Britain's leader more unreservedly than at any time since the early years of the Second World War matched with a prime minister who gave absolute priority to the American connection. But was it also the last hurrah of the special relationship?

It is hard to believe that there will ever again be an American president and a British prime minister who will form quite as close a personal association. That is because it depended on a number of factors, not all of which are likely to be found together again.

First, there was the friendship between them. Although this was a more potent force with him, it eased all dealings between them. It would still not have counted for all that much if they had not both been highly ideological politicians sharing the same ideology. That established a basis of political trust on his part, which transcended mere personal liking. This in turn mattered so much because of his style of governing.

Having set the direction, he relied upon others to help with the policies. He knew where he wanted to go; he often did not know how to get there. This method of leadership gave particular scope for persistent advice from Thatcher. He did not resent it as another president might have done. On the contrary, Reagan himself would quite often want to know what position she took before he came to a decision. All of this meant that during the Reagan years Thatcher was unusually well placed to influence policy before it was determined.

Because of the American system of decision-making, in which policy is time and again battered out in painful compromise among different agencies, different strong-willed presidential advisers, different interest groups and different power-brokers in Congress, it is often too late for a foreign government to have much effect once a position has been reached. To be part of the interagency power game is an inestimable advantage. It is always easier for the British to do that than the representatives of any other government: they can merge so comfortably into the Washington scene. In the Thatcher–Reagan years a customary asset was multiplied by the blessing, but also by the lethargy, of the President.

The final special factor is that both of them were political children of the war and immediate post-war years. Their instincts were implanted at a time when the special relationship was the central feature of foreign policy for both countries. An administration official remarked that whereas in the past people in Washington used to ask what the allies thought, in Reagan's Washington they asked simply what Thatcher thought. Future presidents and future prime ministers are unlikely to think in such predominantly Anglo-American terms.

For all the rhetoric of hands-across-the-sea, our common heritage of language, literature, law and so forth, the intense association between the United States and Britain that we have known for the past half-century was not the product of peace and the gentle virtues. It was forged in the pressure of the Second World War. It was given durability by the post-war Soviet threat. Danger made it; would quieter times cherish it?

Britain is becoming more European. Because of the spread of English among the professional classes throughout Western Europe, language is not the same barrier that it used to be for opinion-formers. Even without a Channel tunnel, younger people have grown up accustomed to going over to the Continent in a way that was unknown to previous generations. They are still attracted to the United States as an exciting and friendly place, but Europe is near and sophisticated. They have never known the drama and tension of the war years. Emotions that are natural to Thatcher's generation come to them only through the medium of television plays and documentaries. Younger people have not had the experience of Americans as comrades in shared peril or as benefactors in the same way.

There has been a significant shift in the British world view. A Gallup Poll in 1969 found that 34 per cent of the British people believed that America was most important to Britain, 34 per cent thought the Commonwealth was, but only 21 per cent Europe. When the same question was asked in 1986 Europe scored 39 per cent, America 29 per cent and the Commonwealth only 26 per cent.

The evolution of British attitudes requires Britain to be more involved in Europe in future, but this matches a trend in American thinking. If Britain is to remain of consequence to whoever rules in Washington, not just to the Bush administration, it will have to be fully engaged in the European Community.

Britain is a trading nation politically as well as economically. Its success depends upon doing political business effectively in a number of areas at the same time. Thatcher was able to play a larger role in the 1980s because she had the confidence of Gorbachev as well as Reagan. Gorbachev valued the relationship with the leader of a medium-sized Western European power because she was known to be close to the President of the United States. She was of more help to Reagan because of her dialogue with Gorbachev. Because she had clout with both Reagan and Gorbachev she commanded the respect of other European leaders.

Britain has not for many years had the power to be politically and economically interesting to the United States just for itself. It cannot afford to be on the sidelines of world affairs: it must be in the international market-place. This means that to cherish the American special relationship in the 1990s Britain must be seen to be part of Europe and, paradoxically, to give less of an absolute priority to the United States.

But this begs two questions. What kind of Europe? And will the Americans still be interested in Britain anyway?

The United States has a relationship with a number of countries, each of which is unique in its own way. It is increasingly obsessed by the economic might of Japan. Germany is seen as the power that counts in Europe. Israel has a claim to a particularly intense form of loyalty. Canada is more closely interwoven with American life than ever after the Free Trade Agreement of 1987.

How do these compare with the British special relationship? Israel has too limited an international role to count in these terms, and one of the most common American characteristics is a capacity to forget Canada.

Despite the occasional talk of an American–Japanese economic duumvirate, it is fear and resentment that Japan inspires in American breasts above eveything else. It is a fear that is not always precisely related to the facts. At the end of 1988 British investment in the United States was nearly double Japanese investment: 102 billion dollars compared with 53 billion dollars. British investment was still rising faster. Yet it was the Japanese takeover that was seen as a threat. The British stake passed almost unnoticed. It was the purchase of the Rockefeller Center by the Mitsubishi Estate Co. of Tokyo that upset Americans. Because the United States played the dominant part in the political and economic rebirth of Japan after the war there is an emotional dimension to the competition between them. It is like an ageing man dreading being outstripped by his protégé.

These concerns are given a bitter edge by the hard, practical grievances over Japanese trading practices. When Americans threaten the world with trade protection it is nearly always the Japanese they have in mind. In fact the two countries are more closely entwined than they will always acknowledge. They need each other. The American bond market would be highly vulnerable without Japanese investment, and Japanese industry depends on its exports to the United States.

Because the economic decisions of one matter so much to the other there is much contact and consultation between the two governments. Their roles are so critical to the stability of the international economy that there is scope for much further cooperation between them. At the moment it is only in the field of military security that they operate as partners rather than rivals, and even there they are only limited partners.

Logic suggests that the partnership should become closer and more constructive. Politics points in the opposite direction. There is not the confidence necessary for the kind of cooperation across a range of issues around the world that the United States has enjoyed with Britain for many years.

Germany looms ever larger in American thinking. It is already and will increasingly be the European state with which the United States will have to deal more than any other on European issues. That is a simple factor of power. For that reason German–American relations are bound to remain of the first importance. How well they progress will be critical for all of us, but they offer the challenge of a problem rather than the stability of an instinctive partnership. German unification could not be resisted and ought to be welcomed; but it poses a range of questions for its allies, partners and neighbours – as well as for itself.

It is partly because the United States is uncertain about Germany that it pays so much attention to Germany. German–American cooperation, no matter how well it may work, is also likely to be confined largely to Europe.

The United States is a world power with interests around the globe. Among European countries only Britain, France and the Soviet Union have worldwide diplomatic representation. Only they see themselves as having a world role; the Germans do not. In the Middle East, Africa and much of Asia, on some issues that have been rumbling on for years and on others that cannot be foreseen, the British connection will be more helpful to the United States than any other.

Britain's natural role in the future will be as the principal point of contact, the gateway to Western Europe for the United States, other

English-speaking countries and Japan. Britain is fitted for this part by custom and language. It would also suit American interests.

Relations between America and Europe may well deteriorate as economic issues loom larger in international relations. Whereas Europeans have looked upon the Americans for half a century as their ultimate protectors, in future they will see them not only as commercial partners – with a large and lucrative market – but also as commercial rivals, perhaps jealously protecting that market. Equally, Americans will be both attracted and disconcerted by Europe's growing economic strength. It will be in everyone's interest to contain this rivalry, to prevent trading disputes becoming a habit. International economic stability requires European–American cooperation, but that certainly cannot be taken for granted.

The United States will need friends in the European Community, and over a period of years it will have more in common with the British than anyone else. The Germans will be preoccupied with making unification work and with their own responsibilities as the wealthiest power in Europe. The French will be too protectionist.

Britain will also be the invaluable partner in keeping a scaled-down Nato as the safeguard for Western security. It ought to be possible to do the job with far fewer arms than at present, but the job will still need to be done. Negotiations should reduce Soviet military capability, but not eliminate it. The Soviet Union is likely to remain the most formidable military power in Europe; and where there is power, there needs to be a balance of power. Britain and France will remain the European members of Nato most aware of the continuing responsibility – and France has for years remained outside Nato's military structure. The alliance will matter less than in the past, but Britain will matter more within it.

So a Britain that was active and positive in the Community would still have much to contribute as a partner to the United States; but it would need the freedom of manoeuvre to operate in its own right. This points not to a federal Europe, but to a Community of nation states combining closely together. Some erosion of national sovereignty is inevitable. It is impossible for a country to operate effectively in the modern world without giving up some sovereignty. But there is a vast difference between a Community which takes away only as much national sovereignty as is necessary to perform its tasks and a tightly integrated United States of Europe.

Developments elsewhere in Europe point in that direction anyway. Sooner or later, and it is likely to be sooner rather than later, other countries to the East, and probably to the North as well, will be clamouring to join. The larger the EC becomes, the less tightly can it be controlled from the centre. Such a Community would offer scope for Britain and others still to have close relations of their own outside.

The worst mistake for Britain would be to repeat the error of trying to prove that it is truly European by distancing itself from America. It is always liable to lose some clout in Europe by seeming too pro-American: de Gaulle's jibe that Britain is America's Trojan horse lives on. Thatcher has inevitably suffered from that. It is a price worth paying to maintain favoured relations with what will still be the world's greatest superpower. The natural advantages of history are there to be used.

That applies to both countries. The United States benefits from a reliable friend and partner with a worldwide role. As Dean Rusk, Secretary of State to Kennedy and Johnson, once said: 'We have to have somebody to talk to in the world.' For all America's other relationships, Britain still best fills that role.

REFERENCES

1 ALLIES IN WAITING

Page

1 President Reagan recalled: in an interview with the author in Los Angeles, 17 July 1989.

1 Michael Deaver . . . remarked: interview with the author in Washington DC 19 December 1988.

1 Charles Price . . . made much the same point: interview with the author in London, 22 December 1988.

2 She (Margaret Thatcher) cannot recall: interview with the author in Downing Street, 8 January 1990.

2 an address . . . to the Institute of Directors: at the Albert Hall, London, 6 November 1969.

2 She (Thatcher) told the author in Downing Street, 8 January 1990.

2 She was still able to recall: interview with the author, Downing Street, 9 January 1990.

2 On the first morning of his visit: 27 November 1978.

5 According to Deaver: interview with the author in Washington DC, 19 December 1980.

7 This second meeting: 27 November 1978.

2 THATCHER LEADS THE WAY

13 The Institute of Economic Affairs: run for its first 30 years by Ralph Harris (now active in the House of Lords as Lord Harris of High Cross). An exuberant extrovert, an active churchman and an accomplished conjurer. At his side throughout that time was the quieter Arthur Seldon, a strongly committed free market economist. For many years they were lonely figures challenging the conventional economic wisdom of the day.

14 speech to the Institute for Socioeconomic Studies in New York: 15 September 1975.

15 William Simon and James Schlesinger: Simon – Secretary of the Treasury under Nixon who subsequently pursued a highly

271

Page

successful Wall Street career. Schlesinger – Defence Secretary under Ford and Energy Secretary under Carter.

20   He (Brock) was immensely impressed with its quality: interview with the author in Washington DC, 12 January 1989.

21   Michael Baroody . . . recalls: interview with the author in Washington DC, 19 December 1988.

21   Brock claimed: interview with the author in Washington DC, 12 January 1989.

3 PARTNERS IN POWER

26   David Gergen . . . made a similar point: interview with the author in Washington DC, 24 October 1988.

29   the remarkable personal correspondence they exchanged: published in full in three volumes by Princeton University. *Churchill and Roosevelt: The Complete Correspondence*. Edited with a Commentary by Warren F. Kimball. A magisterial work and essential source for anyone interested in the Churchill–Roosevelt relationship.

30   According to Churchill's doctor, Lord Moran: *Winston Churchill: The Struggle for Survival 1940–1965*. Taken from the diaries of Lord Moran. Published by Constable in Britain and by Houghton Mifflin in the United States.

33   the judgment of his (Macmillan's) official biographer, Alistair Horne: *Macmillan 1957–1986, Volume Two of the Official Biography*, published by Macmillan, p. 281.

33   according to McGeorge Bundy: interview with the author in New York, 5 July 1989, from which all Bundy quotations in this chapter are taken.

34   Ted Sorensen . . . confirms: interview with the author in New York, 5 July 1990, from which all Sorensen quotations in this chapter are taken.

34   In his (Macmillan's) memoirs: *At the End of the Day*, published by Macmillan, p. 216.

34   Lord Harlech . . . discussed: conversation with the author in London, 5 January 1984.

36   according to Harry McPherson: interview with the author in Washington DC, 28 October 1988.

4 IN REAGAN'S WASHINGTON

42   as Deaver put it: interview with the author in Washington DC, 19 December 1988.

46   remarked to Robert McFarlane: author's interview with McFarlane in Washington DC, 7 October 1988.

Page

5 ARMS AND THE LEADER

51 how much he (Reagan) refers to them: interview with the author in Los Angeles, 17 July 1989.
51 he (Reagan) reflects: interview with the author in Los Angeles, 17 July 1989.
52 Reagan, looking back: interview with the author in Los Angeles, 17 July 1989.
53 corroborated by Michael Deaver: interview with the author in Washington DC, 19 December 1988.
53 Donald Regan claims in his memoirs: *For the Record: From Wall Street to Washington*, published by Harcourt Brace Jovanovich.
53 But . . . in conversation: interview with author in Alexandria, Virginia, 24 January 1989.
53 the story that Reagan tells: interview with the author in Los Angeles, 17 July 1989.
57 Haig recalls: interview with the author in Washington DC, 14 December 1988.
58 she (Thatcher) balks: interview with the author at Downing Street, 8 January 1990.

6 REAGAN SENDS A SIGNAL

61 Nowadays he (former Congressman Jim Jones) is a Thatcher admirer: interview with the author in Washington DC, 30 June 1989.

7 NATO IN DISARRAY

69 as Perle recalls: interview with the author in Washington DC, 30 July 1988.
71 McFarlane, the chief American negotiator, believes: interview with the author in Washington DC, 10 January 1990.
71 according to Max Hastings and Simon Jenkins in their authoritative study: *The Battle for the Falklands* published by Michael Joseph in Britain and by Norton in the United States.
75 In his memoirs Haig: *CAVEAT: Realism, Reagan and Foreign Policy*, published by Macmillan.

8 THE FALKLANDS

84 Laurence Eagleburger remarked: interview with the author in New York, 10 November 1988.
85 He (Haig) records: *CAVEAT* pp. 284–5.
85 He (Haig) states: *CAVEAT* p. 285.

Page

85   As he (Haig) looks back now: interview with the author in Washington DC, 14 December 1988.

86   Sir Nicholas Henderson wrote: in *The Economist*, 12 November 1983.

86   Reagan still recalls: interview with the author in Los Angeles, 17 July 1989.

90   Eagleburger even goes as far as to say: interview with the author in New York, 10 November 1988.

92   Henderson has written: in *The Economist*, 12 November 1983.

92   McFarlane tends to believe: interview with the author in Washington DC, 5 December 1988.

92   Haig believed: interview with the author in Washington DC, 14 December 1988.

93   He (Reagan) points out: interview with the author in Los Angeles, 17 July 1989.

94   McFarlane . . . later assessed: interview with the author in Washington DC, 5 December 1988.

9 AT THE SUMMIT: FROM VERSAILLES TO WILLIAMSBURG

105   Shultz speaks: interview with the author at Stanford, California, 3 November 1989.

105   he (Robert McFarlane) remembered: interview with the author in Washington DC, 10 January 1990.

106   Shultz himself acknowledges: interview with the author at Stanford, 3 November 1989.

107   Reagan recalls: interview with the author in Los Angeles, 17 July 1989.

107   David Gergen recalls: interview with the author in Washington DC, 6 June 1989.

109   Reagan recalls: interview with the author in Los Angeles, 17 July 1989.

111   David Gergen remarked: interview with the author in Washington DC, 24 October 1988.

10 TESTING THE BEAR

114   Thatcher maintains: interview with the author at Downing Street, 8 January 1990.

119   as McFarlane puts it: interview with the author in Washington DC, 10 January 1990.

122   McFarlane has no recollection: interview with the author in Washington DC, 10 January 1990.

122   Shultz points out: interview with the author in Stanford, 3 November 1989.

Page

123 According to McFarlane: interview with the author in Washington DC, 10 January 1990.

11 THE GRENADA INVASION

126 Deaver recalls: interview with the author in Washington DC, 19 December 1988.

126 Robert McFarlane ... confirms that: interview with the author in Washington DC, 10 January 1990.

126 When Reagan was asked: interview with the author in Los Angeles, 17 July 1989.

126 McFarlane says: interview with the author in Washington DC, 20 October 1988.

128 Reagan is able to claim: interview with the author in Los Angeles, 17 July 1989.

130 Reagan himself believes: interview with the author in Los Angeles, 17 July 1989.

131 Lord Harlech made clear: conversation with the author in London, 5 January 1984.

133 McFarlane recalls: interview with the author in Washington DC, 10 January 1990.

133 Adelman adds privately: interview with the author in Washington DC, 2 November 1988.

135 Ambassador David Abshire recalls: interview with the author in Washington DC, 10 January 1990.

12 THE SECOND TERM BEGINS

140 Reagan recalls: interview with the author in Los Angeles, 17 July 1989.

13 A COUP AT CAMP DAVID

146 she (Thatcher) said: interview with the author at Downing Street, 8 January 1990.

146 Thatcher remembers: ibid.

147 in the judgment of Frank Carlucci: interview with the author in Washington DC, 25 July 1989.

147 according to Max Kampelman: interview with the author in Washington DC, 21 July 1989.

147 McFarlane says: interview with the author in Washington DC, 5 December 1988.

148 Thatcher explained: interview with the author at Downing Street, 8 January 1990.

149 she (Thatcher) says: interview with the author at Downing Street, 8 January 1990.

Page

149 To McFarlane: interview with the author in Washington DC, 7 October 1988.

157 said McFarlane: interview with the author in Washington DC, 7 October 1988.

14 IN CHURCHILL'S FOOTSTEPS

161 'Do you realise we are making history?' Moran diaries, *Winston Churchill: The Struggle for Survival 1940–1965* published by Constable in Britain and Houghton Mifflin in the United States.

165 Allen Wallis . . . has recorded: in the Cameros Family Lectures on 'A Just Society', The University of Rochester, 25 October 1989.

166 says Adelman: interview with the author in Washington DC, 2 November 1988.

167 McFarlane recalls: interview with the author in Washington DC, 7 October 1988.

168 Thatcher now describes: interview with the author at Downing Street, 8 January 1990.

171 he (McFarlane) says: interview with the author in Washington DC, 5 December 1988.

173 Thatcher remembered: interview with the author at Downing Street, 8 January 1990.

173 Max Kampelman . . . explained how: interview with the author in Washington DC, 21 July 1989.

173 according to McFarlane: interview with the author in Washington DC, 10 January 1990.

174 Kampelman reflects: interview with the author in Washington DC, 21 July 1989.

16 THE LIBYAN GAMBIT

191 Thatcher recalled: interview with the author at Downing Street, 8 January 1990.

18 REYKJAVIK: 'IT WAS LIKE AN EARTHQUAKE'

214 'It was like an earthquake': Thatcher interview with the author at Downing Street, 8 January 1990.

214 in an interview for *The Times*: with the author, published on 28 March 1986.

219 Thatcher speaks: interview with the author at Downing Street, 8 January 1990.

224 'it was the most productive summit': interview with the author at Stanford, 3 November 1989.

Page

19 DOING BUSINESS WITH GORBACHEV

234 according to Frank Carlucci: interview with the author in Washington DC, 25 July 1989.

20 INTO THE SUNSET

245 Carlucci recalls: interview with the author in Washington DC, 25 July 1989.

249 struck Shultz: interview with the author in Los Angeles, 3 November 1989.

256 Reagan's answer: interview with the author in Los Angeles, 17 July 1989.

21 THE BALANCE SHEET

261 the telling expression of McGeorge Bundy. Interview with the author in New York, 5 July 1989.

270 As Dean Rusk ... once said: quoted to the author by Professor Richard Neustadt on the basis of a memorandum of a conversation in the State Department.

INDEX

Note: Entries under Reagan and Thatcher refer to personal attitudes and their partnership together, events appear as main headings.

ABM (Anti-Ballistic Missile) Treaty (1972), 149, 152, 154, 157–8, 162, 170–2, 216, 218, 222, 262
Abrahamson, General James, 150
Abshire, David, 135
Acheson, Dean, 35
Achille Lauro, hijacking of, 189, 190
Acland, Sir Antony, 204, 207, 209, 223, 255
Adam Smith Institute, 13
Adams, Tom, 127
Adelman, Kenneth, 25, 133, 166–7, 170, 221
Adenauer, Konrad, 35
Afghanistan, Soviet invasion of, 72, 130, 169
Agnew, Spiro, 6
Alexander, Sir Michael, 174, 175, 231
Allen, Richard, 3, 23, 25, 41, 50, 103
American Enterprise Institute, 13
Andropov, Yuri, 116, 146
Anglo-Irish Agreement, 198, 201
Annenberg, Walter, 78
Argentina, 76, 77, 78–82, 84–7, 89–93, 100, 103, 223–4, 247–8
Armacost, Michael, 209
Armilla Patrol, 236, 237
Armstrong, Anne, 132
Armstrong, Sir Robert, 193
Atkinson, Caroline, 43

Attali, Jacques, 110–11
Austin, General Hudson, 127

Baker, Howard, 239
Baker, James, 25, 50; as Bush's Secretary of State, 253–4, 257; disagreement with Haig, 80, 98; as Treasury Secretary, 177, 180, 181, 183, 184, 239, 243
Baldwin, Stanley, 221
Band, Stephen, 221, 223
Barber, Stephen, 22
Baroody, Michael, 21
Biaggi, Mario, 200
Bishop, Maurice, 127
Botha, P. J., 202–3
Boyson, Sir Rhodes, 12
Brady, James, 43, 49
Brewster, Kingman, 7, 132
Brezhnev, Leonid, 72, 86, 116, 146
Bridgeton, The (US tanker), 235
Brighton bombing, 163
Britain in Europe movement, 15
British Airways, 141–4, 152, 165
Brock, Bill, 19–20, 21–2
Broder, David, 43
Brook-Shepherd, Gordon, 122
Brzezinski, Zbigniew, 103
Buchanan, Keith, 162
Bundy, McGeorge, 33–4, 35, 36, 261

279

Burgess, General Sir Edward, 231
Burt, Richard, 69, 109, 153, 154
Bush, George, 79–80, 100, 114–15, 152, 247, 248, 250, 252–5, 256–7
Butler, Robin, 151, 152, 153
Butler, Stuart, 67
Byrd, Robert, 234

California, Reagan as Governor of, 2, 3, 6, 7
Callaghan, James, 7, 8, 29
Camp David, 153–60, 162, 165, 168, 170–1, 221–5, 256
Canada, 267
Carlucci, Frank, 147, 224, 234, 235, 237, 245
Carrington, Lord, 18, 78, 104–5, 134–5
Carter, Jimmy, 7, 17–18, 28, 29, 68, 103, 132, 200, 260; and deregulation, 67, 188; and the Soviet invasion of Afghanistan, 72, 74, 169
Cartledge, Sir Bryan, 229
Casey, William, 41, 88, 112
Castro, Fidel, 127
Catto, Henry, 257
Centre for Policy Studies, 13
Charles, Eugenia, 127
Chernenko, Konstantin, 146, 159
Chicago, University of, 13
China, People's Republic of, 3, 150–1
Chirac, Jacques, 231, 232
Chissano, Joaquim, 233
Christian Science Monitor, 162
Churchill, Winston, 29–33, 77, 83, 93, 147, 161, 162, 166, 221, 260, 261
Clark, William (Judge), 79, 88, 93, 98–9, 100, 103, 110–11, 137–8, 163, 198
Clinton, Bill, 259
Cockfield, Lord, 102
Commonwealth, British attitudes to, 266
Commonwealth conferences, 16, 17, 202, 263
Connally, John, 40
Conservative Party (British), 5, 6, 11
Cooper, Sir Frank, 18

Cradock, Sir Percy, 204, 207, 209
Crowe, Admiral William, 196, 221, 235
Cuban missile crisis, 34–5, 131–2
Czechoslovakia, 72

Daily Telegraph, 2–3, 22
Dart, Justin, 4
Deaver, Michael, 1, 25, 42, 53, 88, 97, 98, 107, 108, 126
Deedes, William (now Lord), 3, 22
Delors, Jacques, 250, 257
Deukmejian, Governor George, 185
Diefenbaker, John, 35
Dobrynin, Anatoly, 113
Doherty, Joseph, 199
Dole, Elizabeth, 142
Dole, Robert, 251
Donlan, Sean, 198
Dukakis, Michael, 246–7
Dulles, John Foster, 33

Eagleburger, Lawrence, 48, 84, 88, 90, 128
Eagleton, Tom, 201
Eastern Europe, 15, 123, 249
Eden, Anthony, 33, 76–7
Eekelen, Willem van, 235
Eisenhower, Dwight D., 33, 36, 76–7
Elizabeth II, Queen, 97, 106–7, 133–4
Enders, Tom, 86
Europe, 15, 269–70
European Common Agricultural Policy, 66
European Community, 73–4, 249–50, 255, 256–7, 266–7, 269–70
European Monetary System, 184, 243, 255
Export–Import Bank (Exim), 165

Falklands War, 39, 71, 76–94, 95–6, 105, 132, 197, 223, 262, 263
Fanfani, Amintore, 35
Feulner, Edwin, 13
Fieldhouse, Sir John, 220, 235–6, 238
Financial Services Act (1986), 188
FitzGerald, Garret, 138, 163, 164, 198
Fitzwater, Marlin, 228, 256
Fletcher, Yvonne, 190

Foley, Tom, 200
Foot, Michael, 97
Ford, Gerald, 3, 5, 6–7, 8, 20, 40
France, 7, 24–5, 76, 91, 96, 109–10,
    110–11, 131, 195, 196, 238, 242,
    268, 269
Frankfurt airport, terrorist attack at,
    189
Friedman, Milton, 12
Friends of Ireland, 200
Frost, David, 256

Gadaffi, Colonel, 190, 191, 195
Galtieri, General Leopoldo, 76, 77–8,
    79, 80
Gaulle, Charles de, 35, 46, 97, 249,
    270
General Belgrano, sinking of, 91, 92
Genscher, Hans-Dietrich, 56, 174, 231
Gergen, David, 26, 107–8, 111
Germany, 56–7, 182, 189, 191, 193,
    238, 242, 254, 267, 268, 269
Ghorbanifar, Manucher, 205, 206, 209
Gingrich, Newt, 259
Giraud, André, 232, 235
Giscard d'Estaing, V., 7
Goldwater, Barry, 9
Goodall, David, 193
Gorbachev, Mikhail, 121, 146–9, 159,
    172–3, 214, 215, 229–30, 240–1,
    245–6, 256, 264, 267
Gordievski, Oleg, 122, 123, 173
Graham, Katherine, 41
Greater London Council, 259
Grenada, invasion of, 125–32, 145,
    194
Gromyko, Andrei, 116, 117, 156, 157
Guadaloupe economic summit (1979),
    47
Gulf, British minesweepers in the,
    235–9

Habib, Philip, 99
Haig, Alexander, 25, 39, 50, 75, 98–9,
    102–5, 129, 134; and arms control
    negotiations, 55–6, 57, 170; and the
    Falklands War, 39, 79–80, 81, 83,
    85–6, 88, 89, 90, 91, 92, 95
Hailsham, Lord, 194
Hannaford, Peter, 3–4

Harlech, Lord, 34–5, 131–2
Hartington, Lord, 34
Hastings, Max, 71
Hattersley, Roy, 5
Hayek, F. A., 11–12, 14
Healey, Denis, 73, 228
Heath, Edward, 5, 6, 9, 24–5, 139
Helms, Jesse, 199, 234
Henderson, Sir Nicholas, 18, 79, 86,
    90, 92
Heritage Foundation, 13, 22
Heseltine, Michael, 106, 118, 167, 176,
    227
Hinckley, John, 49
Hindawi, Nezar, 210
Hine, Sir Patrick, 231
Holt, Harold, 36–7
Home, Lord (Sir Alec Douglas-Home),
    2
Hong Kong, 150–1, 256
Hoover Institution (California), 13
Horne, Alistair, 33
Howe, Admiral Jonathan, 128
Howe, Sir Geoffrey, 118, 202, 236; and
    arms control negotiations, 220, 232;
    as Chancellor of the Exchequer, 61,
    63, 65, 67, 179–80; and the
    European Monetary System, 243,
    255; and the Grenada invasion,
    125–6, 128, 130–1; and Irangate,
    209, 210; and Libya, 189, 193; and
    SDI, 158–9; and Shultz, 105, 122,
    142, 174
Hume, John, 138, 200
Hungary, 72, 123, 146
Hunt, Sir John (now Lord), 18
Hussein, King of Jordan, 82

IMF (International Monetary Fund), 8,
    66
India, 30
Ingham, Bernard, 151, 153, 178–9,
    223, 256
Institute of Directors, 2, 14
Institute of Economic Affairs, 13
Institute of Socioeconomic Studies, 14
International Court of Justice (IJC),
    201–2
IRA (Irish Republican Army), 137, 138,
    163, 164, 198, 199

Iran, US hostages in, 17–18, 23, 25, 27–8, 78
Iran–Iraq war, 211, 235–9
Irangate, 204–13, 214, 221, 223, 227, 241, 242, 263
Ireland, 136–8, 163–4, 197–201
Israel, 76, 99, 206, 209, 267

Japan, 66, 109, 110, 267–8
Jellicoe, Lord, 93
Jenkins, Simon, 71
Johnson, Lyndon B., 36–7
Jones, General David, 88
Jones, James, 61–2
Joseph, Keith, 13

Kaifu, Toshiki, 110
Kampelman, Max, 147, 173, 174
Kaunda, Kenneth, 17
Kean, Tom, 259
Kemp, Jack, 62, 67
Kemp-Roth, Bill, 62
Kennedy, Edward, 200
Kennedy, John F., 23, 33–6, 40, 68, 132, 260–1
Kennedy, Joseph, 34
Kennedy, Kathleen, 34
Kennedy, Robert, 34
Kerr, John, 152, 153, 221, 223
Key West Citizen, 5
Khashoggi, Adnan, 209
Kimche, David, 206
Kinnock, Neil, 211, 228
Kirkpatrick, Jeane, 81–2, 84, 86, 88, 93, 94, 95
Kissinger, Henry, 24–5, 39, 103, 110
Kohl, Helmut, 7, 109, 119, 175, 182, 231, 232, 254
Korean War, 15
Kornienko, Georgy, 117
Kosygin, Alexei, 16–17
Kuwaiti tankers, US reflagging of, 235, 236
Kvitsinsky, Yuli, 115

Labour government (Britain, 1970s), 8, 27, 28
Labour Party (British), 5, 97, 98, 107, 130–40, 243, 259
Laker Airways, 141, 143, 144, 152, 164–5, 262

Lawson, Nigel, 13, 62, 179, 180, 181, 183, 184, 187–8, 228, 239, 243, 255
Lebanon, 99, 129
Libya, US bombing raid on, 189–97, 200–1, 204, 207, 208, 210, 215, 227, 262, 263
Linhard, Robert, 218
Lippmann, Walter, 14
London, Reagan in, 1, 2–4, 97–8, 246, 247
Louis, John, 78, 126, 133
Louvre accord, 183–4, 243
Lugar, Richard, 199, 200, 201
Luns, Dr Joseph, 99, 134, 135
Luxembourg, 238

Machel, Samora, 233
Macmillan, Harold, 24, 25, 33–6, 68, 132, 216, 260
Marshal Chiukov (Soviet tanker), 235
Maynard, Roger, 143, 152
McFarlane, Robert, 46, 69, 71, 105, 165–6; and the Falklands War, 92, 94; and the Grenada invasion, 126–7, 133; and Irangate, 204, 205, 206; and the Soviet Union, 119, 120, 122, 123
McGovern, George, 201
McPherson, Harry, 36–7
Meese, Edwin, 25, 38–9, 41, 88
Mellor, David, 236, 237
miners' strike (Britain, 1984), 139–40
Mitterrand, François, 51, 91, 96, 107, 109, 111, 182, 195, 220
Mondale, Walter, 181
Mont Pelerin Society, 11, 12, 13, 14
Moore, Major-General Jeremy, 92
Moran, Lord, 30, 161
Moynihan, Patrick, 200
Mozambique, 233–5, 262

Nakasone, Yasuhiro, 110
Nasser, Gamal Abdel, 77
National Security Planning Group (NSPG), 80, 87–9, 93
Nato, 15, 55–7, 71–3, 106, 110–11, 238, 243–4, 254, 269; see also Nuclear Planning Group
New Ireland Forum, 138, 163
New York, Thatcher in, 48

New York Times, 208
Nicaragua, 201–2, 262
Nidal, Abu, 190
Nimrodi, Yaacov, 206
Nir, Amiram, 209
Nitze, Paul, 115–16, 169, 217
Nixon, Richard, 6, 9, 20, 24–5, 38, 39, 40, 103, 110
North, Oliver, 205, 206
Northern Ireland, 137–8, 163, 197–201, 262
Nott, John, 69, 70, 105
Nuclear Planning Group (NPG), 55, 56–7, 113, 232, 239
Nunn, Sam, 172
Nyerere, Julius, 17

O'Neill, Sir Con, 15
O'Neill, Tip, 164, 200
O'Regan, Michael, 137
Observer, 162
Ottawa economic summit (1981), 50–4, 60, 64, 71, 182
Owen, David, 3

Palliser, Sir Michael, 18
Parsons, Sir Anthony, 81, 82, 117, 204
Pattie, Sir Geoffrey, 169
Pearl Harbor, Thatcher visits, 151
Pearson, Lester, 36, 264
Pereira, Vasco Futscher, 134
Peres, Shimon, 209
Perle, Richard, 46–7, 55, 57, 69, 73, 83, 159, 170, 175, 215, 216, 218, 219, 224
Peru, Falklands War peace plan by, 90–1
Phillips, Kevin, 5
Pirie, Madsen, 13
Plaza agreement, 183, 184
PLO (Palestine Liberation Organisation), 189, 251, 252
Pohl, Dr Karl Otto, 183
Poindexter, John, 204, 205, 209, 215, 222, 223, 224
Poland, 71–4
Portugal, 4
Powell, Charles, 151, 152, 153, 154, 155, 177–8, 189, 221–2, 223
Powell, Colin, 224

Pravda, 4
Price, Charles, 1, 132, 133, 134, 144, 153, 209, 222, 223, 235, 252
Prideaux, Group Captain, 225
Prior, James, 60
Ptarmigan (battlefield telecommunications system), 185–7
Pym, Francis, 69, 89, 105
Reagan, Maureen, 234
Reagan, Nancy, 4, 41–2, 49, 50, 97, 108, 120, 152
Reagan, Ronald: attempted assassination of, 49–50; character, 1–2, 45–6, 174, 258, 261; and nuclear weapons, 58, 114, 154, 166, 264; partnership with Thatcher, 258–65; style of leadership, 23–6, 120–1, 258–60
Regan, Donald: as Chief of Staff, 165, 177, 227; as Treasury Secretary, 40, 44, 45, 62, 63, 96, 179–80, 183, 184, 185
Rentschler, James, 48
Renwick, Robin, 128
Republican Party (US), 19–22
Reykjavik summit (1986), 109, 168, 214, 216, 217–21, 225–6, 233, 241, 247
Richardson, Elliott, 132
Ridgway, Rozanne, 219, 221, 222
Rifkind, Malcolm, 117
Road to Serfdom, The (Hayek), 12
Rogers, General Bernard, 231
Rogers, William, 103
Rome airport, terrorist attack at, 190
Roosevelt, Franklin D., 29–33, 59, 77, 147, 260
Rowland, Tiny, 208–9
Rusk, Dean, 270

SALT (Strategic Arms Limitation Talks/Treaty), 54, 55, 56, 169–70, 215–16
Sands, Bobby, 137
Saudi Arabia, 66
Scargill, Arthur, 139, 140
Schlesinger, James, 15
Schmidt, Helmut, 7, 47, 51, 52, 72
Schwimmer, Adolph, 206
Scoon, Sir Paul, 127

SDI (Strategic Defence Initiative), 113–14, 149–50, 151–2, 153, 154, 155–60, 166, 167, 168, 170–1, 172, 175–6, 186
Second World War, 29–33, 15, 172, 182, 266
Secord, Richard, 206
Seidon, Elliott, 142–3
Seitz, Raymond, 219
Sheinwald, Nigel, 152, 153
Shevardnadze, Eduard, 215, 217, 253
Shultz, George, 40, 104, 105, 252; and arms control negotiations, 156, 157, 170, 171, 173, 175, 215–16, 219, 220, 223; and the Soviet Union, 112–13, 114–15, 116–17, 119, 120, 122
Siberian pipeline issue, 53, 71, 72–5, 83, 96, 99–100, 101–2
Simon, William, 15, 40
Slater, Rear Admiral Jock, 225
Sofaer, Abraham, 171
Solzhenitsyn, Alexander, 5
Sommer, Peter, 152, 153, 222, 223
Sorensen, Ted, 34, 35, 36
South Africa, 202–3, 263
Soviet Union, 4, 112–24, 229–30, 245–6
Sprinkel, Dr Beryl, 64
Stahl, Lesley, 212
Stalin, Joseph, 32
Star Wars, see SDI (Strategic Defence Initiative)
START (Strategic Arms Reduction Talks), 54
Steel, David, 131
Stephens, David, 225
Stockman, David, 44, 45, 60–1, 62, 63
Stoessel, Walter, 88
Storm Birds, The (Brook-Shepherd), 122
Strauss, Franz Josef, 7
Streator, Edward, 78
Suez crisis (1956), 33, 76–7, 92, 131
Sunday Express, 249
Sunday Times, 251
Syria, 189, 204, 210

Takeshita, Noboru, 110
Tehran conference (1943), 32

Texaco Caribbean (US supertanker), 237
Thatcher, Denis, 41–2
Thatcher, Margaret: attitude to foreign affairs, 16–17, 177; character, 49–50, 258, 261; partnership with Reagan, 258–65; style of leadership, 23–6, 100–1, 120–1, 258–60; views on Soviet Union, 16–17, 54–5
Thomas, Derek, 128
Thomson, Sir John, 131
Time magazine, 54–5
Times, The, 14, 162, 196, 211, 214
Tindemans, Leo, 134
Tokyo economic summit (1986), 208, 209
Toronto economic summit (1988), 248
Trudeau, Pierre, 51, 109, 140
Truman, Harry S., 33

Ullman, Richard, 110
United Nations, 81–2
Uruguay Round, 182
Ustinov, Marshal, 240

Vance, Cyrus, 103
Versailles economic summit (1982), 95–7, 99
Vienna airport, terrorist attack at, 190
Vietnam War, 37, 196
Volcker, Paul, 63

Wall Street Journal, 61
Wallis, Allen, 13, 165
Walters, Alan, 13, 66
Washington, Thatcher visits, 17–18, 41–8, 100–1, 256
Washington Post, 43, 61–2, 211
Watkins, Alan, 162
Weinberger, Caspar, 25, 40, 106, 113; and arms control negotiations, 55, 57, 170, 216; and the Falklands War, 81, 83, 84, 85, 87, 88, 89, 93, 94, 105; and Libya, 191, 195–6
Weir, Reverend Benjamin, 205
Westland affair, 227
WEU (Western European Union), 235, 238
Whitelaw, Lord, 193–4, 207

Williamsburg summit (1983), 106–11, 115, 136
Wilson, Harold (now Lord), 36, 37, 264
Woerner, Manfred, 231
Wright, Sir Oliver, 128, 204, 228
Wyman, Jane, 42

Yalta conference, 32
Younger, George, 106, 189, 193, 220, 232, 235, 237, 238, 239, 240

Zakheim, Dov, 83
Zimbabwe, 16, 18